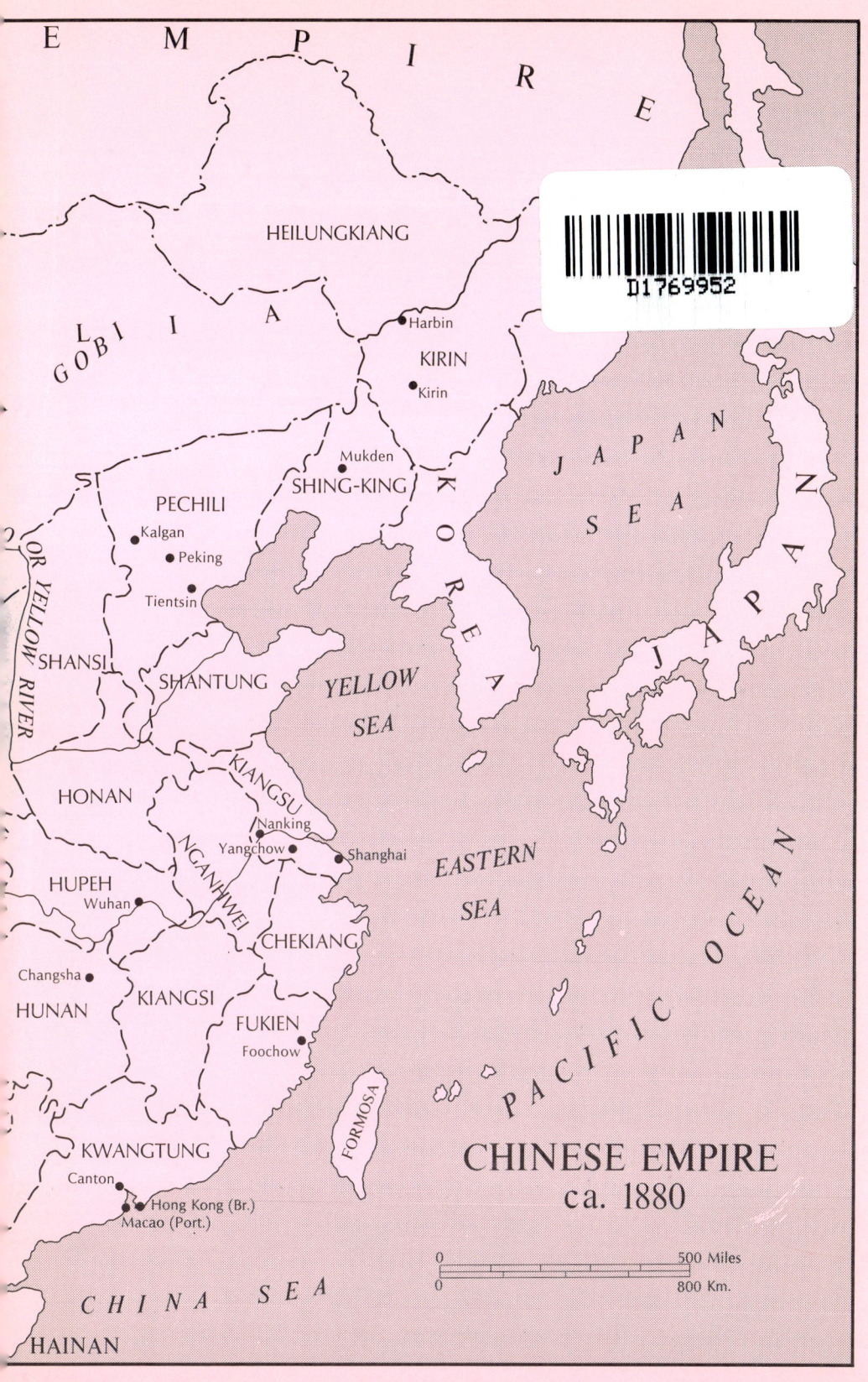

# TSO TSUNG-T'ANG AND THE MUSLIMS

## Statecraft in Northwest China, 1868-1880

by
Lanny B. Fields

THE LIMESTONE PRESS
Box 1604
Kingston, Ontario K7L 5C8
1978

© 1978 by The Limestone Press. All rights reserved.

International Standard Book Number 0-919642-85-3

Central Asia series: No. 1

Printed and bound in Canada by:   Brown & Martin Limited
Kingston, Ontario

For my wife, Aye,
with all my love.
          Lanny

CONTENTS

Illustrations

Maps

Introduction

Acknowledgements

| | | |
|---|---|---|
| CHAPTER I | TSO TSUNG-T'ANG'S UPBRINGING AND EDUCATION | 1 |
| | Family Background | 1 |
| | Education | 6 |
| | Hsian-shang nung-jen (Husbandman of the Hsian River) | 9 |
| | Geographical Interests | 10 |
| | Military Matters | 11 |
| | Statecraft as an Educational Discipline | 12 |
| CHAPTER II | THE IMPORTANCE OF SOCIAL TIES IN TSO TSUNG-T'ANG'S CAREER | 13 |
| | Tso Tsung-T'ang's Connections with the First Generation Statecraft Group | 15 |
| | Second Generation Connections | 20 |
| | Other Helpful Relations for Tso's Northwestern Campaigns | 25 |
| CHAPTER III | THE HUNAN STATECRAFT GROUP AND TSO TSUNG-T'ANG | 29 |
| | The Statecraft Tradition | 30 |
| | Sources | 34 |
| | Statecraft Personnel | 37 |
| | Some Salient Statecraft Concerns | 38 |
| | Tso as a Statecraft Adherent: Background for the Northwest | 42 |
| CHAPTER IV | NORTHWEST CHINA: BACKGROUND AND INTEREST GROUPS | 45 |
| | Background | 46 |
| | Northwest China: Economic Decline and Political Corruption | 50 |
| | The Tributary System and Its Connection to the Northwest | 52 |
| | Interest Groups in Northwest China | 55 |
| CHAPTER V | THE NEW TEACHING (HSIN CHIAO) MOVEMENT AND ITS ROLE IN THE NORTHWEST MUSLIM REBELLIONS OF 1862-1878 | 62 |
| | Important Features of Central Asian Islam | 63 |

|  |  |  |
|---|---|---|
|  | The Hsin Chiao in Kansu (1761-1871) | 67 |
|  | Networks and Interest Groups | 73 |
| CHAPTER VI | THE NORTHWEST CAMPAIGNS | 77 |
|  | The Campaigns: Problems | 77 |
|  | The Campaigns (II): Chinese Turkestan | 82 |
|  | Reconstruction | 84 |
|  | International Questions | 89 |
| CHAPTER VII | EVALUATION | 92 |
|  | Military Aspects | 92 |
|  | Political Concerns | 98 |
|  | Economic Programs | 102 |

| | |
|---|---|
| CONCLUSION | 105 |
| Notes | 107 |
| Chronology | 174 |
| Bibliography | 177 |
| Index | 201 |

## ILLUSTRATIONS

Three portraits of Tso Tsung-t'ang

Tso Tsung-t'ang and foreign visitors

The Arsenal at Foochow (1873)

Machine to raise water, Lanchow

Bridge across Yellow River, Lanchow

The ruins of Soochow

## MAPS (Endpapers)

The Chinese Empire (ca. 1880)

Northwest China - Ethnolinguistic groups

INTRODUCTION

Tso Tsung-t'ang (1812-1885) an extremely important and dynamic Chinese scholar-official ably served the Ch'ing government in four decades of the nineteenth century (1850s to 1880s). He died in office one of the most powerful, honored statesmen in the empire. Tso even favorably impressed the scathingly critical Westerners in China, some of whom fancifully compared him with Europe's Napoleon and Bismarck.

Many of these same Western observers scoffed at or otherwise ridiculed China's backwardness, corruption, and inefficiency. Perhaps the most glaring example of China's hopelessness in their eyes was the scholar-officials' tendencies to venerate the past and seek therein for answers to China's current problems. These Westerners therefore often failed to appreciate the complexity with which Chinese scholars regarded the interrelationship of past with the present, and the foreigners largely missed the richness of theory and practice embedded within China's massive body of written records. Things such as top-soil rotation methods, military strategies, and statecraft techniques awaited discovery by Tso Tsung-t'ang and others.

Chinese statecraft (ching-shih) possesses a long, important history. H.G. Creel persuasively argues that Shen Pu-hai developed a theory and application of statecraft more than two thousand two hundred years ago. Among Shen's most important discoveries was hsing-ming, a merit rating technique whereby a person's job performance would be rationally measured by an existing standard.[1] This and other methods were successfully used by a group later known as the Fa-chia (School of Law and Statecraft) which applied them on an empire-wide scale during the Ch'in dynasty (221-207).

The Fa-chia was seriously discredited by the fall of Ch'in but their invaluable techniques and bureaucratic model continued to be used in the Han, Three Kingdoms,

---

[1] The terms hsing-ming and ming-shih as well as the phrase "the ming-shih technique" will be used interchangeably in this manuscript. They will stand for the longer phrase tsung-ho ming-shih which translates "to make reality conform with the norm" or "to compare actuality with what it is supposed to be and regulate it accordingly." I am indebted to Professor K.C. Liu for these renderings.

Sung, Yuan, Ming, and Ch'ing periods. In the latter dynasties especially statecraft practices blended with Confucian theories. Thus the evolving statecraft tradition contained both Fa-chia and Confucian traits. Some Confucian thinker-practitioners such as Wang An-shih, Ch'en Liang, Chang Chu-cheng, and Tso Tsung-t'ang gave great emphasis to institutional solutions for dynastic problems while others such as Ku Yen-wu and Tseng Kuo-fan stressed moral cultivation over administrative initiatives. Neither group, however, ignored the other aspect.

Tso Tsung-t'ang is fascinating because he joined what later became a two-generation statecraft group centering geographically on Hunan and personally around T'ao Chu, Ho Ch'ang-ling, Tseng Kuo-fan, Hu Lin-i, and others. These scholars lived in a time of dynastic decline and tried to implement a reform program to revitalize the state. Although this group was one part of a larger late-Ch'ing statecraft movement, it is the central focus here because of Tso Tsung-t'ang's membership therein. It is interesting to note that not only did this Hunanese statecraft group generally experience ideological and political unity they also bound themselves together in a maze of kinship and quasi-kinship connections.

One significant example of statecraft practices came with Tso Tsung-t'ang's campaigns against the Muslims in Northwest China. He served there for thirteen years his longest tenure of office anywhere, and for twelve of those years (1868-1880) Tso confronted problems relating to the Muslims and Russians. He fought, rebuilt, and built anew in that distant region. By 1880 Northwest China returned to Ch'ing control and four years later Chinese Turkestan became a province. Present Chinese control of the Northwest owes much to Tso's efforts.

The Muslims who controlled most of the region before Tso arrived were united more by their hatred of the Ch'ing government than by other factors. Indeed the Muslims were often fragmented by ethnic, linguistic, social, and religious differences. Rather than speak of a single Muslim rebellion in Northwest China like previous scholars one might better state that many Muslim rebellions existed. One of the politically most important Muslim groups in Kansu was the Hui-hui (Tungan) sometimes called the Chinese Muslims although the latter term signifies more a tolerance of Chinese cultural practices than ethnic derivation. Ma Hua-lung, a Tungan, headed the New Teaching (Hsin chiao) movement which numbered adherents in Chinese Turkestan, Kansu, Shensi, and elsewhere. Ma became one of the most powerful religious-political leaders in the Muslim rebellions of the 1862-1878 period.

Northwest China contains a wide variety of ethnolinguistic groups including Tibetans, Han Chinese, Mongols, Manchus, Turkic peoples, and others. Chinese Tibetans, or

Mongols might be Buddhist, Confucian, or Islamic in religious orientation so that the resulting diverse and complex socio-economic patterns often defy understanding and interpretation. Other factors such as harsh climatic conditions or rugged terrains frequently challenged Tso Tsung-t'ang's strategic ability. He prevailed against these obstacles and his success in surmounting them owed much to his personal tenacity, organizational ability, and statecraft orientation.

Peace returned to Shensi, Kansu, and Chinese Turkestan in the 1860s and 1870s with a terrible human cost. Millions of people perished either in the fighting or from famine-related disasters. Fields lay unplanted for years at a time. Travelers through the area in the 1870s and after usually describe scenes of destruction, poverty, and de-population. All groups suffered to some degree from the fighting but the Muslims seemed to have endured enormous sacrifices and tragedies. Centers under the Hsin chiao's influence or domination experienced widespread devastation as Tso considered them the most ardent supporters of rebellion. The few survivors of his siege warfare tactics faced either exile or relocation to other less strategic parts of Kansu. Some even preferred suicide to capture. A balanced assessment of Tso Tsung-t'ang's tenure of office there is most difficult.

Previous studies of Tso Tsung-t'ang and mid-nineteenth century Northwest China have focused on personality or military questions rather than his statecraft theories and methods. Furthermore such efforts usually ignored the complex socio-economic diversity there. The network-interest group mode of analysis should therefore add another perspective. Tso Tsung-t'ang's Northwestern campaigns provide a case study for the domestic impact of the Hunanese statecraft group as well as the continuing vitality of the wider Chinese statecraft tradition. A consideration of this group's foreign policy dimensions must await a later time.

ACKNOWLEDGEMENTS

    I wish to express my deep thanks to many people and institutions for helping to make this study possible. Special thanks goes to Professor S.Y. Teng who guided it through the dissertation phase at Indiana State University. I met John K. Fairbank but once, yet it was he who suggested that I explore Tso Tsung-t'ang's connections to the Hunanese statecraft group. Joseph Fletcher, K.C. Liu, Chang Hao, Roger DesForges, and Jonathan Lipman read all or parts of the manuscript and offered many helpful suggestions. I would also like to thank John Killigrew, Morris Rossabi, Wolfram Eberhard, and DeWitt Ellinwood for support and encouragement. The Interlibrary Loan departments at Indiana University and SUNYA rendered me invaluable aid in locating sources and obtaining information. The Research Foundation of the State University of New York gave financial assistance in aid of publication. Finally, I wish to thank my wife, Aye Aye Khaing Fields, for her untiring support, encouragement and assistance. To her this book is affectionately dedicated.

                                                L. F.

CHAPTER I

TSO TSUNG-T'ANG'S UPBRINGING AND EDUCATION

Chinese elites customarily felt that the traditions handed down in a family or clan could significantly influence the behavior of later generations. These "family instructions" were designed to encourage conduct by family members which would serve as models for others.[1] This chapter will show that Tso Tsung-t'ang's clan produced several generations of capable scholar-officials, filial children, and upright individuals who often involved themselves in matters of public welfare. They did so despite many decades of economic difficulties. Thus Tso's programs of relief and assistance in his official career, his national reputation for incorruptibility, and his ability to use knowledge for practical purposes stemmed in part from the desire to perpetuate the clan's reputation. Furthermore as the statecraft group promoted similar attitudes and practices, Tso's early and continued association with it owed much to his family and personal background.

Tso's initial educational training adhered to the customary path of memorizing the Confucian Classics but expanded in the 1820s to include less conventional subjects like geography, agriculture, military affairs, and administrative matters. Although he failed to attain the coveted <u>chin-shih</u> degree and thus a relatively rapid and high-level appointment, the persistent quest for utilitarian knowledge equipped Tso Tsung-t'ang with a background suitable for handling the complex, technical matters confronting the Ch'ing bureaucrat. The statecraft outlook and training thus provided a basis to serve effectively throughout the Chinese empire in a career which spanned four decades.

Family Background

Tso Tsung-t'ang was born in Hsiang-yin, Hunan, on November 10, 1812.[2] His father, Tso-Kuan-lan (1770-1830), a poor but respected scholar, raised the family, including his sons: Tsung-yu (1798-1823), Tsung-chih (1804-1872), and Tsung-t'ang by income earned from teaching.

The Tso clan had a tradition of producing honored and able individuals.[3] For example, Tso Tsung-t'ang's great grandfather, Feng-sheng (eighteenth century), grandfather, Jen-chin (1738-1817), and father all attained some distinction as scholars. The great grandfather gained the status, student of the <u>hsien</u> (<u>hsien hsüeh-sheng</u>), and the grandfather became a student of the Imperial Academy (kuo-tzu chien-sheng). In addition Feng-sheng was cited in a local history as having authored a literary work.[4] Tso Tsung-t'ang's father earned the licentiate (hsiu-ts'ai) and was mentioned in the district's gazetteer as the editor of a scholarly piece. Tsung-t'ang and his brothers worked hard to continue their clan's educational tradition. Indeed, Tsung-chih and Tsung-t'ang, each brother joined by his eldest son qualified for the provincial graduate (chü-jen) ranking, a feat which certainly gave much local prominence to the clan.[5] Tsung-t'ang was the only son to gain national fame but Tsung-chih gained a province-wide reputation as an outstanding poet in his lifetime. In addition, Tsung-chih became greatly interested in ancient Chinese literature which he pursued in his leisure time. This brother also served in the Chinese government but at low administrative levels.[6]

Biographical accounts of Tso Tsung-t'ang such as those of Ch'in Han-ts'ai, Chu Wen-djang, and William L. Bales often focus on their subject's egotistical behavior.[7] This personal characteristic may have emerged partially because of the family's local reputation noted above but more importantly reflected Tsung-t'ang's strikingly self-assured manner. Even at an early age Tsung-t'ang's parents resorted to the tactic of making their son the object of jokes and other forms of ridicule to undercut his great pride.[8] In a more positive respect, however, Tsung-t'ang's ambition to become an important official in the bureaucracy animated him to read widely and include geography, military tactics or strategies, as well as agriculture in his educational background. Tso Tsung-t'ang therefore ranged far beyond the scope of the Four Books, Five Classics, their commentaries, and the eight-legged essay form. Although he abandoned the examination route in 1838, Tso continued to believe that if a person studied diligently in a wide-ranging manner then his reputation would force the state to seek him out.[9] Later as a successful official Tso encouraged others to emulate his "unconventional" path to governmental service.[10]

Bragging, arrogance, and a combative nature did occasionally hinder his career and may even have hampered his military campaigns. In the late 1850s, for example, Tso's difficult personality so irritated his co-workers in Lo Ping-chang's staff (mu-fu) that they initiated impeachment proceedings against their colleague. Tsung-t'ang's perilous legal and political situation alarmed Tsung-chih who pleaded with his younger brother to curb his tongue. Instead the timely intervention by high officials saved Tsung-t'ang from a trial and possible disgrace.[11] Much later in Northwest China, Tso dogmatically tended to follow his own course of strategy or tactics then clashed with subordinates like Liu Tien and Liu Chin-t'ang who ventured independent opinions about his battle plans.

Thus Tso gained a "reputation" for being difficult to work with, something which hindered his search for talented subordinates and ultimately weakened his administration there. Even family members criticized Tsung-t'ang's incessant bragging about his successful Northwestern campaigns when he returned home for a visit in the 1880s. In these later years Tso Tsung-t'ang, although an honored statesman, had become a partially blind, frequently ill, lonely old man; a somewhat pathetic figure.[12]

Members of the Tso clan, Tsung-t'ang's immediate ancestors, gained recognition for manifesting public-spirited behavior. In the 1750s, for example, a severe famine hit the Hsiang-yin district. Tso Tsung-t'ang's grandfather pawned his clothes and some valuables to purchase foodstuffs for the hungry people.[13] This type of action although clearly not unique in China, received notice in a local history and certainly must have provided a positive model for Tsung-t'ang.[14] The latter responded in a similar fashion in 1848-1849, when a series of floods devastated the countryside near the family home. Personal possessions were again pawned to provide food, shelter, and medicine for the destitute. This characteristic concern for and assistance to stricken people reappeared throughout Tso Tsung-t'ang's long service in the government. During and after hard-fought, bloody campaigns, for example, Tso energetically attempted to revitalize the war-torn areas. While serving in Kansu, Tsung-t'ang once wrote to his son that he gave primary consideration to avoid having a single person starve to death in an area under his jurisdiction.[15]

The Tso clan equally tried to inculcate proper filial behavior among its members.[16] Tso Tsung-t'ang himself lamented the declining moral conditions of the times and demanded that his own family set outstanding examples of proper conduct. One occasion for this kind of behavior came after the death of his beloved first wife because Tso repeatedly urged his children and other family members to conduct themselves with exemplary propriety.[17] Improper behavior might lead to criticism and damage the family's reputation. Several decades earlier in the late 1820s and early 1830s, Tsung-chih and Tsung-t'ang carefully observed the customary mourning periods for a four year time as mother and father died within two years of each other. This meant that the brothers had to forego the examination route at a time of extreme financial difficulty for the whole family.[18]

The wife of Tso Tsung-t'ang's eldest brother and the young bride of his nephew were cited by the gazetteer of the Hsiang-yin district for their meritorious behavior following the deaths of their husbands. The nephew's wife additionally received an Imperial commendation for the same action.[19] Tsung-t'ang's eldest son, Hsiao-wei, also gained posthumous Imperial recognition for his exceptional conduct in attempting to revive his dying mother. In an act of extreme personal sacrifice, Hsiao-wei cut flesh from his arm then mixed it with his mother's medicine in the desperate hope that the additional nourishment would arrest her decline and facilitate a recovery. The remedy failed, and Hsiao-wei's mother passed away. Later, after the funeral, Hsiao-wei, although seriously ill himself, traveled to Northwest China in order to comfort his grieving father. The latter was in the midst of his campaign against the Muslim rebels and could not return home. The arduous trip to the Northwest fatally undermined Hsiao-wei's own health, and Tso's eldest son died soon after returning home to Hunan. Before Hsiao-wei's own death, his wife, a daughter of Tso Tsung-t'ang's teacher and close friend, Ho Hsi-ling, severed flesh from her arm so that Hsiao-wei might be revived and recover.[20] One of the statecraft group's concerns centered on seeking to change the declining customs of the areas in which they lived or served through the personal examples of their lives and the publication of actions manifesting exemplary behavior.[21]

The relatively unfavorable economic position of the Tso clan significantly influenced Tsung-t'ang in several respects. As an infant, Tso reportedly cried a lot because he was given insufficient nourishment. Similarly the lack of family servants in his younger years forced Tsung-t'ang to help with the chores of the family.[22] All this helped promote an austere lifestyle which characterized his career and general conduct. Tso Tsung-t'ang, for example, refused to sanction the hiring of a wet nurse for his children, and later, even when a high official in Northwest China, he insisted on living in a simple, unostentatious manner. Tso frequently lived with his troops, a factor which bolstered morale.[23] A vigorous and active youth might have provided the physical characteristics necessary to withstand the exhausting work, rugged terrain, and harsh climate in Northwest China. When Tso began serving there he was already in his mid-fifties.[24]

Tso Tsung-t'ang suffered numerous incidents of humiliation growing out of his family's difficult economic situation. After marrying his first wife, Tso's inability to provide a home forced the newly-married couple to live in the quarters of his wife's family for over a decade. This development troubled Tso who began saving his teaching salary. Finally after many years of sacrifice, Tso accumulated enough money to purchase his own farm near the ancestral home.[25] Tso Tsung-t'ang's rather simple living habits particularly when coupled with the familial tradition of public-spirited conduct reinforced his later tendency to serve in an honest way. For example, as was pointed out by J.O.P. Bland and other Western observers in the nineteenth century, on several occasions Tso refused offered gifts or customary gratuities.[26] This tends to underline Tso Tsung-t'ang's assertion that he seldom sent more than five per cent of his own salary home or otherwise spent it for personal needs. Tso preferred to use most of the balance to assist the troops and personnel under his command.[27] He supplemented as best he could the meager incomes of his subordinates. Near the end of his public career in the 1880s, Tso's reputation for personal integrity spread throughout the empire and even impressed the sceptical writers living in China.[28] Finally Tso Tsung-t'ang's activist personality animated his tendency to seek out and master subjects of a practical nature so that his knowledge might one day be put into practice. This trait and concern characterized other individuals in the statecraft tradition such as Shen Pu-hai, Chu-ko Liang, and Chang Chu-cheng.

Tso Tsung-t'ang's two wives often possessed many of the above-mentioned traits. His first wife, Chou I-tuan (1812-1870), a highly educated person, left behind a collection of poetry. Her educational training which was extensive began at seven. Chou possessed an exceptional memory for it was noted that she could easily and quickly locate passages from works in the extensive family library. She seldom erred in selecting the appropriate volume.[29] In their leisure time, Chou and Tso would often discuss academic matters at length. On one occasion she assisted him in drawing maps when he studied the geography of the Chinese empire.[30] Although a frail person, Chou helped her husband and family secure an economic livelihood in the late 1830s by sewing and washing clothes in the neighborhood.[31] Some years later when Tso and his family moved to their homes in Hsiang-yin, Chou settled in then took charge of matters relating to sericulture, her special interest which complemented Tso's own attention to agriculture. One of her poems speaks of her happiness at that time in the 1840s.[32] From most indications it seems that Tso Tsung-t'ang deeply loved his first wife. In a movingly personal tribute to her, he proclaimed that the two of them remained extremely close throughout their lives.[33]

Tso and Chou raised several daughters but were unable to produce a male offspring. In his desire to have an heir, something very important for properly filial children, Tso took a second wife, Chang Ju (1814-1889). Chang came from a poor family and originally served as Chou I-tuan's maid servant. Although fragmentary information about her exists, the available records note her "sincerity." Apparently Tso and Chou confidently relied on her, and one source stated that the personal relations between the two wives evidenced propriety and reasonable behavior, something deemed unusual apparently for this type of social situation. Following the first wife's death in 1870, and despite the fact that Tso "respected" Chang, he refused to elevate her position to fill that of his departed wife. The former must not have complained, openly at least, about her situation because people came to believe that Tso Tsung-t'ang possessed a good method for governing his family.[34] It might also be noted that for most of the years after 1870, Tso was home only for extremely brief periods of time.

Tso's complex personality defies simple classification. Although characterized as very honest Tso occasionally employed individuals of a questionable reputation. One example involved Chou K'ai-hsi, a former student who served with Tso in Chekiang and later in Kansu. In both areas, Chou's abrasively harsh but effective administrative techniques alienated co-workers and other officials who brought complaints. These people charged Chou with official misconduct in Kansu then demanded that he be investigated. Tso strongly came to Chou's defense in a memorial pointing to Chou's record of able service and attacked the motives of his accusers. The case was dropped, and Chou later died in combat.35 Of course, Tso Tsung-t'ang's energetic efforts did reflect the actions of a teacher protecting a former student and protege, but they indicate other considerations as well. Tso certainly remembered his own misfortunes stemming from difficulties with his co-workers in Lo Ping-chang's staff. Furthermore Tso's own administrative techniques embodied a key element of the statecraft tradition, that of rating officials by their performances in office rather than focusing solely on their personality or character traits. This perspective probably originated with Shen Pu-hai and was used by Chu-ko Liang, Chang Chu-cheng, as well as by the nineteenth century statecraft group members.36

Tso has been criticized for harboring violent anti-foreign sentiments. The record, however, shows that throughout his long career, Tso hired and rewarded numerous foreign nationals for their meritorious service to the state.37 Foreigners helped him raise loans, buy the latest Western equipment, train Chinese to operate machinery, and to build and fire accurately the latest-style artillery. Tso was also criticized for seeking to ingratiate himself with the Empress Dowager, Tz'u-hsi. A study of his life and personality, however, shows him to be a plain-spoken, blunt individual with a manner which angered many high officials.38 Tso Tsung-t'ang utilized the best means at his disposal to serve his country, at times sparing neither himself nor his family.39

Education

Tso's formal education began at four with tutoring by his grandfather, a scholar of some note in the district. Two years later when the grandfather died, Tso's father, Kuan-lan, assumed these duties. In those youthful years Tso studied the Analects (Lun-Yu) and the Mencius (Meng Tzu) as well as the other important Confucian Classics necessary for the aspirant to a position in the government.40 Tso Kuan-lan continued to guide his sons' educations until his death in 1830. Initially the father manifested a stern and quite severe attitude with his children and demanded that they exert themselves to the utmost. With the death of the eldest son in 1823, however, this rigorous routine ceased. The more relaxed atmosphere apparently did not change the study habits of the surviving sons, Tsung-chih and Tsung-t'ang because the two young men energetically continued studying for the local examinations.[41] Both became provincial graduates in the 1830s.

Tsung-chih and Tsung-t'ang adopted highly critical perspectives with the works they jointly read as well as with each other. Usually the brothers would discuss and debate points that they learned, and occasionally disagreement led to heated arguments.[42] Further, Tsung-t'ang's Chronological Biography (Nien-p'u) gives examples of the analytical approach pursued toward such highly-regarded scholars as Ku Yen-wu (1613-1682) and Ku Tsu-yu (1631-1692), two early Ch'ing thinkers.[43] Ku Yen-wu in particular was highly regarded as a statecraft adherent. A sceptical manner although not unique to members of the statecraft group does seem to be an important characteristic of their approach to education. They surveyed all aspects of the Chinese classical tradition and mined even the discredited, hated Fa-chia tradition for useful ideas and techniques concerning political administration.[44]

Along with their critical, eclectic approach, the statecraft thinkers sought out material useful for the effective management of a bureaucracy. After acquiring such knowledge they would soon try to apply it. Although the Lun Yu may be interpreted to show that Confucius felt that utilitarian-minded people were too narrow in their outlook to be proper officials,[45] certain passages from the same work reveal the Master and his students encouraging one another to learn then put their knowledge to practical use.[46] Of course, Confucianism was not completely hostile to the practical application of what the scholar learned. Two key phrases frequently appearing in the writings of Tso and his statecraft colleagues are useful writings (yu yung chih shu) and useful knowledge (yu yung chih hsüeh).

In his desire to acquire the background necessary for the effective management of government rather than limit himself to the subjects required for the examination system, Tso Tsung-t'ang moved counter to the prevailing intellectual trends of his day. As noted by that person and others, their fellow students concentrated instead on memorizing the accepted interpretations of the Confucian Classic, on practicing the eight-legged essay forms, and on improving their calligraphy. Proper brushmanship became increasingly important for the aspiring scholar to pass the civil service examinations after the mid-eighteenth century.[47] The statecraft group as well as others attempted to replace self-centered goals by more public-spirited ones.[48] When Tso began the study of agriculture and geography many of his colleagues ridiculed his "misguided" efforts. Yet Tso Tsung-t'ang like Kung Tzu-chen ignored his fellow students' remarks and maintained his pragmatic direction.[49] The statecraft group in the nineteenth century was consciously aware that its practical orientation sharply differed from the prevailing intellectual fashions.

After the death of Kuan-lan in 1830, Tsung-t'ang's education continued in a somewhat different manner. In one work, Tso indicated that a close family friend, the father of Hu Lin-i, took over the education, but the extent of that contact is uncertain.[50] More clearly, however, this young scholar's interest in pragmatic subjects intensified through the encouragement of a high Ch'ing official, Ho Ch'ang-ling, who had returned home to observe the mourning period for a parent.[51] A few years prior to this, Ho edited an extremely important work, The Collected Essays Relating to Statecraft in the Present Dynasty (Huang-ch'ao ching-shih wen-pien).[52] Although the significance of this work will be explored below, it should be noted that Ho Ch'ang-ling encouraged Tso Tsung-t'ang's study of geography and agriculture by lending him manuscripts about them from his private library collection. Then Ho would engage Tso in conversation about the books when the latter returned them.[53]

Ho Hsi-ling, brother of Ho Ch'ang-ling, exerted an equally important influence on Tso's education and life. Hsi-ling, a chin-shih like his brother, Ch'ang-ling, served in the bureaucracy as a Censor and Commissioner of Education. While at home in retirement, Hsi-ling was made director of the Ch'eng-nan Academy (Ch'eng-nan shu-yüan), one of the two most important education centers in Hunan in the 1820s and 1830s, the other being the Yüeh-lu Academy (Yüeh-lu shu-yüan). Tso attended the Ch'eng-nan Academy and studied under Ho Hsi-ling who used many different teaching methods and covered many new subjects. Ho encouraged his students to have great ambitions, stressing that this meant serving one's emperor rather than oneself. This principle appealed to Tso who had earlier expressed similar sentiments. Together teacher and students would explore the essential works of the Han and Sung Confucianists then Ho would encourage the students to apply the principles learned. The teacher demanded careful thought, vigorous criticism, and hard work of his charges. Ho Hsi-ling also promoted the study of statecraft (ching-shih)[54] as well as self-cultivation with special emphasis on self-control and introspection leading to the manifestation of virtuous conduct.[55] One of the concepts emphasized in theory and practice at the academy was the comparison of name and reality (ming-shih). Although ming-shih is a technique used to run a government, it also may be used by an individual seeking to improve his behavior and character. In the latter sense one examines one's daily conduct to expose insincere and incorrect actions or attitudes with the intention of correcting them and satisfy the expected mode of behavior. This method developed by the <u>Fa-chia</u> was used by the Confucianists as a form of self-cultivation seeking not to project a surface manifestation of good behavior but rather a total realization of a person's innate goodness.[56] <u>Ming-shih</u> may be employed in this latter sense to "rate" the character and personality of another individual as well as oneself.[57]

Ho Hsi-ling and Tso Tsung-t'ang, teacher and pupil, soon came to admire each other. The elder statesman grew impressed with the knowledge and ability of his young charge. Tso's systematic and disciplined manner of study especially pleased him.[58] On one occasion Ho wrote that Tso "does everything very well...he really has something of substance in his mind" and further that "when I watch his manners with people and the way he talks, he seems to have good manners" thus "at that time I already thought that he was different from other people."[59] The two men became and remained good friends.

<u>Hsiang-shang hung-jen</u> (Husbandman of the Hsian River)

Tso Tsung-t'ang not only studied agriculture but practiced it as well. Interest in the theory and practice of agriculture probably stemmed from Ho Ch'ang-ling who enjoyed researching it himself. Ho, for example, had published the work <u>Soil Rotation Theory</u> (Ch'u-t'ien shuo). This particular farming technique encompassed the rotation by spreading of topsoils in order to conserve their moisture levels.[60] One ideal time to rotate would be "when the spring rains come then you should wear rainproof clothing and rotate the soil. When rotating the soil one should dig deeply and cut it into small pieces."[61] Another beneficial effect of topsoil rotation was that relatively infertile, highly acidic, or greatly alkalinic land could be improved by spreading complementary soils over them.[62] Tso read many works about soil rotation theories then later experimented with the technique. He not only authored his own book on <u>ch-u-t'ien</u> but also applied it to the Northwest Chinese topsoils during his service there in the 1870s.[63]

In 1838, Tso Tsung-t'ang failed the Metropolitan examination for the third time then vowed never again to take that test. He immediately returned to Hunan where he began to devote himself increasingly to agricultural pursuits. Tso studied texts and experimented whenever possible which was difficult owing to the lack of farmland. The latter problem was remedied after 1843, because as mentioned above, the Tso family accumulated sufficient money to buy a modest estate in Hsiang-yin. The following year the Tso household moved to their new home,[64] and thereafter Tsung-t'ang proudly styled himself as the "Husbandman of the Hsiang River."[65]

Acting thus in the capacity of a farmer, Tso happily grew or tended mulberry trees, tea, and bamboo.[66] Doing much of the work himself, Tso tended nearly one thousand trees and encouraged his wives to raise silk worms.[67] Tso has been credited with being the first in his area to practice the cultivation of tea but this claim is difficult to verify from the available material.[68] The period of the 1840s and the early 1850s before the devastating Taiping Rebellion, seems to have been the most tranquil and satisfying time in Tso's life. This therefore partly explains Tso Tsung-t'ang's reluctance to leave Hsiang-yin and serve his country when the Taiping rebels threatened Changsha, the capital of Hunan.[69]

In the Northwest, Tso had ample opportunities to apply his farming knowledge and techniques. Tso himself, for example, insisted that the recruiters for his forces pay special attention to securing men who were not only physically fit but also experienced in horticulture or related areas. He even occasionally instructed his troops in the most effective use of different planting methods. While in Northwest China Tso devoted considerable time and energy aiding destitute peasants and otherwise encouraging them to return to and work in their war-ravaged fields.[70] In addition Tso Tsung-t'ang introduced a new type of rice never before seen in Kansu and brought the sweet potato into that region of China for the first time.[71] Pavel Piassetsky, a Russian traveler in Northwest China during Tso's tenure of office there, met Tso and was surprised to find the famous general carefully tending a large garden which the visitor toured.[72] Tso's promotion of agriculture in Shensi, Kansu, and Chinese Turkestan in the 1860s and 1870s reflected his larger plan to revitalize the region's economic structure by means of a rapid but permanent economic recovery and development to underlay political stability.

## Geographical Interests

Matters relating to geography also deeply interested Tso Tsung-t'ang especially because they constituted an integral part of the knowledge which an aspiring student of military affairs needed to assimilate. Although Tso studied geography prior to his acquaintance with Ho Ch'ang-ling, the latter also maintained a collection of geographical works which he lent his young Hunanese friend. Ho again discussed these materials at length with Tso. Among the authors considered by Ho and Tso were the abovementioned Ku Yen-wu and Ku Tsu-yu.[73] Ku Yen-wu took particular interest in geography because of its application to military affairs. He traveled extensively and took notes relating to the many strategic places in the Chinese empire because he one day hoped to use the information gathered to overthrow the recently-installed Manchu regime. Ku Tsu-yu also explored the relationship between geography and military affairs. The accuracy of his information earned him the admiration of later scholars.[74]

Tsung-t'ang himself carefully studied geography; both he and his wife, for example, drew numerous maps to enhance the regions studied. Some of these productions were done to scale using five different colors in the process. Other maps were of individual provinces.[75] Employing a comparative methodology enhanced by an historical perspective, Tso followed the rise and fall of successive dynasties which he then linked with the seizing and holding of strategically-vital mountains, rivers, and towns. In this way he was able to integrate politics with topography and military theory. The material collected in this way with the accompanying notes filled several large volumes, most of which were unprinted save for <u>Aspects of Geographical Maps</u> (Wei yu-ti-t'u shuo). Hu Lin-i, a friend and later a famous general, used some of Tso Tsung-t'ang's geographical writings in his own publications.[76] This methodical analysis and historical perspective provided Tso with a solid background for understanding the military significance of places within Northwest China as well as of the entire region itself. Tso's writings from that period (1867-1880), show his extensive knowledge of many of the places where he fought. Tso would discourse at length about a strategically important city.[77]

<u>Military Matters</u>

Tso Tsung-t'ang's reputation conventionally rests on his successful military exploits against the Taiping, Nien, and Muslim forces. His dazzling victories in Chinese Turkestan from 1876-1878, for example, particularly impressed Western observers. They marveled at his armies' ability to travel and fight across long distances in short periods of time; they admired his ability to conquer extremely hostile terrains and climates; and they lauded his soldiers' efforts in fighting, farming, harvesting crops, then moving elsewhere to fight anew.[78] Some of these admiring commentators even compared Tso Tsung-t'ang favorably with von Moltke and other great Western strategists of the nineteenth century.[79]

Tso studied military history and theory in his younger days with his customary thoroughness. At that time as well as in his later years Tso especially admired Chu-ko Liang, one of China's most able generals and politicians.[80] Chu-ko served Liu Pei, the ruler of the Shu-Han state in the third century A.D. Together they built a relatively stable administration which lasted for decades. Chu-ko also played a key role in quelling some non-Han Chinese tribes in the South and in keeping the enemies of Shu-Han generally on the defensive. Through all these efforts Chu-ko Liang relied on careful and thorough planning to achieve success on the battlefield while lessening the taxation and conscription burdens on the population. Whenever possible Chu-ko employed stratagems and persuasion rather than force to nullify his opposition's power.[81] Before and during each campaign Tso also planned carefully and thoroughly to lighten the burden on the population under his administration. He diligently studied the writings and campaigns of Chu-ko Liang then commented favorably on Chu-ko's efforts saying, for example, that the practice of persuading rather than destroying an enemy was preferable.[82] Tso did lament the fact that in the nineteenth century conditions in China were much more complex than in Chu-ko's day and moreover that people at the later time seemed to respond less positively to orders given by an official.[83] Therefore his successes in Chinese Turkestan under more difficult conditions led Tso to consider himself as the greatest general in Chinese history.[84]

Tso also read the writings of Sun Tzu and was probably influenced by that thinker as well.[85] Like that earlier Chou strategist Tso frequently employed spies, so that when a Muslim leader sent a man to assassinate Tso, the latter thwarted the plot, retained the man in his own camp and thereby learned much about the Muslim forces opposing him.[86] Tso furthermore read biographies of China's greatest military heroes and often hand-copied special passages as maxims to follow.[87] Later in the 1840s Tso commented about the empire's military affairs. He wrote with a critical, perceptive eye and occasionally farsightedly about the Opium War and then similarly about the Taiping Rebellion of the 1850s.[88] In this study less attention will be devoted to the military side of Tso Tsung-t'ang's campaigns as this has been covered at length elsewhere.[89] I will focus instead on the rehabilitative aspects of Tso's Northwestern campaigns, especially those relating to domestic matters.

Statecraft as an Educational Discipline

Statecraft will be treated in depth below but deserves some mention here because of its connection with Tso Tsung-t'ang's education. Agriculture, geography, and military affairs usually interested statecraft adherents who made them important parts of their education. Although one author stated that Tso turned to statecraft concerns only after rejecting the examination route in the late 1830s, a careful analysis of Tso's Chronological Biography, however, shows clearly that Tso interested himself in statecraft several years prior to that time.[90] This subject continued to be useful to Tso during his long career as a scholar-official. Even before Tso met Ho Ch'ang-ling, the general editor of the Huang-ch'ao ching-shih wen-pien, the statecraft manual, Tso knew of the work. Interest in the theory and practice of statecraft characterized a group of scholars in the Tao-kuang era, and Tso Tsung-t'ang participated in the discussions and debates with them.[91]

Tso associated himself with T'ao Chu, Ho Ch'ang-ling, and Ho Hsi-ling, three Hunanese practitioners of statecraft in his youthful days, a crucial time in his life. Even Tso Tsung-chih, Tsung-t'ang's elder, scholarly brother who seemed more preoccupied with less practical matters like writing poetry, once wrote a memorial tribute to a former teacher in which he commented favorably as well as at length about his interest in statecraft. In addition Tsung-chih served as a government official and interested himself in astronomy then used both Chinese and Western observational techniques.[92]

Tso Tsung-t'ang's family traditions and educational upbringing forged an effective foundation on which to serve the Ch'ing government. A crucial concern for him, however, was how and in what capacity he might serve.[93] Having attained the chu-jen degree which did not necessarily guarantee employment, and after withdrawing himself from the competition for the chin-shih degree, Tso entered a time of limbo with respect to governmental work. A minor position in the local area or one on the staff of a high official seemed to be his only options. Tso therefore entered a long period of relative isolation (1838-1853).[94] During these years Tso did not seek solace in Buddhist or Taoist mysticism, but instead remained active though secluded in the manner of the great statesman he admired, Chu-ko Liang. Like this illustrious predecessor, Tso Tsung-t'ang awaited the proper occasion to be summoned.[95]

CHAPTER II

THE IMPORTANCE OF SOCIAL TIES IN TSO TSUNG-T'ANG'S CAREER

Chinese interest in questions relating to friends, family, and governmental power began very early.[1] The Confucians, for example, joined these three elements in their concept of the five social relationships: ruler-subject, father-son, husband-wife, elder brother-younger brother, and friend-friend.[2] One's position or positions within this hierarchical social order became an issue of crucial importance because security and even power could result from the establishment of a proper set of connections. People therefore sought to tie themselves with as many influential figures as possible.[3]

During the first millenium of the imperial era (221 B.C.-906 A.D.) great families usually owning sizeable tracts of land often dominated the political and economic spheres of Chinese society. In times of stable rule vigorous monarchs could check and contain their influence but in the later stages of the dynastic cycle these families developed into local or regional power centers which fragmented political and economic power thereby hastening a regime's collapse.[4] The early Sui and T'ang rulers sought first to weaken and then destroy the remaining influence of the old great families by limiting the size of their land holdings coupled with the regularization of the examination system as a central means of recruitment for the bureaucracy. Not only did the intended results occur but comparable new power groups failed to emerge from the examination process.[5]

After the elimination of the previous landed-family network elite groups sought to give themselves security through many different ways one of which was by the establishment of ties of a personal nature.[6] An ambitious person would seek to develop ties with influential officials and other important people who might offer protection and assistance. Marriage of their children sometimes resulted to cement these connections. Power, of course, was also very fragile because it was based on a family's continued retention of a political office. In the remaining centuries of the imperial period some families joined themselves in the above-mentioned manner. Such groupings if widespread, however, might incur the suspicions of a government which tolerated no challenge to its presumed monopoly of political power.[7] This "normal" antagonism became even more pronounced at certain times in the Ch'ing dynasty because the ruling Manchus, a minority ethnic group, feared that the Han Chinese majority might one day join together to overthrow their regime.[8]

One remarkable set of relationships emerged from provincial as well as professional associations most of which began in the 1820s and 1830s. At that time and somewhat later, high officials in the Ch'ing bureaucracy such as T'ao Chu, Lin Tse-hsü, and Ho Ch'ang-ling worked together in attempting to solve the enormous problems besetting the regional administrations of Central China and other parts of the empire. These friendships lasted throughout their lives and constitute the core of what should be called the first generation Hunanese statecraft group.[9] Ho Ch'ang-ling as mentioned earlier edited the Huang-ch'ao ching-shih wen-pien, the statecraft manual of the Ch'ing period which greatly influenced the thinking and actions of many scholar-officials in the Tao-kuang period. The zenith of the first generation group's power probably occurred in the late 1830s when the controlled positions of regional influence in Central and Southwest China.[10] With the death of T'ao Chu in 1839 and the disgrace of Lin Tse-hsü during the Opium War a few years later, the group's influence waned.

Significantly, however, the original statecraft group established a complex of ties with a number of promising young Hunanese scholars. Many of these relationships included marriage connections and student-teacher associations. The central core of the second generation group included Tso Tsung-t'ang, Hu Lin-i, and Tseng Kuo-fan whose writings showed a keen interest in the theory and practice of statecraft as well as the debts which they felt were owed to the first generation, Hu, Tseng, and Tso rapidly became important figures in the crisis era of the 1850s and 1860s and their influence helped shape Chinese politics until Tso's death in 1885. Owing to their close interrelationships and statecraft backgrounds these Hunanese formed a cohesive and well-prepared elite group which helped defeat the deadly Taiping challenge. Thus there is a social and intellectual basis for the relative solidarity of the anti-Taiping generals which will be examined below. Both statecraft generations provided a major impetus to Chinese politics for over six decades.[11]

## Tso Tsung-t'ang's Connections with The First Generation Statecraft Group

Tso's relations with this primary group commenced with the Ho brothers, Ho Hsi-ling and Ho Ch'ang-ling of the Shan-hua district in Hunan province. These two scholar-officials both attained the chin-shih degree and came from a family with a lofty academic reputation because a third brother, Ho Kuei-ling also reached the chin-shih level in the Tao-kuang period.[12] A family which could boast of having three such sons in the same generation was quite remarkable.

Ho-Hsi-ling, the middle brother, seems to have had the greatest impact on Tso Tsung-t'ang. As mentioned above, Hsi-ling was Tso's teacher and considered his pupil to be outstanding. Tso admired his teacher and the two men grew quite close, perhaps in part because Tso had recently lost his father.[13] Much of Tso's early correspondence was to Ho Hsi-ling.[14] Later Tso's frustration because of his inability to produce a son was alleviated with the birth of a male child in 1846, something which so overjoyed Hsi-ling that he betrothed a daughter to Tso's offspring.[15]

As has been noted in the previous chapter, the eldest of the three Ho brothers, Ho Ch'ang-ling strongly influenced the education of Tso. Ho, a successful official, served ably in the Kiangsu area and later was a governor then governor-general in the Southwest. Ho returned to Hunan about the time of Tso's father's death and continued then expanded Tsung-t'ang's interest in and knowledge of works related to statecraft.[16] In addition Tso was given the added dimension of Ho's bureaucratic experience.

Tso similarly owed Ch'ang-ling much for stimulating his interest in geography and agriculture, two extremely useful subjects for his campaigns in Shensi, Kansu, and Chinese Turkestan. One program of particular importance to Tso Tsung-t'ang was Ho's efforts to eradicate the production of opium in Kweichow in the 1840s. Growing that substance was prohibited by law, and Ho attempted to find a substitute crop by creating a special bureau to produce cotton fabrics.[17] Tso Tsung-t'ang planned and implemented a much more extensive scheme involving cotton, wool, and Western machinery. As will be seen below he sought to replace opium by these products. Hu Ch'ang-ling's association with Tso followed a pattern which he established for other capable Hunanese scholars; Ho in effect would sponsor and encourage them.[18] This person's influence ranged from geography to the theory and practice of statecraft.

The consideration of Tso Tsung-t'ang's connections with important Ch'ing officials continues with a treatment of those associated with T'ao Chu. This powerful bureaucrat from Hunan worked together with Ho Ch'ang-ling in Kiangsu in the 1820s and thus knew the latter quite well.[19] In addition T'ao and the Ho family were joined through marriage ties.[20] As a high-ranking official in the Ch'ing government for three decades, T'ao acquired an extensive amount of administrative experience. Some of his most impressive accomplishments were his reforms in Kiangsu during the 1820s and 1830s.[21]

Tso first met T'ao while teaching at the Lu-chiang Academy (<u>Lu-chiang</u> <u>shu-yüan</u>) in Liling, Hunan. One time during Tso's period of service there T'ao passed through the area and spent the night at the academy. Tso's stature was highly regarded, and he was given the honor of composing a couplet for the occasion. The poetic piece so impressed T'ao that the two men were formally introduced. Most accounts record "that the two men spent the entire night until the next morning discussing a wide range of topics."22 Although the accuracy of the quotation may be questioned T'ao and Tso did become friends because Tso later made a special trip to visit T'ao Chu in his administrative headquarters at Nanking. Once again the two spent several days together.23 T'ao who was noted for his ability to evaluate and select able people for governmental service said on one occasion that Tso was a great genius who would one day become very famous.24

Apart from a mutual intellectual attraction many other things linked these two remarkable people. Both for example, came from relatively impoverished economic backgrounds but through the cultivation of their powerful ambitions to become famous officials, they managed to circumvent these potential handicaps. Each worked hard in youth and enjoyed reading about subjects of a practical nature or with a statecraft orientation. They preferred emphasizing these pursuits rather than the more "conventional" ones like perfecting their calligraphy or mastering various eight-legged essay patterns. A similar regard for money involving honesty, careful spending, considerable saving, and the adoption of a simple life style characterized T'ao and Tso.25

Although T'ao Chu died suddenly of illness in July 1839, he managed to indicate to his friend and relative, Ho Hsi-ling that he wished for Tso to educate one of his sons, T'ao Kuang,26 who later became Tso's son-in-law.27 This position in the T'ao household provided the struggling young scholar with numerous benefits. He gained access to T'ao Chu's enormous collection of manuscripts as well as other materials relating to administrative topics. In addition a degree of financial security materialized which soon enabled the thrifty Tso Tsung-t'ang to purchase a family home.28 Finally during his stay in the T'ao residence, Tso revived his friendship with Hu Lin-i, one of T'ao's sons-in-law.29

If Ho Ch'ang-ling provided the statecraft manual and thus some of the inspiration for the Hunanese statecraft group, certainly T'ao Chu's gathering of highly talented individuals in his mu-fu30 and his vigorous championing of reform while an official offered a worthy model for the second generation group.31 T'ao also held some of the most important posts held by the first generation.

Lin Tse-hsü, another great statesman of the early nineteenth century influenced Tso Tsung-t'ang in several respects. Although different from most statecraft members under consideration here in that he was born in Fukien rather than in Hunan, Lin became friendly with T'ao Chu and Ho Ch'ang-ling when all three served in the Kiangsu region in the 1820s.[32] T'ao and Lin collaborated on many projects at that time, and the two men shared similar perspectives on most of the political and economic issues they faced.[33] Ho Ch'ang-ling's practical experience as well as his extensive knowledge about economic matters made him invaluable to Lin and T'ao so that several of their reforms relied on Ho's expertise.[34] Lin Tse-hsü may have learned about Tso Tsung-t'ang from either Ho Ch'ang-ling or T'ao Chu because both men already admired him as a talented person. Whether or not this is accurate Lin certainly knew about Tso from Hu Lin-i who was working in Kweichow at the same time as Lin in the 1840s. Hu recommended to Lin that Tso be hired for Lin's <u>mu-fu</u> and the offer was made.[35] Tso, however, with many excuses declined the opportunity to join the staff of an illustrious statesman.[36]

Despite this rebuff Lin in the winter of 1849 while returning home to Fukien because of illness took a detour through Changsha specifically to call on Tso Tsung-t'ang.[37] The two men upon meeting immediately discarded all formalities, moved the boat upon which Lin resided to a secluded spot, and spent the entire night in spirited conversation. Despite the usual attention to the problems currently facing China, the thrust of the talk shifted to Northwestern China. Lin's exile there in the 1840s, owing to imperial disfavor caused by the worsening military position of China in the Opium War, provided the venerable statesman with considerable knowledge and experience about the entire frontier region. While in the Northwest, for example, Lin even aided the government in quelling a Muslim rebellion, one covering large parts of Shensi and Kansu.[38] After a time in their conversation that evening Lin Tse-hsu realized that Tso's vast geographical and military knowledge of Northwest China made him an individual particularly suited to serve there, and if this possibility happened then Tso might continue or revive many of Lin's own projects.[39] Lin thereupon presented to his young guest all the material which he had collected pertaining to that remote area.[40] Tso kept these documents and utilized them in a profitable way in his later campaigns there. This meeting thus greatly influenced Tso who remembered it with gratitude in his later years.[41]

Tso's debt to Lin manifested itself in several concrete ventures which will be indicated here. Lin Tse-hsü's prohibition of opium consumption and production like that of Ho Ch'ang-ling deeply impressed Tso who attempted the same thing in Shensi and Kansu in the 1870s.[42] As indicated above Lin also helped suppress a large Muslim disturbance in the Northwest. In that regard Lin devised a system of controls for the defeated Muslims, undertook an extensive survey of the various kinds and numbers of different ethnic groups there, opened wells then reclaimed land in Chinese Turkestan, and instructed the local inhabitants in techniques of silk weaving.[43] Tso, of course, knew of these varied efforts and later followed in Lin's path with respect to most of them.[44] When acting in the capacity of governor-general in Nanking during the early 1880s, Tso decided to express his gratitude to Lin Tse-hsü and T'ao Chu by building a temple honoring their tenure in Nanking where both worked so many decades before.[45]

Wei Yüan is the last notable of the first generation Hunanese statecraft group who will be considered here. Wei, a Hunanese native, worked closely with Ho Ch'ang-ling, T'ao Chu, and Lin Tse-hsü in the Kiangsu region in the 1820s and 1830s.[46] Wei, for example, assisted Ho with the task of editing the Huang-ch'ao ching-shih wen-pien, noted above as an important statecraft work. Wei wrote its introduction and included some of his own writings in it as well.[47] A short time later Wei was assigned the responsibility of collating a report on the sea transport of tribute rice to Peking in 1826, a project sponsored by T'ao Chu and the other statecraft group members. This activity proved most successful, and the report was to be a record to guide future efforts. The resulting document, Complete Archives about the Sea Transportation in Kiangsu (Kiangsu hai-yun ch'uan-an) was published in the names of Ho, T'ao, and others although Wei should be credited with providing the major impetus behind its compilation.[48] During this time and later Wei served in T'ao's mu-fu and rendered important service to him. Another area of reform was that of the salt monopoly in the 1830s, and again Wei's suggestions on many aspects of that program proved useful.[49] Tso's later attempts to revitalize the salt monopoly in Shensi and Kansu contained some elements of the Kiangsu program.[50]

Wei had developed some close connections with Lin Tse-hsu in Peking prior to their work in the Yangtze region. Later in the 1840s just prior to his exile to Chinese Turkestan, Lin met with Wei Yüan then handed him the materials which had been collected in Canton relating to the Western countries. Lin urged Wei to edit these documents, and two of Wei's most famous works, A Record of Imperial Military Exploits (Sheng-wu chi) and the Illustrated Gazetteer of the Maritime Countries (Hai-kuo T'u-chih) used some of this information.[51] Tso Tsung-t'ang knew both works very well and even wrote a preface for a later edition of the Hai-kuo t'u-chih.[52]

The Sheng-wu chi proved to be extremely useful during Tso's campaigns and programs in Shensi, Kansu, and Chinese Turkestan because in it Wei not only discussed the strategies employed by the great Manchu emperors, K'ang-hsi, Yung-cheng, and Ch'ien-lung in that region but also imparted a considerable amount of information about the Muslims living there particularly about those affiliated with the troublesome New Teaching (Hsin-chiao).[53] In addition Wei argued that the complete incorporation of

Chinese Turkestan into the Chinese empire as a province would immeasurably strengthen the Ch'ing government's control of that vast but strategically important territory. When Tso Tsung-t'ang became a high official of that region in the 1870s, he realized the significance of Wei's earlier arguments in favor of making Chinese Turkestan into a province. He praised Wei as one of the most important statecraft thinkers.[54] Therefore the ultimate success of Tso in convincing the Manchu regime to create the new province in the Northwest owed much to Wei Yüan's inspiration.[55]

## Second Generation Connections

Hu Lin-i one of the great scholar-generals in the anti-Taiping campaign provided invaluable assistance to his friend and relative Tso Tsung-t'ang on many different occasions. He perhaps more than any other person in the second group influenced and comforted Tso. The Hu clan much in the manner of the Tso clan nourished a long tradition of producing concerned and filial individuals. Hu Lin-i's grandfather, Hu Hsien-shao, for example studied matters relating to statecraft in a thorough manner and urged the clan members to set aside some of their lands' income to be used in aiding its poorer members. He built nurseries for orphans as well. In times of famine Hu Lin-i's relatives donated money to assist in the relief of the destitute, and they constantly tried to improve the moral climate of their native place by setting good examples and pointing out others' trangressions.[56] Hu Lin-i's father continued this pattern of enlightened conduct and even built an academy (shu-yüan) to revitalize the scholarly traditions of the district.[57] Even in the nineteenth century's era of decline, a kind of idealistic Confucianism was implemented by some families to reduce the social tensions in the countryside. The proper starting point for these scholars was of course the smallest social unit, the family.

The fathers of Hu Lin-i and Tso Tsung-t'ang knew each other quite well from their school days together in Changsha.[58] In addition Tso Tsung-t'ang and Hu Lin-i could feel close because they were born in the same year (1812) and studied with the same teacher (Ho Hsi-ling).[59] Furthermore when the two lived for a time in Peking during the 1830s they became better acquainted. There they joked a lot and dreamed about becoming famous statesmen.[60] The final consolidation of their friendship came, however, through the ties they established with T'ao Chu. Hu was a son-in-law of T'ao, and Tso tutored one of T'ao's sons who became Tso's son-in-law.[61] T'ao managed to join to his household two talented young men who were to become very important officials in the 1850s and after. Both these scholars spent some months together in the T'ao estate in 1842. The description resembles those of

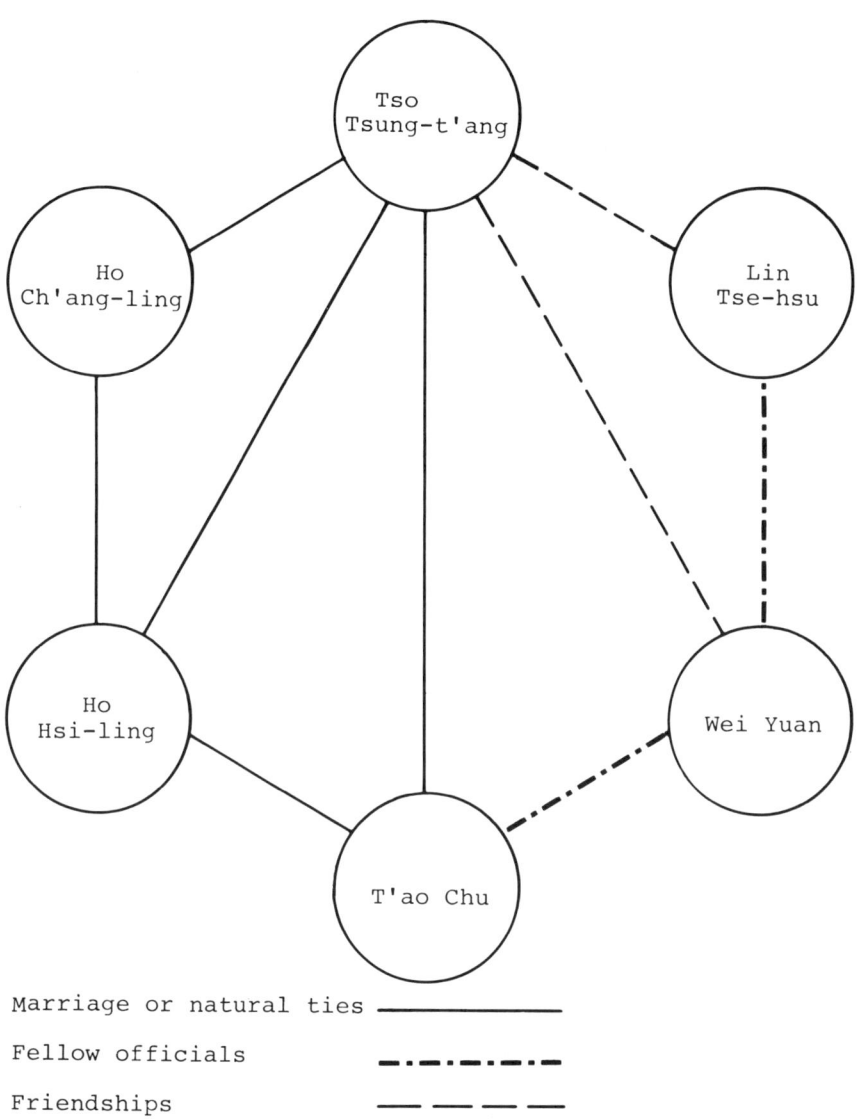

*Tso Tsung-t'ang's ties to the First Generation Statecraft Group*

Tso's earlier contacts with Lin Tse-hsu and T'ao Chu: Hu and Tso are said to have devoted several days and nights to discussing various subjects related to all periods of Chinese history, although more than likely their main topic was the current state of the Opium War.62

Hu Lin-i and Tso Tsung-t'ang now intimate friends soon tied their relationship in a closer way when they arranged for the marriage of two relatives.63 During the crucial stage of Tso's early career this new relative provided the means for the establishment of valuable contacts with high officials and also recommended Tso for jobs with several people. In 1848, for example, Lin Tse-hsü on Hu's advice summoned Tso but the latter refused. During the early years of the Taiping rebellion, Hu similarly pressed Chang Liang-chi, the Hunan governor to secure a post for Tso Tsung-t'ang, and Chang who desperately needed qualified personnel offered Tso a position. Tso not wishing to associate with people whom he considered corrupt and being one who enjoyed the life of a farmer in the manner of Chu-ko Liang refused to leave his family.64 In the manner of that early hero Tso might also have expected his summoner to make repeated efforts to secure his services.65 After the situation in Hunan became extremely critical, however, Tso finally left his family retreat and joined Chang's mu-fu. There he was given full responsibility for the conduct of military operations against the Taiping forces. Later when Chang left Hunan for another post in 1853, Tso retired. Lo Ping-chang, the new governor who also learned of Tso's accomplishments from Hu and others, managed to entice this "recluse" to join his own administration.66 Once again Tso was given command of the province's military affairs. His administrative talents were so useful that with Lo's assent Tso Tsung-t'ang gradually assumed many of the governor's duties. Indeed in many respects Tso was the de facto governor for the next five years.67

While on a journey to Peking in 1859-1860, after having broken his earlier vow never to retake the Metropolitan Examination, Tso was intercepted by a message from Hu Lin-i strongly advising Tso to halt his trip to Peking and move immediately to Tseng Keu-fan's headquarters. There he would find new employment. Hu had in the meantime persuaded Tseng to permit Tso's entrance into his staff. Even the Hsien-feng emperor learned of Tso's outstanding talent through Hu and others.68 Thus within a short time after coming to Tseng's camp Tso received an imperial command to raise five thousand Hunanese troops and use them against the Taiping forces.69

Hu aided Tso in several other ways. Throughout the 1850s, for example, Hu mediated as it were in disputes between Tseng and Tso, two opinionated and stubborn individuals. Hu's position of closeness to both men made his posture of "neutrality" a viable one. Certainly both respected his stature.[70] Following Hu Lin-i's death in 1861, Tso and Tseng continued quarreling over tactics, strategy, and personnel matters. As long as the Taiping threat continued both managed to subdue their tempers then after the fall of Nanking, the Taiping capital, a serious dispute began which led to the sundering of their friendship.

Even when financial crises threatened to engulf the Tso household Hu often provided monetary assistance. On one occasion while serving in Kweichow, Hu learned that Tso Tsung-t'ang's family faced economic hardship owing to a crop failure. Hu then dispatched a subordinate with funds so that the Tso family could survive the winter. Tso Tsung-t'ang gratefully remembered this incident many years later.[71] Again when Tso needed to raise an army to campaign against the Taiping rebels, Hu assisted in the securing of money for the maintenance of the family in Tso's absence.[72] Tso therefore deeply lamented Hu Lin-i's death in 1861 and wondered who remained to understand and console him in difficult times.[73]

Tseng Kuo-fan also grew interested in the ideas and methods of statecraft in the 1830s.[74] In a letter to Ho Ch'ang-ling, Tseng said that he had spent too much time in mastering the elements of the Sung learning and perfecting the flowery-style writing techniques, but declared that he would henceforth devote considerable attention to wide reading and the attainment of practical knowledge which would be useful to society (ching-shih chih ts-ai), and that he would make reality conform with the norm (tsung-ho ming-shih). He saw this as the essence of statecraft and as will be seen below his assessment was quite accurate.[75]

Tseng one of the chief statesmen of the T'ung-chih period adopted or extended many of T'ao Chu's reforms in Kiangsu.[76] Unlike T'ao, however, Tseng's power in the 1860s transcended provincial boundaries so that he could push through reforms and programs with less hindrance than his predecessors.[77]

The relationship between Tseng and Tso has occupied the attention of scholars for a long time.[78] The suggestion that Tseng and Tso might have argued in 1864 and then split in order to soothe the growing anxieties of the Manchu court seems most interesting but lacks convincing supportive evidence.[79] Considerable information does exist to show that a friendly relationship did continue between Tso Tsung-t'ang and Tseng Kuo-ch'uan, Kuo-fan's younger brother long after the feud between Tso and the elder brother began. Tso, for example, wrote numerous friendly letters to Tseng Kuo-ch'uan in the 1867-1881 period.[80] Furthermore Tso composed a warm tribute to the wife of Tseng Kuo-ch'uan after her death.[81] On his part Tseng Kuo-ch'uan after the death of Tso requested and received permission from the court to construct memorials to Tso in the areas where he served.[82] While in Nanking in the 1880s Tso cordially received some of Tseng Kuo-fan's relations who had come to see him. He treated them like his own children.[83]

The dispute between the T'ung-chih statesmen reflected many things. Tso was a man of great age and pride, one who felt himself superior to Tseng and others. Tso also resented the fact that he had to serve under Tseng in his mu-fu. Furthermore even after gaining his own command Tso's position was generally subordinate to that of Tseng in the Ch'ing bureaucratic structure.[84] Coupled with this are the "natural" antagonisms of two powerful bureaucrats who can request or order one another to render assistance but who need the court to enforce some commands. The Manchus seeing their power waning during the anti-Taiping struggle were delighted to see high officials railing against each other rather than united against the ruling group. Thus in this atmosphere of growing resentment and tension a memorial by Tso detailing the mistakes of Tseng in a characteristically blunt manner was perhaps interpreted as being full of ridicule.[85] Subordinates on both sides seeking to glorify their respective leaders magnified harsh statements or gave them exaggerated interpretations; positions hardened on both sides when pride and reputation predominated.[86] Although the friendship was severed, ties with other family members were not. One reason for this latter side was that marriage connections between the Tso and Tseng families, though indirect, did exist as will be seen more clearly below.

Kuo Sung-t'ao was another interesting person with some ties to Tso Tsung-t'ang. Kuo came from the same district (Hsian-yin) as Tso and knew the family quite well.[87] Kuo greatly respected Tso Tsung-chih and married his daughter to Tsung-chih's son.[88] This then established one link between the Tso and Tseng families because Kuo's eldest son married Tseng Kuo-fan's fourth daughter.[89] Despite the kinship tie between Sung-t'ao and Tsung-t'ang their personal relations grew worse leading to a breaking of their friendship.[90]

Kuo also had an interest in the ching-shih way of thinking. He studied in the Yueh-lu Academy, one of the important statecraft centers in Hunan.[91] He familiarized himself with the Huang-ch'ao ching-shih wen-pien, and his younger brother, Kuo Lun-tao developed a keen interest in matters relating to statecraft.[92]

The statecraft-kinship pattern presented here continues with a consideration of Lo Tse-nan. Lo studied with Tso Tsung-t'ang at the Ch'eng-nan Academy and under Ho Hsi-ling.[93] Thereafter Lo became noted for his teaching methods which included stressing the application of learning to practical ends.[94] Tseng Kuo-fan praised

*Tso Tsung-t'ang*

*Tso Tsung-t'ang [early 1880]*

# ERRATA

p. iii Contents line 5  Hsiang-shang for Hsian-shang.
"           6  Hsiang for Hsian.
p. viii Acknowledgements line 4  Indiana University for Indiana State University.
p. 9 Section heading  Hsiang-shang nung-jen for Hsiang-shang hung-jen.
p. 9 par. 3 line 17  ch'u-tien for ch-u-t'ien.
p. 16 par. 3 line 12  Ho Ch'ang-ling's for Hu Ch'ang-ling's.
p. 22 par. 3 line 5  Tseng Kuo-fan's for Tseng Keu-fan's.
p. 24 par. 3 line 3  Hsiang-yin for Hsian-yin.
p. 27 Fig. 2  Lo Tse-nan for Lo Tee-nan.
p. 30 par. 1 line 6  decision for descision.
p. 36 par. 6 bottom line  t'i yung for ti-yung.
p. 38 par. 1 line 5  Sung Cheng-pi for Sung-Cheng-pi.
p. 41 par. 2 line 6  Ch'ang-ling for Ch'iang-ling.
p. 57 par. 4 line 4  (755-763) for (775-763).
p. 58 par. 3 line 3  delete they.
p. 61 par. 2 line 7  them for tham.
p. 75 par. 3 line 18  An-liang for An'liang.
p. 86 par. 2 line 6  Tseng Kuo-fan for Tsen Kuo-fan.
p. 103 par. 4 line 2  Mesney for Mesney's.
p. 107 note 2 line 1  nien-p'u for nien-n'u.
p. 107 note 3 line 3  HYHTC for YHYTC.
p. 108 note 11 line 3  acquired for acquited.
p. 112 note 60 line 1  ch'üan-chi for ch'ian-chi.
p. 118 note 22 line 1  Chung-hsing for Chung-gsing.
p. 119 note 40 line 1  San-ming-chen for San-ming-chan.
p. 125 note 4 line 7  Feng Kuei-fen for Fen Guei-fen.
"        line 8  Liang Chiang for Lian Chiang.
p. 127 note 33 line 3  for Hao read Chang.
p. 128 note 41 line 2  for Beaslet read Beasley.
p. 138 note 45 line 5  CTPTSKSKHFFL for CTPTSKSHFFI.
p. 139 note 51 lines 1-2  Ch'ing for Sh'ing and Crowley for Browley.
p. 149 note 41 line 2  Musulmans for Kusulmans.
p. 149 note 43 line 1  Ma Ming-hsin's for Ma Ming-hain's.
p. 150 note 50 line 2  kenkyu for kenRyu.
p. 152 note 76 line 1  ts'ao-t'ang for ts-ao-t'ang.
p. 153 note 92 line 2  Hui-fei fang-lüeh for Hui-fei fang-lueh.
p. 156 note 8 line 4  Hupei for Hupeg.
p. 157 note 9 line 4  Hunanese for Hunan.
p. 157 note 15 line 1  Ch'ing for Ch'iang.
p. 159 note 37 line 1  tsou-kao for Tsou-kai.
p. 159 note 38 line 1  CTPTSKSKHFFL for CTPTSKSKHFFI.
p. 174 Chronology 1830  Ho Ch'ang-ling for Ho Ch'iang-ling.
p. 175 "  1874-1875  rages for ranges.

*Tso Tsung-t'ang near end of career*

*Tso Tsung-t'ang and foreign visitors [early 1880s]*

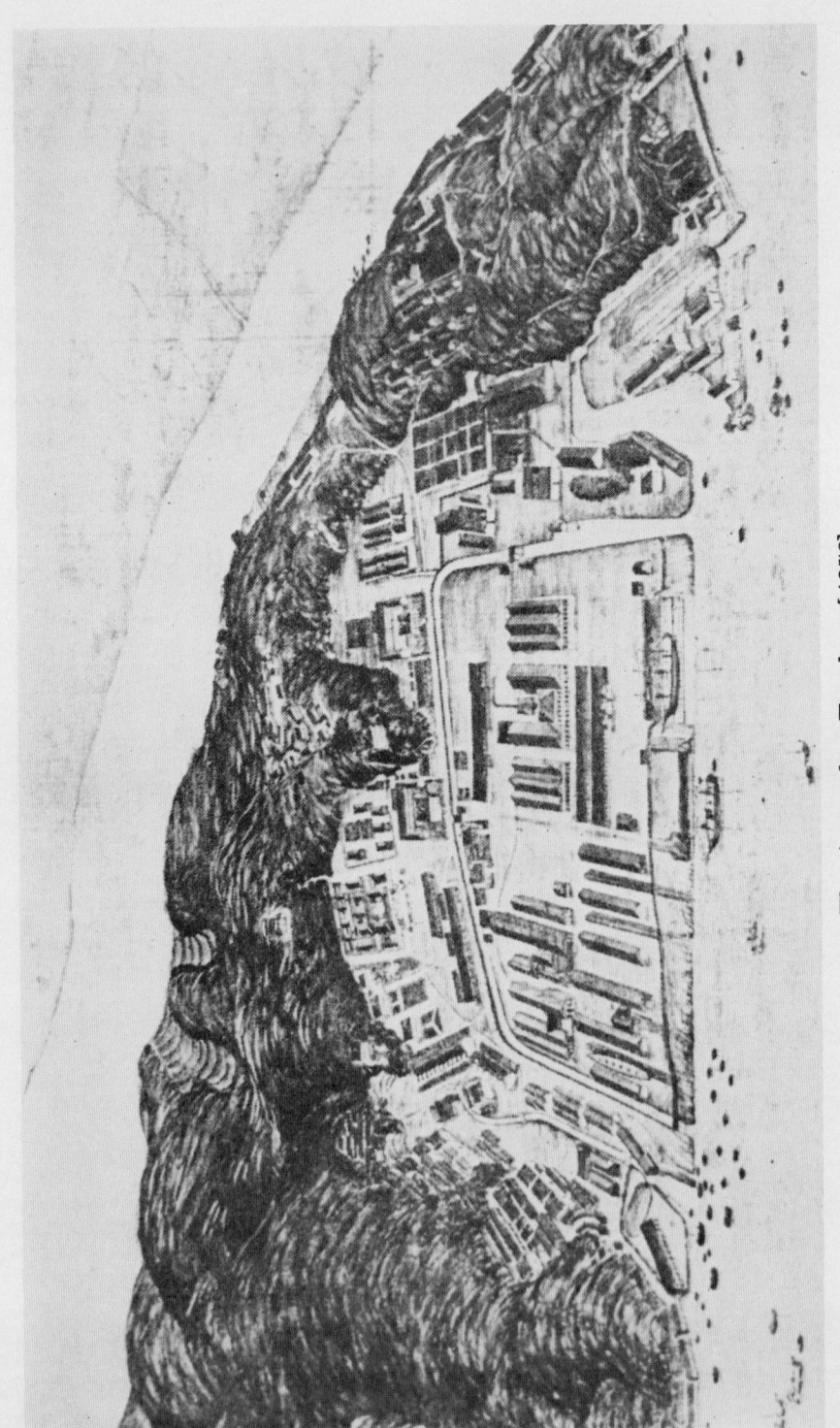

*The Arsenal at Foochow [1873]*

*Machine to raise water, Lanchow*

*Bridge across Yellow River, Lanchow*

*The ruins of Soochow*

Lo Tse-nan for his knowledge of and interest in statecraft. In one letter to Lo, Tseng also noted some earlier statecraft adherents and indicated that certain statecraft concepts were still useful.[95] Lo's character and scholarship so impressed Ho Ch'ang-ling that he asked Lo to tutor his son.[96]

Lo Tse-nan provides another connecting link between the Tso and Tseng families, one that was very indirect. Tseng's third daughter married a son of Lo while another son of Lo married a sister of Hu Lin-i.[97] Thus the Lo, Tseng, Hu and Tso families all had marriage connections.

Lo's political impact stems in part from his personal endeavors in the anti-Taiping struggle where he ably served Tseng Kuo-fan. After Lo's death in 1856, his students like Liu Jung and Liu Tien continued to serve the government in Tso's forces.[98] Wang Chin, another student also contributed to the Ch'ing effort in the 1850s. Wang organized the troops fighting under him in a manner different from Tseng Kuo-fan in his Hsiang Army (<u>Hsiang-chün</u>). After Wang's death in 1857, the leadership of his fighting force passed to a younger brother. When Tso began to raise his own army he patterned it on Wang's model and even used some of Wang's old troops. This fighting element became a crucial part of Tso's force, the Ch'u Army (<u>Ch'u-chün</u>).[99] Tso Tsung-t'ang greatly admired Wang Chin and frequently corresponded with him until he died. Eventually Tso betrothed his son, Hsiao-t'ung to Wang's daughter.[100]

The second generation statecraft group's interconnections are much more complex than those of the first generation predecessors yet they essentially shared the same fundamental intellectual outlook which stressed the importance of statecraft techniques and practical knowledge for solving the problems which the empire faced.[101] The social ties entwining them with the first generation group stemmed primarily from Tso and Hu. Perhaps the relative social, intellectual, and political cohesion of this group helps explain the effectiveness of their successful response to the great challenge of the Taiping, Nien, and Muslim Rebellions in the mid-nineteenth century. Certainly the social dimension as outlined above is important to an understanding of the unity of the anti-Taiping leadership.

Other Helpful Relations for Tso's Northwestern Campaigns
----

One important scholar-official who influenced Tso Tsung-t'ang was Hsü Sung. Like Lin Tse-hsü, Hsü Sung fell into disfavor with the Manchu court and traveled to Chinese Turkestan as an exile. During his seven year stay in that region Hsü Sung was granted permission to travel about and collect material about Chinese Turkestan's topography. In 1815-1816 especially Hsü journeyed from Aksu to Karkand then reached Kashgar. From these and other trips Hsü gathered much information about the area's history, ethnography, and geography.[102] He wrote or edited many works including <u>An Account of the Waterways of the Western Region</u> (<u>Hsi-yu shui-tao-chi</u>) and Notes on the <u>Hsi-yu chuan of the Han Shu</u> (<u>Han Shu Hsi-yu chuan pu-chu</u>). At this time a Muslim rebellion led by an <u>akhund</u> broke out, and Hsü was closely associated with the government's efforts to quell it. He learned much about the Muslims thereby.[103] Tso made Hsü's acquaintance while in Peking during the 1830s, and Hsü must have become deeply impressed with Tso's ability because he supplied the young Hunanese scholar with his published works, including those relating to Northwest China.[104] These works and the talks with Hsü gave Tso an immense fund of material and first-rate information to complement that which he later received from Lin Tse-hsü.

Wang Po-hsin directly aided Tso Tsung-t'ang's Northwestern campaigns by offering valuable advice and encouragement. Wang had worked with Lin Tse-hsü in Yunnan and Kweichow then later with Tso on Chang Liang-chi's staff in Hunan. After Tso's appointment as commander of the Shensi-Kansu theater in 1866, and while on his way to that territory in the following year, Tso stopped at Wang's home in Hupeh in order to seek his advice. The latter had traveled extensively in Shensi and Kansu to investigate the customs of the Muslims and other ethnic groups there.[105] In their talks Wang urged Tso to plan for a prolonged campaign and to concentrate his attention primarily on destroying the main Muslim strongholds. Wang also promoted a plan whereby the Muslims and Han Chinese would be segregated as far as possible. Wang felt that these two groups' inability to dwell peacefully together created the conditions for later rebellions. He also favored the establishment of a military colonist system there so that the army could support itself, reduce expenses, and spark rehabilitative operations.[106]

Another individual who significantly helped Tso by giving sound advice was Liu Jung, a fellow Hunanese and former student of Lo Tse-nan.[107] As an ex-governor of Shensi, Liu offered Tso a succinct analysis of the various problems faced by officials residing there.[108] Liu further argued that Shensi should first be cleared of rebels so that it could be used as the central base of military operations for the Kansu theater. Furthermore as the latter province housed the two central foci of the Muslim opposition, Chin-chi-pao and Hochow, they both must be effectively neutralized as soon as possible. Liu also stressed that it was vital to secure substantial supplies before embarking on these campaigns.[109] Tso Tsung-t'ang carefully noted the advice of Wang and Liu thereby incorporating many of their suggestions into his own strategic and tactical planning for the Northwestern campaigns.[110]

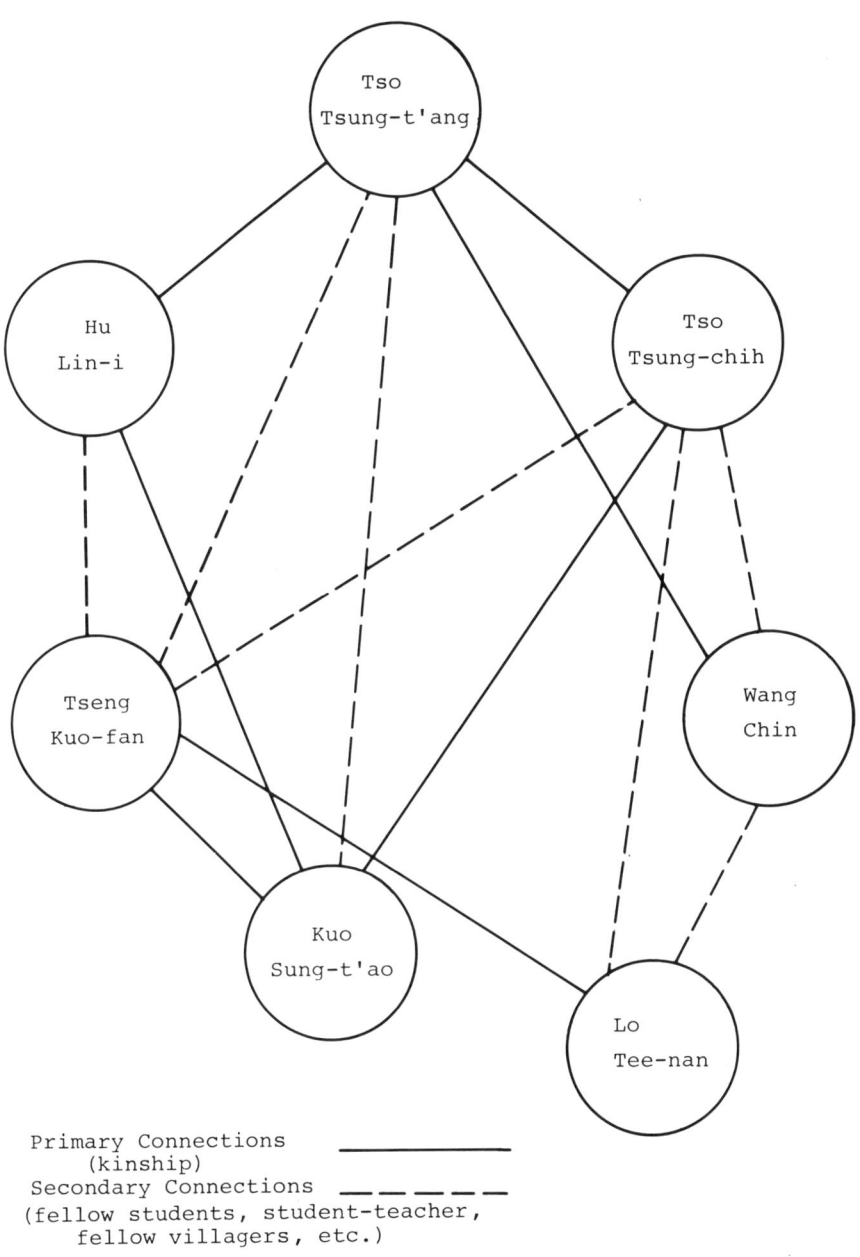

*Tso Tsung-t'ang's ties to the Second Generation Statecraft Group*

As may be seen from the above, friends played a crucial role in the life and career of Tso Tsung-t'ang. They supplied financial assistance, opportunities for employment, chances for advancement, and support when he was imperiled by the judicial process. In Tso's as with many other cases, any one of several elements might serve initially to link him to another: the fact that they lived in the same village, studied in the same school, worked for the same official, or were friends of relatives or friends. From these initial contacts close friendships were formed even with a "difficult" person like Tso Tsung-t'ang. The latter seemed to get along better with his generational elders than with his peers. Nevertheless as has been seen matrimonial ties frequently solidified friendship connections, creating one intricate web of attachments.

Through these relationships, most of them with statecraft officials or scholars, Tso gained considerable insight into the bureaucracy and how to deal with problems affecting it, and useful information and perspectives relating to the peoples and problems of the remote Northwest. This background information significantly aided his efforts there, as will be seen in Chapter VI.[111]

CHAPTER III

THE HUNAN STATECRAFT GROUP AND TSO TSUNG-T'ANG

Thomas Metzger in his work, <u>The Internal Organization of Ch'ing Bureaucracy</u>, briefly raises the question of the existence of a statecraft movement operating in nineteenth century China and then rather quickly dismisses such a possibility.[1] This perspective squares with a central concern of his which is to emphasize the Ch'ing state's positive, dynamic aspects. Thus he argues that a government largely staffed by specialists or semi-specialists could solve or at least effectively cope with the increasingly numerous and complex problems. Ch'ing bureaucrats rather than being useless generalists were able themselves or through others to maintain the system's operation.[2]

In this chapter and elsewhere it will be argued that indeed a Hunanese statecraft group did exist in the nineteenth century, and that it was a self-conscious, closely-knit, two-generational reform movement. This group drew on a long tradition of revitalization or restoration efforts by officials rather than emperors,[3] but in terms of reforming techniques, it often preferred those of the current dynasty.[4] Certainly numerous bureaucrats could effectively handle the difficult matters facing them, and there did exist other scholars with specialized, technical knowledge or skills who could be called upon for advice and assistance. During the Tao-kuang era signs of decline appeared with increasing frequency along with evidence of a bureaucracy unable to function effectively, and talk of reform became a central preoccupation of young Hunanese scholars who were further stimulated by the appearance of the <u>Huang-ch'ao ching-shih wen-pien</u>, a large collection of essays compiled and arranged to aid officials.[5] Statecraft adherents studied practical subjects like geography and agriculture and then endeavored to apply their learning. These preoccupations though not unique often brought ridicule from their contemporaries who mastered calligraphy and the eight legged essay instead.[6] Although persisting in their "unconventional" practices some <u>ching-shih</u> people like Tso Tsung-t'ang and Lo Tse-nan failed in the examination route and only secured important political positions when the Taiping rebellion engulfed the empire.

The <u>Huang-ch'ao ching-shih wen-pien</u> which catalyzed the Hunan statecraft group was designed to be "objective" in its philosophical approach to reform. The editors, Ho

Ch'ang-ling and Wei Yüan, both Hunanese, dispassionately selected what they felt to be the best, most useful essays relating to bureaucratic management but also presented a range of options concerning which techniques to employ. In this manner the official was to form his own descision in selecting a particular option.[7] This accounts for the variety of individuals and opinions represented in that work. Ho and Wei stressed not the philosophical position of the individual but rather the potential of his method.

One striking feature of the statecraft group considered here was its social cohesiveness. Provincially it centered largely in Hunan and was initially confined to elites who served together in the Lower Yangtze area of the Chinese empire in the 1820s and 1830s. T'ao Chu, Ho Ch'ang-ling, Lin Tse-hsü, and Wei Yüan are the most important figures of the first generation group and through a series of marriage ties which were explored above T'ao and Ho became interrelated with a second generation group which included Tso Tsung-t'ang, Tseng Kuo-fan, and Hu Lin-i, all of whom rendered outstanding service to the Ch'ing government during the Taiping rebellion and after. With their ching-shih perspectives and social cohesion both generations worked parallel to and supportive of the Imperial court. In following their sequential development and particularly when confined to domestic problems, one is struck by the commonality and continuity of the two groups.[8] During six decades of political influence the statecraft groups demonstrated the continuing vitality of the Chinese past in solving internal problems.

Below the statecraft tradition in Chinese history will be investigated; the sources central to the nineteenth century group will be discussed; some key individuals will be noted; and its central concerns and techniques will be explored. Finally Tso Tsung-t'ang's role as a ching-shih adherent will be examined; first as a student and then as a practitioner of its methods during his service in Hunan, Chekiang, and Fukien. This should then establish the administrative basis for his campaigns in Northwest China from 1868-1880.

The Statecraft Tradition

Early in their recorded history the Chinese began organizing relatively sophisticated political institutions. One recent study details the rather complicated governmental structure created in the Western Chou era long before similar Western Instutions appeared.[9] Indeed the Chinese invented techniques for establishing and controlling bureaucracies, some of which the West later borrowed. One such important device was the Civil Service examination system, a rather objective and professional means of bureaucratic recruitment which the Chinese gave to the British.[10] As H.G. Creel pointed out in his monograph on Shen Pu-hai; some "ancient" Chinese practices have their analogues in the practices of businessmen today. Western thinkers of the mid-twentieth century period speak a "language" close to that of Shen Pu-hai over two thousand years ago.[11]

As a state minister of Han in the fourth century B.C., Shen applied his administrative techniques and successfully avoided the serious problems which plagued most of the other states. Creel like most scholars sees Shen and his contemporary, Shang Yang as forerunners of the Fa-chia, but in an impressive argument says that the term "Legalism" should not be used to translate Fa-chia. He shows rather that two Fa-chia branches existed, one of Shang and Han Fei Tzu stressing the importance of strict rewards and punishments defined by law for controlling a territory; and the other, that of Shen emphasizing that techniques rather than force should be used to run a bureaucracy. Legalism would therefore better characterize the former than the latter.[12] Although Creel does not name Shen's wing, it seems that the term statecraft might best describe it.[13]

When Ch'in conquered the other states in the late third century B.C., it used the Fa-chia system to establish and run a centralized empire. Although collapsing after less than two decades in power, Ch'in left a two thousand year legacy of a centralized state run by an imperially-dominated bureaucracy. The administrative techniques advocated by Shen exerted an influence in Chinese history as will be seen below.

What constituted the basis of Shen's thought and why did it appeal to later statesmen? Shen, both a theorist and practitioner, conceived himself to be a practical man for whom theory unrelated to practice would have little appeal. A crucial aspect of his program involved using impartial methods for selecting and evaluating officials. The former involved selecting the most qualified person for a post regardless of his virtue. This practice later became the basis for the examination system. After employing able people the bureaucratic head then demands effective and efficient performances from his subordinates. This implies a merit-rating procedure which Ch'in possessed including inspectors and annual reports for officials.[14]

Shen used the term hsing-ming to refer to the evaluation process; an equivalent term employed with greater frequency in later centuries was ming-shih.[15] These terms mean rectification of names or comparison of name and reality, and in this context refer to the process employed by the Fa-chia to promote efficiency within the government. After a fixed period of service someone would check the office holder's record; if he failed to perform according to the job expectations (hsing does not correspond to ming) then he would be fired or demoted. When the ming squared with the hsing then he should expect to be rewarded.[16]

Embodied within the rating procedure was a concept of seeking appropriate information then checking and evaluating it. That presupposes the existence of categories by which to measure something. Ming thus also means category, and with such things you can organize material to give it meaning. As early as 800 B.C. the Chinese employed a kind of auditing then a few hundred years later statistics came to be used. Finally sometime thereafter the concept of statistics appeared.[17] Statistics thus aided the ruler in running a country and his bureaucracy. Effective organizational methods using statistics and budgeting also characterized the Hunan statecraft group in the nineteenth century.

How should a bureaucratic head conduct himself to best control his subordinates? He should keep himself well informed through as many different information sources as possible but must avoid entangling himself in petty details.[18] When all runs smoothly and efficiently than problems may either be anticipated or at least dealt with when relatively minor.[19] Finally the head must strive to conduct himself as objectively as possible being stern, fair, and not too familiar with his own subordinates.[20]

Shen Pu-hai's impact reached through Chinese history despite Confucian hostility towards the Fa-chia. H.G. Creel considered two Han Dynasty rulers particularly adept at and committed to Shen's ideas. Han Wen-ti came to power when the monarchy was weak, but managed through skillful ruling to pass a strengthened throne to his successor. About a century later Han Hsüan-ti came to the throne and managed the empire so well that one scholar considered him to be one of the best during the entire period. Both rulers admired and employed Shen's writings and techniques. In addition Hsüan-ti especially concerned himself with agriculture and built many ever-normal granaries to aid starving people.[21]

Important ministers in various periods of Chinese history also indicated an interest in and utilization of Shen's methods. Chia I who ably served Wen-ti in the second century B.C. had a great respect for Shen.[22] Ch'ao Tso who also aided Wen-ti admired and frequently employed Shen's practices like the hsing-ming.[23] Chu-ko Liang, the eminent Shu-Han minister and one of the most admired men in Chinese history is respected as much for his achievements in administration and statecraft as in military affairs. Hsing-ming was a crucial element in his rule too.[24] With a practical mind this person used ideas and knowledge from all sources; Chu-ko was eclectic and borrowed from the Confucians as well as the Fa-chia.[25]

Chang Chu-cheng, a Ming Dynasty Confucian-<u>Fa-chia</u> reformer particularly admired the methods of Shen Pu-hai and Shang Yang. Chang developed no philosophy nor considered himself a part of any school because he thought such narrowness might obscure the truth. He read widely and admired Han Hsüan-ti as well as Chia I and Ch'ao Tso for their able ruling practices.[26] One of Chang's six principles of ruling was the examination into name and reality (<u>tsung-ho ming-shih</u>).[27] For Chang this meant that the ruler and his ministers must regularly investigate to see that talented people are selected and incompetents are dismissed from the government. The laws must be upheld and problems detected before they became overwhelming.[28] Chang also employed a certain Legalist spirit in his administration. He felt that one central reason for the dynastic decline was the laxity in application and enforcement of the laws. Thus the law must apply equally to minister and subject. Therefore the good ruler must constantly check to see that rewards and punishments were being properly given.[29]

Chang fully exerted himself while a chief minister; to him the state mattered more than one's family. According to Robert Crawford this identity of self with state at times blinded Chang to the errors of his own rule and undercut the objectivity which he tried to inject into the state.[30] His rule, however, is considered to be a bright spot in a time of decline; the frontiers were quiet, domestic affairs were orderly, and the treasury was in good shape.[31] The second generation statecraft group in the Ch'ing tended to look favorably on Chang's rule using his ideas and practices because they like him had to restore a sorely-needed vitality to the empire.[32]

Before turning to the Ch'ing one other statecraft theme needs to be explored. As noted above one characteristic of most if not all statecraft adherents was pragmatism. Shen, Chu-ko, and others sought out knowledge, often in an eclectic manner, to be applied to specific problems. During the Sung era, first Wang An-shih and then later Ch'en Liang as well as others concerning themselves with reform stressed a kind of utilitarianism which promoted the practical application of knowledge. The function of literature was to help solve the problems of the time, and scholarship was judged by its applicability. Just like Tso Tsung-t'ang who greatly admired Ch'an, the latter railed at Confucians who talked much and did little.[33]

The term pragmatism (<u>kung-li</u>) and the utilitarian way of life for which it stood greatly motivated other reformers in Chinese history. Toghto in the Yuan period and Chang Chu-cheng in the Ming commented most favorably on Wang and Ch'en, especially on their <u>kung-li</u> orientations.[34]

Mary Wright in her classic account of the T'ung-chih

Restoration demonstrates that period's claim to being a restoration by comparing it with that of Chou Hsuan-wang (727-782), Han Kuang-wu (25-27, and T'ang Su-tsung (756-762). Here she follows many Chinese thinkers as well.[35] A kind of uneasiness seems to come into the work at this point, however, because the T'ung-chih Restoration occurred in a seeming absence of "an effective central executive power."[36] She then argues that the Imperial role was filled by Prince Kung who with his prestige and ability provided a channel "through which ideas of the Restoration statesmen could be sanctioned and implemented."[37] Granted that Prince Kung provided a certain amount of symbol as well as substance necessary for the revitalization of the Chinese state, but it might also be argued that in addition to the idea of a restoration being fostered by a "strong, able, and virtuous ruler" a parallel tradition existed. This second legacy with both Confucian and Fa-chia tendencies as seen above should be labeled statecraft and often encompasses strong and able ministers who often in the absence of a strong executive (Shen Pu-hai, Chu-ko Liang, and Chang Chu-cheng) or in conjunction with an able ruler (Chia I and Ch'ao Tso) played key roles in the central administration. Significantly it is to and about these ministers that the Ch'ing statecraft practitioners referred in their writings.[38] Thus the nineteenth century statecraft group who played a significant role in the T'ung-chih era consciously modeled themselves on ministers who played major roles in the resurgence of state power in various eras of Chinese history. They thus perpetuated the statecraft tradition.

Sources

Before considering the Huang-ch'ao ching-shih wen-pien, the central statecraft source, some attention will be devoted to earlier works of a statecraft orientation. Shen Pu-hai's works had passed out of existence in the seventeenth century but mention of him did occur in the nineteenth century.[39] Tseng Kuo-fan in a letter to Lo Tse-nan mentions that Ssu-ma Kuang's great work, Comprehensive Mirror for Aid in Government (Tzu-chih t'ung-chien) is the best of the earlier statecraft works.[40] Although it is not known if Ho Ch'ang-ling and Wei Yüan modeled the Huang-ch'ao ching-shih wen-pien on Ssu-ma's source, certain similarities do exist between the two. Ssu-ma's opposition to Wang An-shih's reforms confuses his position as a statecraft reformer, but in his life and scholarship he emphasized actuality and practicality. In attempting to organize his massive work into a convenient and manageable form, he sought to give the ruler the essentials to run the state properly. The Comprehensive Mirror has been praised by later scholars for having a scientific nature and having objectivity as its guiding principle.[41] To be effective the work had to encompass the widest possible scope in time and subject matter.[42]

Near the end of the Ming period, Chen Tzŭ-lung

(1608-1647), a Confucian scholar and member of various political societies compiled the <u>Huang-ming ching-shih wen-pien</u>, a collection of essays relating mainly to political and economic matters.[43] This work appearing in a time of dynastic decline (1638) sought to aid the beleagured bureaucrats by giving expert opinions on vexing problems of the day. Not only that but Chen and his collaborators also attempted to prepare administraters so that they could select classically consistent solutions for the problems facing them. Generally, however, its aimless form and bulky size undercut its effectiveness as an administrative tool, something which Ho and Wei who used the Ming work as a model, managed to avoid.[44] Apart from politics, Ch'en also interested himself in agriculture and military affairs. Interest in this person revived in the early nineteenth century because his collected works were printed in 1803.[45]

The <u>Huang-ch'ao ching-shih wen-pien</u> appeared in 1827.[46] Its editors like those mentioned above gathered and published material to aid the scholar-official. In addition, this work came from a particular environment and influenced Chinese thought and politics for the next century.[47]

The catalyzing element for this document was the service of Ho and Wei in T'ao Chu's staff in Kiangsu. There they confronted corruption, inexperience, and inertia which forced them to consider ways to reverse the situation.[48] They gathered, organized, and printed the hundreds of essays covering a wide range of options for the bureaucrat. He would perform efficiently and become the model for others who in turn and collectively would begin to revitalize the dynasty.[49]

Despite the hopeful scenario mentioned above one irony must have troubled the statecraft reformers at times. Although Ho, T'ao, or Lin might occupy positions of power at the regional level they seldom dominated the court for lengthy periods as did Chu-ko Liang or Chang Chu-cheng. At best they could push for a regional reform. Yet they strove earnestly to accomplish even that minor task because their public-spirited behavior was deeply rooted. Tseng, T'ao, Hu, and Tso died in office working for a difficult cause.[50]

Not only did the editors seek reform they also realized that experience gained from dealing with current problems often transcended that of earlier times.[51] Thus they chose writers and essays originating in the Ch'ing period.[52] These essays did discuss institutions throughout Chinese history but offered critical and utilitarian perspectives from their own dynasty.[53]

Practicality was another criterion for Ho and Wei. Methods presented in their work had to be tested by experience. Thus excessively abstract proposals or those of an impractical nature were excluded. Finally in the best bureaucratic procedure even for today the editors sought to give the widest range of options for a course of action.[54]

One aspect of this statecraft manual is its treatment of <u>ming-shih</u>. Clearly the author, Chang Shih-yuan is concerned with the question of dynastic decline and problems of drought or flooding. Unlike Chang Chu-cheng who would stress the importance of stern laws in the Legalist manner, Chang Shih-yuan says that law "is not of the utmost importance" but rather the importance of individual initiative. Yet in the best statecraft tradition he argues that with a bureaucratic government one must rate the official by <u>ming-shih</u>, the best officials and rulers do this. <u>Ming-shih</u> is a vital part of properly using people.[55] Other essays showing the most current practices of the 1820s were those dealing with the sea transport of tribute rice program which was implemented by T'ao Chu and his advisor, Wei Yüan who authored these writings.[56]

The impact of the <u>Huang-ch'ao ching-shih wen-pien</u> spread throughout the empire in the nineteenth century. It directly influenced many individuals,[57] but more than that brought forth a whole series of successors and imitators. Each of the latter added new material relating to Westerners, their weaponry, and relations with non-Han Chinese peoples near or over the border areas of the Chinese empire.[58] The <u>ming-shih</u> concept used as a device to rate people was included in the <u>Huang-ch'ao ching-shih wen-hsü-pien</u> which appeared in the late 1880s.[59]

Of the various successors of the nineteenth century statecraft editors, Chang P'eng-fei and Jao Yü-cheng are interesting. Chang, a native of Shensi, served in Szechwan which borders Hunan and thus may have had some contact with the second generation Hunanese statecraft group in the 1850s there.[60] Jao spent part of his official career in Changsha in the 1850s, the same time when Tso Tsungt'ang served in Lo Ping-chang's <u>mu-fu</u>.[61] Although it cannot be said for certain, these two people may have met each other there.

The final successor to Ho and Wei's work, the <u>Min-kuo ching-shih wen-pien</u> was published in 1913 thus transcending the Ch'ing dynasty itself.[62] Along with its predecessors the latter work stressed that changing times demanded new methods and included much material relating to the now prestigious Western ways.[63] Indeed in the next year Ch'en Tu-hsiu's <u>New Youth</u> appeared thus initiating the New Culture Movement with its theme of replacing traditional Chinese culture entirely by Western cultural patterns.

In a sense the statecraft manuals seemed to give substance to the <u>ti-yung</u> theory propounded by the Westernizers of the late nineteenth century.[64] Collectively the second generation statecraft group acted as a yung trying hard to shore up the sagging Ch'ing dynasty and its Confucian base.[65] That they successfully overcame many domestic problems and restored a relatively viable and trouble-free administration reflects favorably on the statecraft tradition and its practitioners.[66]

Statecraft Personnel

Since much of Chapter II concerned the nineteenth century Hunanese statecraft group, less attention will be devoted to it. Throughout Chinese history individuals and groups with a statecraft orientation have existed. Some people became important officials while others failed to attain sufficient political power necessary to implement their ideas and programs. In the Sung Dynasty, for example, Yeh Shih (1150-1223) and Ch'en Fu-liang (1141-1207) provided the leadership for the Yung-chia school in Chekiang province. Although Confucian scholars with Ch'en Liang severly criticized Neo-Confucian metaphysics for its Buddhist and Taoist tendencies as well as a lack of concern for the practical application of knowledge.[67] Their interest in statecraft caused them to seek out solutions for the basic economic and military problems of the day. Ch'en Fu-liang intensively studied and wrote about warfare and has been seen as China's first military historian. This group's immediate impact, however, remained relatively minor because their reform proposals were not adopted by the Sung government.[68]

Near the end of the Ming Dynasty other groups appeared in the Chinese empire. One scholar has referred to the growth of a new pragmatism oriented to practical realities which developed in the sixteenth century.[69] Chang Chu-cheng is but one representative of this tendency but he has been considered above. Ni Yuan-lu, however, has generally received little attention from scholars. Ray Huang who studied the thought and programs of this ill-fated official, calls Ni's thought patterns "realist". Ni, a high official in the late Ming era, promulgated a series of sweeping reforms which included economic matters such as the utilization of an auditing procedure, the sea transport of tribute rice, and the curbing of economic abuses.[70] This official professed to be an activist and spoke admiringly of Chang Chu-cheng's political achievements which is interesting because he belonged to a political group which opposed itself to Chang and other reformers. Ni read widely in seeking out practical knowledge; among the topics which he studied and urged to be taught at the Imperial College included agriculture, water control, military affairs, and astronomy. In this way he was distinguished from many other seventeenth century officials.[71]

Another statecraft group came from the early seventeenth century but survived into the Ch'ing era. The earliest political grouping centered around the Tun-lin faction in the first three decades of the century then permeated the Ming government in the last two decades. Some of the leaders in the 1630s included Chien Tzu-lung, Hsia Yun-i, Hsu Fu-yuan, and Sung-Cheng-pi. They authored the Huang-ming shing-shih wen-pien and implemented impressive fiscal reforms as well. A later generation statecraft group survived the Manchu conquest into the 1660s. Among the most eminent in this group was Ku Yen-wu, cited on numerous occasions by his nineteenth century successors.[72]

One interesting pattern emerges when considering the people and groups mentioned above. Granted that a certain number of individuals at a given time develop an interest in and aptitude for statecraft knowledge. Yet it is primarily during times of unrest, uncertainty, or dynastic decline that such people tend to band together and create programs to arrest the decay and revitalize the spirit of the times. Certainly this was the case for Chu-ko Liang, Ch'en Liang, Toghto, Chang Chu-cheng, and the seventeenth century groups. The two generations of Hunan statecraft reformers in the nineteenth century rose from a similar context and defeated the rebel challenges while partially stopping the disintegration at the regional levels.

## Some Salient Statecraft Concerns

Considerable statecraft interest centered on the mu-fu, that indispensible institution of personal influence. Most if not all the major nineteenth century ching-shih practitioners began their careers in a mu-fu or created one after they reached a high position in the government. Indeed the first generation statecraft group's origins are closely tied to the mu-fu created by T'ao Chu during his tenure of office in the Kiangsu area in the 1820s and 1830s. A particular mu-fu often originated when unemployed friends with specialized talents became advisors to a scholar-official who needed assistance to run his burdensome and complex office. Under the pressure of the 1850s crisis years a more formalized institutional structure emerged.[73] In the former sense, the history of the mu-fu extends back at least to the Chou period when wandering scholar-advisors sought out a ruler for employment.[74] The civilians attached to Yueh Fei's army in the twelfth century also may be seen as a later variation of the same process. They were called serving personnel (hsiao-yung shih-chen) and acted as a kind of informal bureaucracy.[75]

Since an official's career depended heavily on his staff's performance he must devote considerable attention to gathering and rating a mu-fu. The Huang-ch'ao ching-shih wen-pien offered some guidance in this matter.[76]

This work as well as individual scholar-officials in the nineteenth century drew either directly or indirectly on the statecraft tradition of Shen Pu-hai because central to his methods of recruitment and evaluation was <u>hsing-ming</u> or <u>ming-shih</u>, the identical techniques as described above.[77] This procedure, of course, embodied an objective professionalism which has been labeled by Max Weber and others as rational.[78]

Johnathan Porter in his study of the private bureaucracy devotes some attention to the means whereby Tseng Kuo-fan recruited and rated his subordinates. The interviewing technique whereby Tseng explored the candidate's personal background, qualifications, and ability to reason effectively, developed into one means of evaluation.[79] Rather than follow a new pattern, however, Tseng essentially adheres to the <u>hsing-ming</u> model developed by Shen Pu-hai and employed by Chang Chu-cheng.[80]

In another section Porter discusses techniques whereby a new staff member would undergo a probationary period during which his competency would be observed and his potential evaluated. If judged capable he would be retained or promoted. Even the "regular" <u>mu-fu</u> personnel underwent a bi-monthly examination which included a part in which the examinee answered questions proposed by Tseng himself.[81] Granted that specific rating techniques may reflect Tseng's own individual perspective, the general process clearly reflects the <u>ching-shih</u> tradition. Central to Porter's concern, however, is the fact that Tseng unintentionally or "unwittingly" implemented a rational and technical institutional development which foreshadowed the "modern" bureaucratic structures of the twentieth centiry.[82] Tseng was not all that unconscious in his employment of rational procedures which had been tested by statecraft adherents for two thousand years. The "modernity" of Tseng's approach is in the timelessness of Shen's original contribution. H.G. Creel vividly illustrates this by using commentary by businessmen, bureaucrats, and scholars of the twentieth century to parallel that of the Chou statesman. The Chinese past proved not to be as barren as those who view it from a Western-oriented perspective might believe.

<u>Hsing-ming</u> or <u>ming-shih</u> go far beyond being devices for evaluation and control.[83] When <u>ming-shih</u> is coupled with a more Confucian concern for appointing virtuous individuals as members of one's bureaucracy a different dimension emerged.[84] Not only is efficiency promoted but also the office holders serve as models for their subordinates and even the commoners. Theoretically at least, they become a part of a dynamic process which not only restores sound governmental practices but additionally strives to regenerate the sagging spirit of the local area reaching eventually throughout the empire itself.[85]

Financial matters occupied the attention of both

statecraft generations in the nineteenth century.[86] The second generation had to finance their own military operations as well as revitalize the economic structures of the areas which they liberated. The former group, however, which existed largely before the mid-century upheavals concentrated largely on increasing the revenues collected by the government.

Although economic reforms constituted an essential goal of these statesmen, they were limited by certain parameters. The first of these was a desire to lessen the peasant's economic burden.[87] A Mencian concern certainly lay behind this objective but equally important was the realization that since the peasant constituted the overwhelming majority of the population, his needs must necessarily be taken into account. A discontented peasantry might undermine the Mandate of Heaven (popular support) and spark massive rebellions like those of the 1850s. The second limitation stemmed from the insistence that prospective changes must raise additional revenue for the state.[88] This pursuit of wealth and power involved a certain Legalist perspective and indeed a tension existed between a concern for the people and the desire to enrich the government.[89] The ideal solution would have been the elimination of corrupt, inefficient practices and personnel so that an additional burden would not have been placed on the tax payer. Given, however, the inability of the economic structure to support even the existing political system as well as the court's reluctance to support a major reform effort such a program seemed either doomed to failure or the attainment of but limited results.[90]

Ho Ch'ang-ling became expert in economic matters as did other statecraft people. As others have shown he and T'ao Chu through a reform of the salt monopoly, improvement in techniques of regulating the tea monopoly, promoting the sea transport of tribute rice, and the use of water control techniques increased the revenue collection by their administration but only for their tenure of office.[91] They and their second generation successors used budgeting and accounting procedures whenever feasible to improve tax collection and resource allocation, and to root out corruption.[92]

One final statecraft concern to be pursued here was their relation to non-Han ethnic peoples. Although Shen Pu-hai's state maintained no important connection with such minority groups, he did stress the importance of maintaining good relations with other states by linking domestic and external politics together.[93] Other Warring States' governments as well as dynasties thereafter continued to deal with non-Han tribes and developed elaborate procedures for such occasions.[94] In order to secure the Shu-Han state Chu-ko Liang fought and subdued various ethnic minorities, some of whom became ardent supporters.[95]

Tso Tsung-t'ang knew of Chu-ko's efforts and attempted to use them in his own campaigns against the Muslims.[96] Chang Chu-cheng also fought against border peoples, especially the Mongols, and managed to secure the Ming frontier regions.[97]

Yen Ju-i (1759-1826), a Hunanese scholar and strategist, should be regarded as an important immediate statecraft forerunner in this area.[98] In his education Yen concentrated on learning about military and geographical subjects. Later his renowned administrative skills caused the Hupeh governor, Ch'iang-ling (1758-1838), to enlist Yen's assistance in fighting the restive Miao tribes.[99] In the course of his service there, Yen developed the policy of creating military colonies (t'un-t'ien); he would force vagrant peoples to enter the army and thereby provide a means for their control. In addition, inhabitants of these colonies could through enforced discipline be changed into "orderly" citizens.[100] These measures appealed to the state because they might raise revenues or at least drain little from the treasury.[101] Similarly the t'un-t'ien by promoting local militarization made it less necessary for the importation of more expensive and often unruly governmental troops.[102] Although noted for their harsh and regimented character, Yen's camps dotted Shensi, Hupeh, Szechwan, and Hunan during the White Lotus Rebellion, and several of Yen's essays appeared in the Huang-ch'ao ching-shih wen-pien.[103]

Another section of the statecraft manual dealt with problems relating to the Miao peoples.[104] Later both Ho Hsi-ling and Tso Tsung-t'ang dealt with the Miao and wrote about them while serving in Hupeh and Hunan respectively.[105]

The Muslims were another group which received attention from the statecraft group. As noted above, Wei Yüan's Sheng-wu chi contained much important information about the Muslims in Northwest China and Ch'ing government efforts to defeat their rebellions in the eighteenth century. Lin Tse-hsü devoted a considerable amount of attention to the Muslims while serving both in the Northwest and Southwest. In both areas Lin sought not only to defeat the Muslim rebels but to remedy the difficult conditions which sparked the revolts like discrimination by the Han Chinese officials and lack of arable land.[106] Similarly as noted elsewhere both Wang Po-hsin and Hsü Sung traveled extensively in Shensi, Kansu, and Chinese Turkestan gathering much information about the different ethnic groups who lived there. Thus in the statecraft tradition much attention was given to the question of the ethnic minorities and their relations to the central government which was often dominated by the Han Chinese. Often, however, as the statecraft reformers came to power during eras of administrative crisis they were more concerned with defeating the ethnic minorities' rebellions than with solving the problems which led to the trouble. Lin Tse-hsü and Tso Tsung-t'ang endeavored to deal with both questions. The latter also drew on the extensive experience of the above-mentioned individuals in his Northwestern campaigns.

Tso as a Statecraft Adherent: Background for the Northwest.

In the decades of his life up to the 1850s Tso Tsung-t'ang manifested a great interest in statecraft knowledge, techniques, and tradition. Tso finally got an opportunity to implement his ideas while serving for nearly ten years in the mu-fu of Chang Liang-chi and Lo Ping-chang, successive governors of Hunan during the Taiping Rebellion. When the rebel forces pushed into Hunan and attacked Changsha, Tso finally responded to the urgings of Chang and Hu Lin-i then joined the former's staff.[107] Tso helped strengthen Changsha's defenses and after the enemy abandoned their siege, he was promoted to the position of head of Hunan's military affairs.[108] As his Chronological Biography and memorials written for Chang indicate, most of this time Tso handled military affairs.[109] Tso in the manner of the statecraft adherent carefully investigated problems before working out their solutions.

Commensurate with his military duties Tso rekindled his interest in weaponry which began in the Opium War period.[110] He wrote memorials which showed a detailed knowledge about ship building, cannon making, and the production of small arms with its ammunition.[111] These tasks continued and expanded under Lo Ping-chang who gave Tso considerable authority to act as he felt necessary. Tso constructed a manufacturing bureau which built ships and cast guns.[112] These endeavors were lavishly praised by Lo and gave Tso invaluable experience which he used to build the Foochow Arsenal in the 1860s and the great Lanchow works in the 1870s.[113]

Tso acquired increased responsibility under Lo and blossomed as a bureaucrat. He and others conceived that Hunan must become the major center of the anti-Taiping effort.[114] In order to realize this goal the province had first to be cleared of rebels and stabilized; then some provincial revenues were to be used to support the armies of Hu and Tseng. Thus the stress that the statecraft group placed on reviving the economic structure was most important to funding the government forces fighting the Taipings. While pursuing his logistical operation Tao began a revision of Hunan's salt monopoly and taxation system.[115] Later he urged that private merchants be encouraged to involve themselves in the salt monopoly by selling them licenses at reasonable rates.[116] Another of Tso's proposals was for the centralization of revenue

collection from the salt and tea monopolies through the
establishment of a single bureau charged with that task.
This type of management proved so successful in controlling corruption and eliminating waste that it was extended
to the likin collection two years later.[117] With his extensive ching-shih background, Tso Tsung-t'ang was growing
into an able official.

During Tso's service with Lo, the Miao tribes on the
border between Hunan and Kweichow revolted against the
government.[118] Tso wrote three memorials on that question
demonstrating his knowledge of the Miao and his debt to Yen
Ju-i from whom he borrowed some ideas and practices. Tso,
for example urged that the military colonist system be revived and asked that local forces be mobilized to fight
the Miao rebels.[119] Later in the Northwest Tso used the
t'un-t'ien system in many areas with great effect.

Tso Tsung-t'ang acquired valuable experience while
working under the two governors thereby constructing a
foundation for actions later in Chekiang, Fukien, Shensi,
Kansu, and Chinese Turkestan. Hu Lin-i, Tseng Kuo-fan,
and the Hsien-feng Emperor, all noted Tso's contributions
to the anti-Taiping effort in Hunan. A famous though exaggerated tribute came from a censor who asserted that the
empire could not last a day without Hunan and that province
could not survive without Tso Tsung-t'ang.[120] Following a
short period in Tseng's mu-fu in 1860, Tso received a
commission to create his own fighting force. After many
months of difficult fighting in Kiangsi and Chekiang, he
was appointed governor of Chekiang, an important position.
More than one year later in May 1863, Tso became governor-
general of Fukien and Chekiang, a position he held until
late 1866.

Military activities occupied Tso for most of the
early months thus permitting him little time to consider
other matters.[121] In this campaign, however, and thereafter this Hunanese attempted to be sensitive to the interests of the peasantry. Like Chu-ko Liang, for example, he understood that warfare terribly burdened the
common people particularly when an army lived off the land.
Therefore Tso paid considerable attention to the establishment and protection of adequate supply lines. This
made it possible to provision his troops largely from governmental supplies.[122] In addition Tso made it a practice
to clear and hold territory rather than fight a series of
mobile encounters. This strategy aimed at securing areas
along with providing continued security so as to prevent
the occurrence of renewed upheaval. Although such policies
may have reflected Tso's individual military concerns, he
clearly realized that the people suffered less in a campaign conducted in this manner.[123] This commander believed that an army should serve the people, otherwise
soldiers would become indistinguishable from bandits.[124]

Rehabilitation of a newly conquered territory always constituted an important priority for Tso, and he initiated several reconstructive activities during and after the fighting.[125] He purged unworthy, corrupt, and avaricious officials while rewarding those who served in an honorable fashion. In this program he carefully investigated each case and used the ming-shih technique very effectively.[126] After clearing Chekiang he reorganized its financial affairs much as he had done earlier in Hunan.[127] His troops commenced feverishly building or repairing buildings, canals, streets, and farms.[128] The latter was especially important because it helped restore productivity to the agricultural sector, a vital revenue-producing source.

After playing a significant part in defeating the Taiping rebels in Fukien and Chekiang, this governor-general restored a large measure of stability there. By 1866 the court decided to use his talent elsewhere and appointed Tso commander of the government's forces struggling against the Muslim rebels in Shensi and Kansu.

CHAPTER IV

NORTHWEST CHINA: BACKGROUND AND INTEREST GROUPS

Northwest China (Shensi, Kansu, and Chinese Turkestan) has traditionally occupied an important part in Chinese strategic thinking. Shensi served as a base area for the Chou, Ch'in, Han, Sui, and T'ang dynasties and thus was a key political and economic center. In more recent centuries, however, with the development of new economic regions elsewhere in the empire, China's rulers moved their capital to the more populous and rich North China Plain. Yet despite this shift the successive regimes' foreign policy orientations centered on the large Inner Asian frontier across which various nomadic peoples continued to come, sometimes to raid, maybe to conquer.

Following the disastrous eighth century defeat of the T'ang forces at the Talas River in the present-day Soviet Union, Chinese political control effectively passed out of the Turkestan region and, with the exception of the Yuan Dynasty, was not to return until the eighteenth century. Then the Ch'ien-lung emperor's armies virtually annihilated the Zunghar Mongol forces. While incorporating northern Chinese Turkestan (Zungharia) into the growing Ch'ing empire, troubles soon developed in Southern Chinese Turkestan (Kashgaria or Alti Shahr), and the Ch'ing troops marched into the latter territory then conquered the resisting Muslim groups. By the late 1750s both parts of Chinese Turkestan became part of the empire.[1] Prior to these significant events, China's rulers tended to view the Northwest in a defensive manner seeking to guard rather than expand the frontier while simultaneously striving to prevent an alliance between two of their traditional main adversaries, the Tibetans and the Mongols.[2] The latter people who often troubled China from the thirteenth to the eighteenth centuries were replaced by the Muslims in the nineteenth century as the group which most concerned China's rulers. Then after the reconquest of Shensi, Kansu, and Chinese Turkestan in the 1860s and 1870s, Tsarist Russia monopolized the Central Kingdom's attention in Inner Asia.

Two major themes will be developed in this chapter. Northwest China's geography and political situation will be discussed in relation to Tso Tsung-t'ang's campaigns there to illustrate the difficult problems he faced and solved. An interrelated concern is to examine the causes of the major rebellions which erupted there in the 1860s. Despite a historical tradition of economic prosperity and power in Northwest China, a general decline in the region's productive capacity seems to have occurred reflected by the fact that revenue from provinces elsewhere in the empire had to be diverted for the support of Kansu and the territories further West. This assistance ceased in the 1850s following the capture or devastation of China's economic heartland by the Taiping rebels. Growing economic hardship when coupled with usual discrimination by Han Chinese bureaucrats against the Muslims as well as the "normal" incidence of corruption and oppression accompanying Ch'ing dynastic decline provided the essential ingredients necessary for Muslim uprisings. In the next chapter, however, a complementary argument will focus on leaders of Sufi movements who seized the momentum offered by the flammable conditions and ignited a series of revolts to oust governmental influence and control. In other words the mid-century uprisings resulted from political, economic, and religious factors.

The second major concern of this chapter is to explore the ethnic diversity in Northwest China. The Chinese traditionally exploited this feature by playing off the Mongols, Tibetans, and Muslims against one another. Mongol forces were for example frequently used to defeat rebellious Muslim troops.[3] By keeping these groups separated and mutually antagonistic the Chinese hoped to maintain their control in areas where they were a demographic minority. Even among the Muslims themselves ethnic diversity, economic competition, political ambitions, and sectarian divergencies tended to fragment the Islamic unity of a rebellion's early phases.[4] Indeed one should look at the various interest groups apart from as well as within the Muslim forces to understand better the reasons for their defeats in the 1870s.[5] Rather than one Muslim rebellion in Northwest China in the 1862-1878 period, there were many.[6]

The term Muslim will be used in this study to denote all groups which adhered in one fashion or another to Islamic beliefs, practices, and customs. This designation will therefore include Uighurs, Kazakhs, Kirgiz, Tungans, Pao-ans, Salars, Tung-hsiangs, Mongols, Tibetans, and others. Mongols and Tibetans, of course, usually followed Buddhist practices. In addition the term Tungan will be used to refer to the Muslim group inhabiting Eastern Kansu and spread throughout other parts of that province and Northwest China. Tungan will also be used interchangeably with Hui-hui and Chinese Muslim.[7]

Background

If it is a truism to note that geographical features play an important role in an area's history, Northwest China seems to provide conclusive proof for this assertion. Mountain ranges, for example, separate Shensi, Kansu, and Chinese Turkestan from the rest of the empire. These barriers penetrable only by passes, separate Shensi and Kansu from Shansi, Honan, Szechwan, and Tibet. In Chinese Turkestan mountain ranges make travel to Tibet, India, and Central Asia extremely difficult. Various passes in this region have at times become strategic points for either defensive or offensive purposes. The great diplomatic struggle over the Ili Valley in the 1880's in part reflected China's realization that if Russia controlled the vital passes there, few barriers existed between Russia and China Proper.[8]

The T'ien Shan are an important dividing element between Northern and Southern Chinese Turkestan. This fact is reflected in one way of designating each area T'ien Shan Pei Lu and T'ien Shan Nan Lu. Tso Tsung-t'ang used his excellent grounding in the Northwest's geographical features when the Chinese forces under his command struck unexpectedly into Kashgaria crossing by a seldom-used passage.[9]

Deserts are another important geographical feature of Northwest China since much of Chinese Turkestan and the surrounding areas contain arid or semi-arid regions with the principal urban areas located on oases. Two important transportation routes between China Proper and Chinese Turkestan must traverse part of the Gobi (Desert). Since many sections of these routes are either devoid of water or lack suitable drinking water, travel by large groups is inconvenient if not hazardous. Furthermore in the hot season people often travel by night. Tso studied these conditions carefully and broke his forces into small units which traveled at night when necessary.[10] He also found that camels were best suited for carrying heavy burdens while consuming tiny amounts of the precious water. Their inability to survive particularly rigorous conditions often limited their usefulness.[11] Tso also partially alleviated his supply situation by having troops travel to one oasis sow grain then move on. A later contingent would stop to harvest the crop then also move onward. This effective solution attracted much attention from Western observers.[12]

The Zungharian Basin, a desert region largely devoid of human habitation occupied most of the area north of the T'ian Shan. Hami, Tihua (Urumchi), and Wusu are the main oasis centers there. South of the great mountains lies the vast Tarim Basin with its six major centers: Turfan, Aksu, Kashgar, Yarkand, Khotan, and Cherchen. Collectively they are known as Alti Shahr (The Six Cities), a term also used for Kashgaria as noted above. Travel in the latter region was most difficult except on horseback, therefore Tso Tsung-t'ang secured a striking force composed largely of cavalry.[13] His forces swiftly overwhelmed the defending Muslim forces there journeying and fighting across hundreds of miles in several weeks. This feat astounded many sceptical Westerners who previously derided China's military prowess.[14]

The isolated nature of the urban centers in Chinese Turkestan tended to inhibit the consolidation and centralization of political control.[15] Yakub Beg established a relatively stable regime after conquering the oases in Alti Shahr in the late 1860s. He was unable to exert fully his power in Northern Chinese Turkestan across the excessive distances involved. This tended to fragment Muslim rule in Chinese Turkestan and weakened local resistance to Tso Tsung-t'ang's reconquest. Furthermore even in the South people often tended to identify with their native cities rather than Yakub's regime. Often they ran or surrendered rather than fight the invading Chinese forces.[16]

Rivers also could influence travel and campaigning in the Northwest. The one main waterway in Shensi and Kansu was the Yellow River. This watercourse generally provided an effective barrier between Shensi and Shansi but could be crossed when the water froze.[17] In Kansu this waterway constituted less of an obstacle and was associated with an elaborate network of irrigation canals which enriched the Ninghsia area.[18] Tso's forces did experience great difficulty in crossing the T'ao River near Hochow when campaigning against the Muslims there. His troops suffered a serious reverse there, but the Muslims used their advantage to negotiate rather than press the military issue.[19]

The primary rivers in Chinese Turkestan are located in or near the Tarim Basin and frequently provide water for the oases there. Crossing them during the rainy season can be quite dangerous because the existing bridges tend to be washed away. These conditions also confronted Tso Tsung-t'ang's armies.[20]

Other geographical elements may hinder travel in this general region. In Kansu, for example, deep ravines cut into the loess hills making journeys quite difficult.[21] The lack of a relatively smooth road surface and the frequency of large stones on the roadbeds caused hardships for draft and other animals especially in the section from Ansifan to Hami.[22] Springtime rains often created mud pits which covered roads and seemed eager to claim wheeled vehicles. These obstacles considerably prolonged the time spent on the road.[23]

Weather conditions similarly influenced and harrassed those moving from station to station. From May through September high temperatures when combined with a lack of suitable drinking water supplies created serious problems. Temperatures above 90 degrees F. were not uncommon.[24] Information provided by Hsü Sung, Lin-Tse-hsü, and Wang Po-hsin alerted Tso to the possible climatic conditions he would face in the Northwest, and he planned as best he could.²⁵ Some things, however, could not be prevented because he became ill and perplexed by rashes, itching, loss of appetite, and an inability to sleep.²⁶

Cold weather plagued travelers and campaigners alike from October to April. One voyager recorded a March temperature of -15 degrees F.²⁷ Terms or phrases like "terrible frosts," "chilled by icy cold" dot Northwestern travel accounts. One person observed that life in this territory became at times a battle against blizzards, hunger, thirst, and a numbing weariness.²⁸

These above-mentioned conditions were often intensified by the appearance of great wind and sand storms. In the winter the gale-like winds probably brought extremely severe wind-chill equivalent temperatures. The cold wind seemed like a knife which cut through the body repeatedly.²⁹ Sand-storms also caused much grief and occasionally nearly blotted out the sun.³⁰ Drifting sand blocked doors of watch houses, hampered travel, or caused people and animals to become lost.³¹

One's patience or stamina in coping with the cold, heat, or wind might be undermined when confronted by the pests native to the region. Several travelers recorded their difficulties with flies and mosquitoes. These insects were particularly vexatious from March to October.³² Terms like "terrible," "torment," and "purgatory of heat and mosquitoes" appear in their writings.

To counter the negative picture of the region thus far presented it must be indicated that at certain times of the year or in certain parts of Northwest China very favorable living conditions existed. Tso Tsung-t'ang once wrote from Hami that he welcomed the interval between the hot and cold months. Then one experienced moderate temperatures and pleasant living circumstances.³³ Favorable climates in the oases areas when combined with irrigation resources brought abundant harvests and a variety of fruits and vegetables.³⁴ A few decades prior to Tso's campaigns, Lin Tse-hsü implemented a program of digging wells and constructing irrigation networks in Chinese Turkestan. His highly successful efforts transformed thousands of previously unused acres into extremely productive land.³⁵ The Ili Valley attracted both the Russians and the Chinese because it contained vast amounts of raw materials and produced bountiful agricultural supplies.³⁶ Under the most favorable conditions Chinese Turkestan was a prosperous area of the empire. Tso Tsung-t'ang certainly argued that in his efforts to justify Ch'ing reconquest in the mid 1870s and to make it a province in the 1880s.³⁷

Apart from agricultural products, Chinese Turkestan's precious minerals attracted much attention from China's rulers. Jade, a stone especially prized by the Chinese was produced there in sizeable amounts then shipped to China Proper. Khotan jade particularly appealed to members of the Imperial Court.[38] When the Muslims first controlled Alti Shahr, however, they abandoned the jade mines worked for the Ch'ing government.[39] People also mined gold in Chinese Turkestan as well.[40] Indeed the Ch'ien-lung emperor cited Chinese Turkestan's immense mineral wealth as an important reason for his conquest of the area.[41]

## Northwest China: Economic Decline and Political Corruption

The economic decay and political corruption found in the Northwest partly reflected the decline phase of the dynastic cycle. One employing the dynastic cycle mode of analysis but one of many ways of interpreting Chinese history would emphasize that the Ch'ing regime after two centuries of control began to follow a pattern of administrative decline similar to the longer traditional Chinese dynasties. In this context then, the general conditions of mid-nineteenth century Northwest China will be presented. Although not the poorest province in the empire in that unlike Kansu and Chinese Turkestan it did not need large subsidies, Shensi's depleted resources coupled with an age-long political and economic decline deprived that province of its former prosperity.[42]

Parts of Kansu often produced large quantities of grain. The Ninghsia region irrigated as early as the sixth and fifth centuries B.C., for example, was one such area. This potentially prosperous region often provided the economic basis for Chinese military occupation and served as the Hsi Hsia Kingdom's base for three centuries. Kansu appears like a fertile strip of land between the steppe lands North and South of it.[43] Although falling into less prosperous times in the early Ch'ing period, Ninghsia revived when the Yung-cheng emperor reorganized its irrigation system. This prosperity must have lasted for little more than a century because a traveler stated that it was a miserable area in which lived some wretchedly poor people.[44] Reports by Chinese officials a few years later tended to confirm this observation.[45] Kansu it must be remembered needed regular contributions from other provinces to meet its financial needs.[46] The loess top soil which covered extensive parts of Kansu and Shensi became fruitfully productive with adequate rainfall but barren when insufficient rain fell.

Chinese Turkestan's economic potential sagged in the early nineteenth century. For several decades prior to 1880 the administrative apparatus functioned well with little corruption and great efficiency. Interest in adequately maintaining the irrigation system of the Ili Valley waned and production declined.[47] In the second, third, and fourth decades of the nineteenth century the subject

Muslims rebelled and caused much destruction.[48] Raids from the Kokand Khanate in 1830 and after caused further disruption. The government responded to these crises by requisitioning supplies from the local inhabitants thus worsening their economic plight.[49] Lin Tse-hsü's well digging and irrigation programs temporarily arrested the decline in the 1840s but uprisings by religious dissidents grew as did the cost of quelling them. Finally in the 1850s the Taiping Rebellion terminated outside funding and left the local administration financially helpless.

Demographic factors also must be considered in relation to the economic and social conditions of Northwest China. During the upsurge of the dynastic cycle under three extremely competent rulers, the K'ang-hsi, Yung-cheng, and Ch'ien-lung emperors, a vigorously efficient rule generally prevailed. Although large amounts of money were needed to finance the latter ruler's many campaigns, the freezing of the land tax by the K'ang-hsi emperor in 1712 benefitted the peasants, at least to the degree of not being crushed by the growing military budgets.[50] Internal security coupled with external expansion which some called the "Pax sinica" probably meant a relatively stable life in the eighteenth century.[51]

Peace, stability, and the widespread use of new foodstuffs such as the potato and maize helped promote a dramatic population rise within two centuries.[52] After a threefold increase by 1850, the pressure on the land assumed catastrophic proportions and played a role in the devastating rebellions of the mid-century era.[53] Locally in Shensi and Kansu the large population forced many Chinese to leave their own overcrowded villages for the less densely populated Muslim and Tibetan territories. The increasingly close contact between the Han Chinese and Muslims sometimes led to angry confrontations or even armed clashes. Cultural differences often provided the spark, and when these incidents reached the attention of the local authorities, the Chinese usually received preferential treatment from the Chinese magistrates.[54]

The population pressure on the land in Shensi and Kansu led to increasingly smaller landholdings by families. Since it became harder to support life by working the tiny plots the land was sold to landlords who by 1800 owned 50-60% of the arable land.[55] Even then with 50% rent levies being common the peasants were forced to borrow money often at very high interest rates to survive.[56] At times when the peasants needed to purchase seed grain speculators forced up the market prices then when the harvest season arrived prices often dropped dramatically. One source speculated that as a result of these conditions only 20-30% of the population kept warm and received adequate nourishment in the winter months.[57] Demographic pressures therefore increased the prospects for conflict in Shensi and Kansu in the nineteenth century.

In the later years of the Ch'ien-lung emperor's reign, the corrupt and corrupting Ho-shen spread his influence throughout the national level and from there to the lower bureaucratic echelons. Even during "normal" times many officials considered service in Northwest China a hardship duty something to be avoided if possible. Officials "unfortunate" enough to serve there sometimes ruthlessly exploited the native people living there while devoting themselves to carefree and luxurious ways. In Chinese Turkestan, for example, bureaucrats occasionally demanded that pretty Muslim women become their concubines. Similarly they ruled through intermediaries called <u>begs</u> (local native officials) who when free from careful administrative supervision also intensified their corrupt and oppressive measures aimed at enhancing their own pleasurable livelihoods. Under these conditions the local people suffered tremendously and needed but a tiny spark to explode in a widespread conflagration.[58]

Chinese military weakness compounded the political problems and led to internal and external catastrophes in the nineteenth century. The Manchu military forces: the Banner system and the Army of the Green Standard generally lost their fighting effectiveness owing to relatively long periods of inactivity and immobility. When rebellions like the White Lotus or the Taiping erupted these units were often ineffective as fighting forces.[59] Simultaneously the growing humiliation of China by the Western powers in the 1839-1860 period exposed the sagging empire as a kind of "paper tiger." The signing of the unequal treaties and the increasing presence of foreigners especially the missionaries in the interior coupled with the central government's inability to control them, angered some.
The immense size and scope of the Taiping and Nien Rebellions clearly revealed the basic decay of the Chinese bureaucracy and prompted ambitious people like Ma Hua-lung, the New Teaching leader in Ninghsia, Kansu to plot for power. Local problems were compounded because the Peking regime when faced by the monumental mid-century rebellions set as the first priority to crush the Taiping and Nien. Therefore funds normally routed to Kansu and Chinese Turkestan evaporated.[60]

## The Tributary System and Its Connection to the Northwest

The Muslim rebellions in Chinese Turkestan (1864-1878) may be viewed from the perspective of tributary relations. Necessity forced China into contact with peoples bordering her fringes, and her hierarchically-conceived and organized ties with them usually reflected her cultural predominance as well as her political influence. Military might also played an important part in any arrangement. When strong the tributary system functioned in a relatively smooth manner. Yet if China's strength visibly deteriorated the traditional modes might operate differently.61

Chinese power flowed into and out of Chinese Turestan and Central Asia. In the 1750s, for example, the Ch'ing armies swept into Zungharia then shattered the Oyirad (Kalmyk Mongol) empire centered in the Ili Valley thus terminating a sixty year period of intermittent warfare between these two groups.62 Chinese troops later captured two khoja (Muslim holy men) brothers of the Naqshbandiyya tariqat (brotherhood).63 One brother journeyed to Peking as a hostage while the other returned to Alti Shahr to rule. The Peking hostage escaped from captivity, returned to join his brother, then jointly the two ignited a military action against the occupying armies. Soon the Ch'ing forces recovered from their initial surprise conducted an expedition into Alti Shahr, crushed the khoja-led resistance, killed both brothers and rapidly incorporated the rest of Chinese Turkestan into the empire.64

During and after this conquest the Ch'ing armies ranged throughout the adjoining Central Asian territories establishing tributary relations with many of the petty kingdoms there. In the succeeding fifty years the Kokand, Bukhara, and Khiva khanates appeared in the area that later became known as Russian Turkestan. Kokand's close proximity to the Ch'ing empire made it the most influential of the three khanates.65 In several respects the growing unrest in Alti Shahr during and after the second decade of the nineteenth century reflects the ascendency of Kokand and its corresponding influence across the border as well as the decline of Ch'ing control there.

Following their eighteenth century conquest of the Northwest, the Manchu regime demanded that the Kokandian ruler submit to their Ch'ing government like a tributary vassal and the latter ruler complied owing in part to its relatively weak political position. In general, however, the Central Asians regarded tributary relations as de facto trading ventures controlled by the Chinese.66 Thus not only did the Kokandian increase his kingdom's wealth and power through lucrative trading ventures he skillfully used Ch'ing support to strengthen his position at the other khanates expense.67 Kokandian influence eventually grew so powerful that in 1798 its ruler began intriguing in Alti Shahr's political situation. Later during the 1820s this Muslim state supported Khoja Jehangir, grandson of Khoja Burhan-al-din one of the two above-mentioned khoja brothers who perished in the fighting against the Ch'ing in 1758.68 After several years of skirmishing and ineffective fighting the Manchu forces tricked then captured Jehangir.69 Other khojas from the same line sparked renewed troubles in 1846, 1857, and played a decisive part in starting the great rebellion of 1864.70

Since many trade routes between Russia and China passed through Kokand she profited from her control of the trade that passed along them. The Ch'ing government attempted to undermine the Kokandian position by sealing the frontier next to Kokand and urging traders arriving in China to seek future alternate routes. The Kokandians responded to this maneuvering by raiding Alti Shahr in 1830 and seizing sizeable quantities of treasure. The Manchus who quickly realized their helpless military situation in Alti Shahr eventually placated the Kokandians by granting them highly profitable trading rights in the region. Thus the Ch'ing court responded in a traditional if not realistic manner. Other enticements dangled before the Kokandian ruler included the granting of the authority to monitor and thereby control all foreigners stationed in Alti Shahr. The Khan also pressed the Manchus for permission to tax merchants there and upon learning of their refusal to yield further launched new raiding expeditions.[71] Kokand continued to menace Chinese Turkestan until its own conquest by the Russians in 1876.

For several decades prior to the mid-nineteenth century Muslim rebellions both Great Britain and Tsarist Russia displayed an active interest in Chinese Turkestan. Great Britain repeatedly dispatched agents northward from her Indian base into Turkestan.[72] William Moorcroft in the second decade of the nineteenth century, for example, spent several months trading there and gathering information. He accumulated large quantities of detailed data on towns, distances between them, weather conditions, ethnographical features, and economic trends. Moorcroft's presence rather alarmed the Manchus who feared that he might seek an alliance with Muslim forces threatening Alti Shahr. Moorcroft was murdered in Ladakh, and British interest in that region waned until the late 1860s.[73]

Russia's frontier troops actively explored the Ili Valley area in the 1840s.[74] Soon thereafter they pressured the Manchus to open Chinese Turkestan to direct Russian trading ventures. The Ch'ing court initially ignored the Russians then reversed itself by concluding the Kuldja Trade Agreement in 1850. This treaty one of the few relatively "equal" documents that the Chinese government signed in the nineteenth century stated that the Russians could send an unlimited number of caravans to Zungharia for six months each year provided that all were accompanied by a Ch'ing military escort.[75] Shortly thereafter the Russians and British began a vigorously competitive mapping operation of the area with the latter relying on Indian Muslims for that task.[76] Following the Tsarist conquest of the Central Asian khanates in the 1860s and 1870s, the tributary system ceased to function in that area and simple power relations prevailed.[77]

## Interest Groups in Northwest China

Analyzing Northwest China's Muslim rebellions (1862-1878) from an interest group perspective is fruitful for several reasons. China's rulers be they Han Chinese, Mongol, or Manchu frequently played off the various groups and ethnic peoples against one another. Tibetans and Mongols, for example, were employed to put down Muslim revolts.[78] Although the Manchus opposed the Han Chinese to the Muslims and Tibetans, these rulers became increasingly sinified and frequently identified with the Han Chinese majority with respect to other minority peoples.[79] Among the Muslims themselves one's identification with one's ethnic origins, geographical location or religious group rather than larger Islamic elements tended to weaken Muslim rebellions against the government. Tso Tsung-t'ang capitalized on the above-mentioned differences by using Tibetans, Mongols, and tribes like the Ch'iang against the Muslim rebels in the 1868-1880 period.[80] Tso also successfully divided the Muslim forces by rewarding those who "sincerely" switched sides and then fought against their co-religionists.[81]

One's allegiance to a particular interest group could be complex in motivation and subject to change. If Muslim rebels scored many early successes against the government or if the government indiscriminately massacred Muslims then the Holy War call carried great appeal.[82] Victories by the regime's forces on the other hand might cause Muslims to desert and return to their native towns or tribal groups.[83] Below the important ethnic groups in the Northwest will be initially considered exclusive of the Muslims. The latter, their history and underlying differences will be treated in subsequent passages.

The Mongols are one important group in Northwest China. Traditionally from the thirteenth century they plagued rulers of China and conquered the empire for nearly one century. One source noted that Kansu became an important administrative and military territory for the Chinese who used it as a barrier between the Mongols in the North and the Tibetans in the South.[84] Near the end of the Ming dynasty under the influence of Hsiao Ta-heng, a Chinese official there, a new policy developed. Hsiao implemented a complex program of sending the Ordos Mongols gifts, fortifying strategic points near their base areas, holding military exercises near the frontier, and keeping a fund of accurate, current information about them. Although the Ming government did not fully benefit from this policy, the Ordos Mongols did submit to the Manchus then persuaded other Mongols to follow their example. The Mongol Banner system grew from this nucleus.[85] Other Mongol groups to the West, however, became strong about the same time as the Manchus but succumbed to the Ch'ien-lung emperor's armies in the 1750s.

The Mongols' relationship with the Muslims ranged from friendliness to antipathy and even overt hostility. This latter sentiment emanated from the Muslim's usual disdain for Buddhism, the main religion of the Mongols.[86] Another element of antagonism stemmed from the constant raiding of various Mongol encampments by the Islamic Tungans who will be considered as a distinct group below.[87] In Chinese Turkestan another type of conflict occurred between the Kirgiz and Kazakhs (Turkic nomads who were Muslim) against the Kalmyk Mongols. This mutual antagonism resulted largely from the economic competition generated from all three groups who tended the same kinds of herds. Here as well religious factors served to reinforce the rivalry.[88] Thus when the Muslims rebelled against the central government in the 1860s, most feelings of potential sympathy which the Muslims and Mongols might have felt for each other because of their common oppression by the state did not materialize.[89] Often instead the aroused fervor of the Islamic forces spared neither the hated Chinese nor the Mongols from loss of life or destruction of property. Again Tso Tsung-t'ang using his knowledge of Chinese military history combined with his knowledge of the existing situation of ethnic complexity frequently employed the Mongols to assist in his Northwestern campaigns.[90] It should also be noted that some Mongols did go over to Islam. One example of the conversion of a whole tribe of Mongols by a Muslim priest will be presented in the next chapter. In addition the Tunghsiang Muslims who were Mongolian and lived in Central Kansu near the town of Hochow (Lin-hsia) practiced a form of Islam which contained certain Buddhistic elements. They kept poultry and also worked in local handicraft industries. Little information about this group exists except that they seemed to keep to themselves save for some raiding expeditions against other groups in Shensi and Kansu.[91]

Another minority people of some importance in Kansu was the Monguors, a tribe with Mongol and Turkic ethnic characteristics. They spoke a Mongol dialect and worshipped as Buddhists.[92] Historically the Monguors supported the central government during the Ming and Ch'ing dynasties. They submitted to the Ming in 1371, and in the Ch'ing era were granted permission to be ruled by their own leaders and fought bravely in assisting the Manchus defeat the Muslim rebellions of 1781, 1784, and 1862-1873. In the latter campaign, however, the Monguors concentrated on defending their own territory against the rebel Muslims.[93]

The Manchus and ethnically-related tribes also played a role in Chinese Turkestan during the eighteenth and nineteenth centuries. Following the Ch'ien-lung emperor's devastating conquest of Zungharia in the mid-eighteenth century much of the region was depopulated. To remedy that situation, provide a degree of stability, and augment the garrison forces, the Ch'ien-lung emperor transferred large numbers of Sibos, Solons, Daurs, and Manchus from the Northeast. Most resided in the Ili area and perished in or fled from the Muslim uprisings of the 1860s. A few hundred survived into the twentieth century.[94]

Among the Han Chinese residing in Northwest China, particularly in Shensi and Kansu, the local elites seemed especially hostile toward the Muslims because of several factors. As "guardians" of Confucianism these Han Chinese resented the "unorthodox" ways of the Muslims as well as the growing number of converts to that faith from the Chinese community.[95] Their social position in the mixed Muslim-Chinese areas seemed challenged by the immense power and prestige wielded by the Muslim religious leaders. Thus these elites remained antagonistic and easily provoked by incidents growing from cultural conflicts. On such occasions they would mobilize the Han Chinese to pressure the local officials to repress the Muslims. Often the latter obliged.[96]

Although more numerous in Kansu than in Shensi or Chinese Turkestan, the Tibetans were an important influence in Northwest China. In religious terms they were largely Buddhist like the Mongols and some Han Chinese and thus faced the Muslim's contempt and hostility. Some small numbers of Tibetans did convert to Islam over the centuries. Like the various Islamic peoples the Tibetans experienced general discrimination by the central government's bureaucrats.[97] These officials did as a general policy attempt whenever possible to forestall close relations between the Tibetans and other minority groups by employing the Tibetans as soldiers against the others in times of political unrest.[98] Thus cooperation between the Tibetans and Muslims failed to materialize during the 1862-1878 rebellions, but unprotected Chinese settlements or travelers might be subjected to plunder by the Tibetans.

Muslims appeared in China during the T'ang dynasty mainly as traders,[99] although some Arab and Uighur troops assisted the Chinese emperor in regaining political power during the An Lu-shan rebellion (775-763).[100] Commercial relations between the Arabs and Chinese began long before that time and continued into the Sung period and after. Many Muslim merchants sailed to Canton crossing the Indian Ocean and the South China Sea while others traveled by the land routes along the Silk Roads through Central Asia. Still more passed through India and Yunnan to China Proper. At those early times in Chinese-Muslim relations the Muslims used medicines, perfumes, and jade as items for trade while residing in special sections of cities like Canton and Yangchow.[101]

Commercial activity intensified in the Sung era but Islam did not become politically and demographically important until the Yuan period.[102] During that time the Mongols conquered North and then later South China. As they were a minority ruling tens of millions of Chinese, the Mongols welcomed non-Chinese into their government. Many Central Asian Muslims joined the government as financial administrators, tax collectors, and astronomers to name but a few. In their positions as tax collectors and money lenders the Muslims came into close contact with the Chinese and began to experience growing Chinese resentment. The primary basis for Chinese-Muslim hostility seemed to be economic rather than religious at that time.[103] Muslims also began to settle in China in larger numbers in the Yuan period. A Mongol prince who commanded a sizeable number of troops stationed in Kansu converted to Islam and his army followed his example.[104] In Southwest China large numbers of Muslims also settled down on a permanent basis. One reason for this was that the province of Yunnan had been recently conquered by the Mongols and was ruled by a Muslim who served as the province's first governor.[105]

A most important Islamic group appeared in Northwest China during the Yuan and Ming periods, the Tungans. This Islamic sub-group inhabited Eastern Kansu in large numbers and might be found scattered in pockets throughout the empire. Historically they probably were among the earliest Muslim inhabitants of China's Northwest then by the Ming period they had lost much of their non-Chinese characteristics. The gradual Sinification process came about through intermarriage with Han Chinese women and the adoption of Han Chinese children; the latter process being successful in times of famine and economic hardship. After the Ch'ien-lung emperor's conquest of Zungharia in the 1750s many Tungans migrated to the Western regions in Chinese Turkestan where they will be found today. The Tungans became politically active in the mid-nineteenth century in the Northwest; and Ma Hua-lung one of the most important religious-political leaders in the 1862-1878 period was a Tungan. Tungans were also known as the Hui-hui or the Sino-Muslims.[106]

A brief survey of the Chinese treatment of the Muslims reveals that their merchants frequently dwelled in segregated portions of the commercial centers. They they lived according to their own customs and beliefs. Despite the tensions noted above China's rulers usually left the Muslims alone in their own segregated quarters. Segregated living seemed to be voluntary in China as elsewhere in Central Asia for hundreds of years under many regimes. In China legal cases involving Muslims alone were handled by Muslim judges.[107] Usually the rulers of China practiced religious toleration though at times Muslims were not permitted to slaughter animals according to their traditional religious practices.[108] They were usually permitted to build mosques in the empire.[109] One extreme negative reaction by the Chinese regarding the Muslims came during the Huang Ch'ao rebellion (874-884) when thousands of Muslims and other peoples were massacred by the Chinese rebels. Later during the Ming dynasty two anti-Islamic features did appear. The practice of referring to the Muslims by using characters with the dog radical occurred then reflecting intensely negative attitudes about them held by some.[110] Similarly the central government issued regulations making it more difficult for Muslims to marry the Han Chinese.[111]

Although these trends commenced in the Ming it is really during the succeeding Manchu period that anti-Muslim activities intensified. The use of the dog radical became quite widespread and lesser officials in the government especially in the border areas discriminated against the Muslims in legal decisions and tax assessment cases. The Yung-cheng emperor admitted that his officials in Muslim-inhabited areas often urged him to oppress the Muslims. This admission came in an imperial proclamation refusing to lift a previous ban on killing beef in the empire. When the Muslims protested his ban he said in the best autocratic manner that all subjects were his children who must obey the laws. He added that he refused to listen to those officials who urged him to proscribe Islam or sanction anti-Muslim activities.[112] Even then the Yung-cheng emperor's ban caused much hardship for the Muslims because beef was a main part of their diet owing to the religious proscription on their eating of pork. Other elements of the Manchu-Muslim interaction relating to the New Teaching movement will be discussed below.

As has been seen above geographical conditions reflected in the immense distances between centers, the deserts and mountains coupled with poor communications reinforced local peoples' tendencies to identify with their native towns or cities.[113] Despite this aspect some general features of the social patterns of Muslims dwelling in Shensi and Kansu do exist. The mosque, for example, was often the community's nerve center. When the size of a village exceeded the distance necessary to hear the traditional call to daily worship then a new center would form. In this cell-like dividing process the mosque corresponds to the nucleus. Within each Muslim territory the common faith often solidified the working relationships of the members into a cohesive socio-economic unit.[114]

Each locality possessed two different sets of leaders: one religious and the other administrative. The religious group dealt with questions concerning Islam and often provided a degree of education for the inhabitants.[115] Power held by this religious leader (akhund) varied with the region, and in Kansu, for example, he retained considerable influence both as an administrator and spiritual counsellor.[116] The council of village elders generally acted as the local administrators; and as elected leaders they concern themselves with economic matters such as the securing of funds to maintain the mosque. They often hired the akhund for fixed time periods and selected new religious leaders when necessary. Thus in this system strong personalities might be prevented from exerting complete control over the village.[117]

In Chinese Turkestan religious figures also tended to be closely identified with their communities. A Yarkand citizen usually saw himself as a Yarkandi rather than a Muslim. He would be suspicious or contemptuous of Muslims from Kashgar or Khotan. Subjects of those cities felt similarly of course.[118] A religious leader's influence thus was often confined to the place of his birth.[119] The Chinese perpetuated this tendency by appointing local administrators, the above-mentioned begs.[120] Tso Tsung-t'ang favored the retention of the beg system despite the tradition of begs acting like tyrants. To forestall the latter situation Tso insisted that the begs be carefully watched and therefore controlled by using the tsung-ho ming-shih technique of the statecraft tradition. He ultimately preferred the establishment of a provincial administration for Chinese Turkestan.[121]

The practice of segregating Muslims away from other peoples including the Han Chinese stemmed from many things. Historically as noted above Muslims grouped themselves in sections of Chinese cities. Partly it emanated from the tendency of the mosque-dominated village to exclude or limit non-Islamic groups. Inter-group hostility or rivalry must have strengthened these occurrences. Han Chinese elites frequently urged local officials to move the Muslims elsewhere.[122] After Muslim rebellions in the Ch'ien-lung era hatreds seemed to multiply and the desire to revenge the killing of a father or brother passed from generation to generation.[123] Tso and others argued that the Muslims preferred to live apart welcoming only converts. Isolation was a way of life as well as mind.[124]

Ethnic diversity among the Muslims in Kansu and Chinese Turkestan promoted divisions which underlay religious unity.[125] In Kansu, for example, Muslims might speak Chinese, Turkic, Mongol, or other languages.[126] The Salar, a Turkic-speaking people who lived in isolation from other Muslims as well as other groups, generally avoided contact with outsiders. They had a reputation for violent actions emanating from disputes within or without the community. Since some Salars converted to the New Teaching in the eighteenth century they have been involved in many anti-government rebellions.[127]

In Chinese Turkestan differences because of ethnic or linguistic divergences weakened religious and political alliances. The Tungans "Chinese" characteristics and their willingness to serve in the local security forces caused their fellow Muslims to distrust and hate them. Nevertheless the Tungans nourished a hatred for the "heathen" Manchus and Chinese.[128] Thus although the Tungans initiated many revolts in the 1860s against the central government and succeeded in overturning its rule, they and their Uighur (Taranchi Muslim) allies quarreled and ended fighting each other.[129] On occasion the Tungans and Uighurs would rise in rebellion but the Uighurs would switch sides and support the Chinese instead.[130]

The Uighurs were the most populous group in Chinese Turkestan. They spoke a Turkic dialect. Some were sent to the Ili Valley in the eighteenth century by the Ch'ing regime in the hope that they would use their agricultural skills to rehabilitate that devastated area.[131] The Uighurs distrusted their Tungan co-religionists and frequently betrayed tham thus gaining a reputation for selling out their allies among the other Muslim groups.[132]

In Shensi, Kansu, and Chinese Turkestan many elements promoted localism and division. There seemed to be a lack of a united frontier spirit wherein communities would band together to confront major problems. Kansu and Chinese Turkestan in particular possessed a complex array of ethnic groups who spoke different languages, adhered to contrasting cultural practices, exhibited diverse racial characteristics, or worshipped different deities. These features intensified mutual suspicions and local cohesion. Despite a degree of economic interchange such commercial relationships rarely united these peoples.[133] In the resulting fragmented situation Muslims might join in an initial outburst of anti-governmental activity but might not sustain their support. Rarely within these Northwestern provinces did the loyalties of the numerous ethnic groups extend beyond the limits of one local or regional center. In the next chapter the tension between fragmentation brought by the interest groups and the networks established within the Sufi brotherhoods will be explored.

CHAPTER V

THE NEW TEACHING (HSIN CHIAO) MOVEMENT AND ITS ROLE IN
THE NORTHWEST MUSLIM REBELLIONS OF 1862-1878

Chinese Islam has many important dates, events, and people associated with it; one major development came in the 1760s when Ma Ming-hsin founded the Hsin Chiao, an Islamic movement with Sufi characteristics and a West Asian character. For the next century Ma and his successors led or participated in several anti-governmental uprisings in which millions perished and large areas of Shensi, Kansu, and Chinese Turkestan experienced extensive, lasting damage. Europeans traveling there in the latter nineteenth and early twentieth centuries saw many ruined villages as well as whole areas devoid of human habitation.

One feature of Ma Ming-hsin's order was its Central Asian character. Ma and his grandfather traveled from their Kansu home to Central Asia where they visited several major Islamic centers. After a several year stay there they returned to Kansu where Ma began preaching his New Teaching among the Salars in the early 1760s. Thereafter his Hsin Chiao manifested characteristics of West Asian Sufism such as veneration of saints, meditation at tombs, and wonder-working. A central feature of the Hsin Chiao was the use of jahr (vocalization) in the dhikr (remembrance) which horrified the established Islamic group known as the Lao Chiao (Old Teaching). Religious dissention ensued and by 1781 the killing of several Muslims finally precipitated governmental intervention on the side of the Old Teaching. Local officials arrested Ma Ming-hsin sparking his followers to rebel and surround the city where he was held. The terrified officials hastily executed Ma then managed to defeat his adherents after some sharp fighting. Leadership of the order passed to many other people over the several years period into the mid-nineteenth century. At that time Ma Hua-lung, the Hsin Chiao head joined the Muslim rebellions of the 1860s and 1870s. Like his predecessor, Ma Ming-hsin, Ma Hua-lung was eventually captured, executed, and his headquarters destroyed; this crippled the Hsin Chiao movement for years.

To understand the New Teaching's initial success and ultimate failure in mobilizing Muslims in a permanent way, the complex socio-economic order in Kansu and Zungharia might be analyzed in terms of a network interest-group mode.[1] Strong personalities coupled with success in battle could rally thousands of discontented Muslims in a brief time. At least eighteen different Muslim groups were active in Shensi alone. As noted above, however, deep divisions underlay the unity of the various Muslin groups. Ultimately the Han Chinese Commander, Tso Tsung-t'ang, recognized the interest-group nature of Northwest China's various groups and effectively employed it against the New Teaching rebels as well as other Muslim groups there.

## Important Features of Central Asian Islam

Scholars like J. Spencer Trimingham have shown how the Sufi tariqats (brotherhoods) such as the Qadiriyya, Naqshbandiyya, and Yasawiyya played a crucial part in spreading Islam to non-Arab peoples. Relying on religious fervor rather than physical force dervishes journeyed to and lived among nomadic peoples like the Kirgiz.[2] One example illustrating this process concerns an akhund of the Hufeye (Khufiyya or Naqshabandiyya) tariqat. Determined to lead the Mongols to the "true" way and thus save them, this person assumed the guise of a veterinarian. He learned Mongol, moved to live among one Mongol tribe, slowly gained their trust, and gained a position of trust among them. Finally the akhund succeeded in making Islam the dominant religious force among them.[3]

To reach the less-educated Central Asian peoples some dervishes employed many techniques including magic[4] Other Sufis went beyond illusionary practices to establish themselves as saints with special links to Allah. To demonstrate their power Sufis performed miraculous acts like curing illnesses, restoring fertility in people, and predicting the future.[5] Once accepted by a group as a wali (saint), his authority and judgement often passed beyond dispute.[6] Therefore the saint in Central Asia approximated the shaman, that ancient yet still powerful religious figure in Central and Northern Asia.[7] In certain instances Muslim saints' tombs might be located on holy sites previously venerated by Buddhists.[8] This ability of Islam to enwrap itself with traditional and familiar sacred patterns greatly facilitated its propagation.

After spreading Islam in Central Asia the wandering dervishes played other social roles. Their continuing travel tended to reinforce the links that Muslims in remote towns or villages maintained with the rest of the Islamic world. More importantly as Hadji (pilgrims who had been to Mecca) they were welcomed and honored as guests in the homes or caravanserais (hostels) of villages or oasis centers. Many hostels became schools, poor grounds, storehouses, and even banks. Some developed into key economic and social centers.[9] If the dervishes were unable to earn a livelihood teaching in a caravanserai, they could still secure money by giving fatiha (blessings), nefes (holy breath), writing spells, or casting out demons for the faithful.[10] New or revivalist movements could be easily spread in Central Asia by these wanderers.[11]

Some holy men established permanent residences in particular spots where they were born, well-known, or especially venerated. When exceptionally pious a Sufi might found his own order, a branch of a parent tariqat located in Mecca, Bukhara, Kashgar, or Yarkand. Bukhara, for centuries a key state of Central Asian Islam, became particularly eminent in the late eighteenth and nineteenth centuries owing to the exceptional piety of its ruling emirs. Muslim pilgrims traveled to Bukhara from all over Asia including China, and in some places a pilgrimage to Bukhara might replace one to Mecca.[12] Following these pilgrims' deaths their burial sites might become respected as holy places. Death therefore did not necessarily diminish a saint's stature because his shrine became a storehouse of the power manifested during his lifetime.[13] Indeed his reputation may grow if the shrine developed into a pilgrimage site where Muslims could journey for relief from illnesses or personal misfortunes and afflications. One traveler reported journeying from Damascus to a tomb in Chinese Turkestan.[14]

Under certain conditions such as a saint's baraka (power) being very strong or the continued relevance of his teachings over time then the shrine's custodian (mutawali) could himself become an important figure. Pilgrims' contributions could make them wealthy and important members of a community.[15] On occasion shrine guardians did use their economic and social positions to start rebellions against the Chinese government.[16]

One intriguing development relating to various Muslim saints' tombs in Central Asia should be noted. Over a period of time some shrines came to be differentiated in the local people's eyes concerning the types of illnesses believed to receive beneficial treatment from a trip there. The mazar (shrine) of Hazret i bouva, for example, attracted those suffering from kidney diseases while Muslims plagued with various skin disorders would travel to Mazar Kottour for relief.[17] Mazar Koktounkyk-Ata gained a reputation for its success in dealing with tuberculosis.[18] Other people with swellings, headaches, paralyses, leprosy, and even rabies depended on specific shrines to alleviate their afflictions.[19]

Apart from disease sufferers some Central Asian mazars attracted specific clientele while possibly excluding all others. Women alone, for example, were welcomed to certain shrines.[20] One's occupation might even be the distinguishing feature in the attraction to a specific holy place because fishermen frequented one mazar while that of Bibi Paradous favored the cobblers.[21] Specific animal groups even received welcomes at certain tombs in that one saint was known as the "father of cats."[22] In Chinese

Turkestan a particular holy spot came to be associated with pigeons, a sanctuary for those birds as well as for human beings.[23]

The social structure of the Sufi brotherhoods could provide numerous benefits for the member. Often each social or economic unit like workers' guilds would have specific Sufi lodges associated with them. On occasion a village, town, or region might have a single tariqat binding them together. In such circumstances the villager might certainly have gained some security from the fact that his individual fate was bound up with that of the brotherhood membership who most likely would assist him in times of need. The common veneration of a saint added a personal touch of intimacy because each disciple had to go periodically and pay respects to this leader. Other benefits for the faithful might come if the saint were successful in curing afflictions, granting wishes, or restoring fertility.[24] In these circumstances the leader's hold on his group would be extremely firm and could lead to affluence on the leader's part because of the obligatory financial contributions from his followers or for varied forms of service.

The successful saint conversely needed to remain highly sensitive to the individual and collective needs of his adherents. He should be obliged to place himself at their disposal and be ready to assist them no matter what the cost in terms of money, time, or energy to himself.[25] The saint should, for example, settle disputes between different families or religious groups. When his subordinates suffered from conditions of political oppression the saint might be pressured to intervene on their behalf, and if intervention failed then the saint might even feel compelled to foment a rebellion.[26] Of course much depended on the will and ability of the religious leader himself. Certainly the Central Asian brotherhoods did play significant political roles to the extent that even strong political leaders like Tamerlane in Central Asia and Yakub Beg in Kashgaria devoted considerable attention to cultivating the sympathy and support of the Sufi orders.[27] They were aware that the tariqats' social cohesiveness could translate into significant oppositional forces.[28]

One important complex of Naqshabandi orders centering on Kashgar and Yarkand in Alti Shahr, the Afaqiyya and the Ishaqiyya, merits consideration both for their Central Asian characteristics as well as their connections to Sufi orders in Kansu. The founder, Ahmad Kasani or the Makhdum-i A'zam was a direct descendant of the Prophet, Muhammed.[29] The Makhdum-i A'zam himself renowned for unusual piety and support of Islam married Bibi-i Kashgari, a direct descendant of the deeply-venerated patriarch of Kashgarian Islam, Sultan Bughra Khan Ghazi.[30] The Makhdum-i A'zam often wandered from oasis to oasis in Central Asia seeking converts. His sons followed his example and achieved great success in Alti Shahr. Their successful proselytization there brought numerous followers and a religious position of enormous scope which began to assume a political nature. Consequently the khoja lines of the Makhdum-i A'zam began to advise the existing leadership in Alti Shahr on state as well as religious matter in the late sixteenth century then assumed direct political rule in the early seventeenth century.[31] The khojas began filling a political vacuum created by the decline of the Shibanid dynasty in the sixteenth century.[32]

One key figure in the rise of one branch of these Naqshabandi khojas was Hazrat Afaq, a third generation descendant of the Makhdum-i A'zam. Afaq's power base centered on the important city of Kashgar where his tomb came to be located. Indeed Afaq's reputation grew throughout Turkestan during his life; after his death, Afaq's tomb attracted pilgrims from distant parts of the Islamic world.[33] Afaq himself proved to be a great traveler and journeyed to Sining in northeastern Tibet in 1671 where he preached then gained the adherence of a Muslim whose son, Ma Lai-ch'ih played an important role in the spread of the Naqshbandi tariqat throughout that region. By the mid-eighteenth century the Naqshbandiyya was the most influential Sufi order in that part of the Northwest.[34] The religious basis for Afaq's venerated position developed during his lifetime when many wonders (kiramat) became attached to his reputation. Afaq reportedly even possessed the ability "to restore the dead back to life," and at the height of his fame people danced wildly or shouted exuberantly when he appeared in public.[35]

The increasing religious and political influence of these Alti Shahr khojas helped lead to the formation of rival factions within this complex by the time of the founder's death. One faction, Ishaniyya, formed around the Ishan-i Kalan (Muhammad Amin), the Makhdum-i A'zam and Afaq emerged as its most important leader. This group was alternately known as the Afaqiyya or the White Mountain Faction. The second faction was founded by Ishaq Wali (Ishaqiyya or Black Mountain Faction), the youngest son of the Makhdum-i A'zam. Like Afaq, Ishaq Wali performed kiramat; he also studied for a time in Bukhara.[36] The Ishaqiyya's religious center and political base was Yarkand, a city which traditionally rivaled Kashgar.[37] Apart from showing the intertwining of religion and politics as well as how political-religious rivalries can be sharpened and maintained by centering on urban areas; the Afaqiyya-Ishaqiyya clashes also had personality aspects associated with them. These characteristics will also be investigated concerning the New and Old Teaching in Northwest China below.

Although the above-mentioned White-Black Mountain rivalry often weakened the khoja position in Kashgaria, the Afaqiyya managed to expand its influence closer to

China and the Zunghar Mongols by annexing the town of Turfan.[38] To strengthen its position against the rival Ishaqiyya, the Afaqiyya also joined with the Zunghars.[39] These ties did lead to Afaqi dominance in Alti Shahr but when the Zunghars warred with the Manchu-ruled Chinese government in the mid-eighteenth century as noted above, the Afaqiyya became drawn into that larger conflict. Finally the Ch'ien-lung emperor's armies destroyed both the Zunghar Mongols and the Afaqi-led rebellions in Alti Shahr. Then the Ch'ing regime ousted the Afaqi line in Alti Shahr.[40]

## The Hsin Chiao in Kansu (1761-1871)

The history of brotherhoods, saint veneration, and meditation at tombs in China is quite long and complex.[41] The most crucial development, however, relating to the active formation of religious factionalism in China Proper was the founding of the New Teaching movement by Ma Ming-hsin in Kansu during the 1760s.[42] Ma Ming-hsin (Muhammad Amin), a Muslim from Anting,[43] Kansu journeyed to the West in the mid-eighteenth century.[44] Two recently-discovered sources state that Ma when seven traveled with his grandfather to Bukhara where they studied for a time. They resumed their journey, visited other places in Asia then returned home.[45] Another source indicated that Ma visited Samarkand as well as Bukhara;[46] yet another argued that Ma only went to Kashgar, Yarkand, and other cities in Alti Shahr then returned home to Kansu.[47] These views are not necessarily incompatible because Ma's trip to Western Asia could certainly have included stops in Samarkand, Kashgar, and Yarkand. After returning to Kansu for a time, Ma Ming-hsin was invited to propagate his new school of Sufism among the Salar Turks of Hsun-hua, Kansu.[48] Many Salars received Ma and his teachings quite well, and he converted many of them. Over the next two decades Ma's influence spread throughout Kansu, other parts of Northwest China, Chihli, and Shantung.[49]

Central to Ma Ming-hsin's teaching was the practice of vocalizing in the dhikr (pan-k'o che-ho-lai-yeh),[50] and his group was called the Jahriyya.[51] One author writing about Islamic factions in Kansu noted that often the most "trivial matters" divided the Muslims into dissenting religious groups.[52] Two things must be said about that statement. One of the most important injunctions for all Muslims is to pray five times per day. To be effective the prayers must be properly performed otherwise the person praying will commit serious offenses against the faith. Quarrels regarding the manner of performing the dhikr have caused many Sufi divisions over the centuries.[53] Another dimension to this is that often the local believers may be ignorant, superstitious people for whom trivial matters of practicing the ritual correctly are vital concerns. Mistakes could lead to misfortunes or very bad luck. Similar beliefs animated religious people in Russia as well as in China.54

Properly identifying the Hsin Chiao remains a problem which plagues scholars even today. Nakada Yoshinobu in 1959, for example, noted that the Hsin Chiao of Ma Ming-hsin may have been a branch of the Yasawi tariqat because he cited Eugene Schuyler's identification of a group known as the Jahriyya which was reportedly founded by Ahmad Yasawi. The name Jahriyya was another term for the Hsin Chiao in China.55 This evidence seems to be too circumstantial, however. T'ang Chen-yu offered many possible identifications for the Hsin Chiao: as a Yasawi tariqat, as a Naqshbandi tariqat, and as an order originating in Yemen.56 Again there was little evidence marshalled to support any designation. Joseph Fletcher's latest article in 1977, argued that Ma Ming-hsin probably traced his line (isnad) back to Ahmad Yasawi as well as to Baha Naqshband then added that one branch of the Naqshbandiyya emphasized vocalization in the dhikr like that of Ma Ming-hsin.57 Some scholars have focused on the reforming nature of the New Teaching to label it as a Wahhabi movement.58 This designation seems incorrect in two important respects. The Wahhabi violently opposed meditation at saints' tombs something characteristic of the New Teaching.59 Similarly the Wahhabi strongly objected to the use of dancing and active behavior by religious adherents during the dhikr.60

In his treatment of the Jahriyya, Schuyler noted that it was the most militant order in Central Asia.61 If this assertion has some basis in fact then when it spread to the Salars and Tungans both of whom were viewed by observers as volatile groups, the New Teaching's seemingly activist, combative nature becomes more readily understandable.

Early in 1781, serious quarrels erupted between the New Teaching and an opposition group known as the Old Teaching. The main cause of dissension between the New and Old groups was Ma Ming-hsin's insistence of vocalization in the dhikr because the Old Teaching insisted on a silent dhikr (pan-k'o hu-fei-yeh).62 Khufiyya another form of Hufeiyeh was both the name of the Old Teaching and the Naqshbandi tariqat in China as well as Central Asia.63 Therefore since the name and practice of the dhikr are identical it is safe to state that the Old Teaching should be equated with a Naqshbandi tariqat.64 During the above-mentioned fighting between the New and Old Teaching in 1781 scores of Muslims died and the Manchu government intervened. Their swift response succeeded because they captured Ma Ming-hsin who was taken to the provincial capital, Lanchow. Shortly thereafter, however, the New Teaching members rallied, defeated the government's forces in the surrounding area then moved to besiege Lanchow, demanding Ma Ming-hsin's release. Apparently these swift developments unsettled the provincial officials because they hastily executed Ma.[65] Fighting continued for some months after Ma's death but concluded after the government mobilized sufficient funds to overwhelm the New Teaching army.[66]

Although the Manchus considered the Kansu situation pacified, T'ien Wu, an akhund of the New Teaching from Eastern Kansu plotted to avenge Ma Ming-hsin and rebelled in 1784. This effort after several initial successes eventually succumbed to the larger numbers and superior resources of the Ch'ing government. T'ien Wu perished in the fighting.[67] After this second instance of trouble involving the New Teaching, the Ch'ien-lung emperor condemned all rebellious Hsin Chiao members and banned its spread. He further ordered that Muslim teachers should not enter China.[68] In addition:

> The Kansu provincial authorities prohibited the conversion of non-Muslims to Islam, forbade Muslims to go outside their own villages for prayers, barred preachers from coming from the outside to teach, prohibited Muslims from adopting non-Muslim babies, brought to a halt the construction of new mosques, and enjoined the Muslims not to bring "false suit" against one another.[69]

These measures when coupled with the sizeable losses among the New Teaching adherents effectively curbed its political activism until the 1860s.

From the 1780s until the 1860s the Hsin Chiao resembled the traditional Chinese secret society in several respects.[70] Both organizations manifested a religious character which tightly bound members to the order as well as to each other. The resulting socio-religious cohesion implied the potential to act in political matters if the group or its members felt threatened by the central government.[71] Similarly the political nature of these groups meant a degree of mutual hostility between them and the regime which would not tolerate the existence of organized oppositional elements. Certainly they had to act or increase their size by means designed not to attract governmental attention. Like many secret societies, when the New Teaching re-emerged into "open" political activity in the 1860s, it played a major role in the Muslim rebellions of that period. Tso Tsung-t'ang studied the history of the New Teaching and ultimately labelled it as a heterodox movement like the White Lotus and other secret societies.[72] Tso ruthlessly suppressed it whenever he got the opportunity during his Northwestern campaigns.[73]

Despite its having to go underground in the face of governmental oppression during the late eighteenth century, the New Teaching movement continued to be active.

The line of leadership was unclear following the death of T'ien Wu owing to the policy of secrecy necessary for survival. Direction of Ma Ming-hsin's Hsin Chiao seems to have passed to Mu Sheng-hua (Mu Pa-pa)[74] who taught then initiated into the Hsin Chiao the grandfather of Ma Hua-lung who was a major figure in the mid-nineteenth century.[75] Little is known about Ma Hua-lung's grandfather except that he probably lived in Chin-chi-pao (Chin-chi-p'u) in Northern Kansu, at one point owing to problems with the Ch'ing regime was exiled to Heilungkiang in Northeast China, and that he was known as the Grand Master of the Shipyard (Ch'uan-ch'ang T'ai-yeh).[76] Again, knowledge about Ma Hua-lung's father, Ma Erh, is equally limited. Ma Erh was also initiated into the New Teaching movement by Mu Pa-pa and Ma Erh became a leader of that underground group. Furthermore he was called pir (lao jen chia or religious head) by the New Teaching adherents, and his tomb was later venerated along with that of his son, Ma Hua-lung in Hung-lo, Ninghsia.[77]

Ma Hua-lung, the next leader of Ma Ming-hsin's Hsin Chiao, rivaled the founder in importance. Ma and his family lived for generations at Chin-chi-pao and were quite wealthy. Owing to this economic status Ma Hua-lang purchased an honorary military title and at another point successfully bribed his way out of a serious legal matter.[78] Some of Ma Hua-lung's financial well being undoubtedly stemmed from his religious position as the New Teaching head because each year all disciples less than 1000 li (more than 300 miles) distant from the Hsin Chiao pir (Ma Hua-lung) had to journey to the pir to pay respects and present appropriate gifts.[79] At the time of Ma Hua-lung's legal troubles much of the bribery money came from New Teaching members in Yunnan and Shensi.[80] Ma Hua-lung like his predecessor, Ma Ming-hsin, also made a journey to the West although little is known about Ma Hua-lung's route.[81]

There is considerable evidence to indicate that Ma Hua-lung continued to follow the religious tradition of Ma Ming-hsin. While alive both men were called saints and pirs[82] and after their deaths their tombs were venerated.[83] Another element common to both was that their disciples had to kneel while paying respects to the pir something that the Old Teaching traditionalists disliked.[84] Both leaders preached that their followers must vocalize during the dhikr with heads waving and used the name, Jahriyya to denote their group.[85] Ma Hua-lung also performed kiramat including curing illnesses, restoring fertility, and foretelling future events.[86] Muslims once hailed Ma Hua-lung as a king and reportedly regarded him as a descendant of Muhammed and his equal.[87]

Ma Hua-lung's considerable religious and economic influence began to assume a definite political character at a time when signs indicated that the Ch'ing dynasty

had declined significantly. The diversion of the central
government's attention to the Taiping, Nien, and South-
western Muslim rebellions coupled with the Anglo-French
sacking of Peking (1860) seemed to present the possibility of permanently seizing territory and create a regional
kingdom.[88] Ma, however, had to take great care to
avoid prematurely forcing the issue of independence as in
the case of Ma Ming-hsin and T'ien Wu. Defeat could mean
personal death as well as the eradication of the power
base. Thus rather than initiate a disastrous course
through an open, direct challenge, Ma Hua-lung preferred
to act secretly in order to weaken the central government's control of Northwestern China. Ma could accomplish
this by covertly aiding various rebel forces while await-
ing the proper time to strike a decisive blow. A similar
strategy was used in the late 1920s during a revolt
in Northwestern China. On that occasion Ma Chung-ying,
a young Muslim under twenty, became troublesome to the
government and fled from probable arrest. The youthful
"rebel" then took refuge in the Sining region under
the protection of Ma Chi, an important local figure. The
latter actively encouraged Ma Chung-ying and his compan-
ions who after some initial victories commanded an armed
force of nearly 50,000 men. Ultimately, Ma Chung-ying
was defeated, but Ma Chi avoided punishment because he had
acted secretly and had not rebelled openly.[89] Ma Hua-lung's
earlier strategy worked effectively in the rebellions'
initial stages because of the Ch'ing government's preoccupation with the Taiping, Nien, and Southwest Muslim
rebellions as well as the combined rebellions in Chinese
Turkestan and Shensi. Much of the dynasty's power there
collapsed. Until Tso Tsung-t'ang's arrival in Shensi in
1867, the government seldom mobilized sufficient forces
even to contain the Muslim rebels.

Initially in the rebellions the fighting assumed
the dimensions of a Muslim-against-Chinese clash rather
than New Teaching against the Chinese. Most evidence indicates that unlike in the seventeenth century when Muslims did cooperate with other anti-regime dissident interest groups, in the nineteenth century the Muslims acted
alone.[90] Mongols, Tibetans, and Han Chinese were equally
attacked and killed by rebel Muslims.[91] Given this situation it later proved relatively easy for Tso Tsung-t'ang
to use other interest groups to defeat the Muslim rebels.

Before turning to the New Teaching movement in Zungharia, a few words should be said about the Hsin Chiao in
the 1870s and after in Kansu. Tso Tsung-t'ang's forces
as will be seen in the next chapter experienced a long,
extremely bitter campaign against Ma Hua-lung's fortress
capital, Chin-chi-pao, then finally captured it along with
Ma Hua-lung and his family in early 1871. Tso did postpone the executions of Ma Hua-lung and other major leaders
in the hope that additional Muslim rebels in Kansu would
surrender. Tso mistakenly thought that Ma Hua-lung's poli-

tical control extended throughout Kansu in a centralized, hierarchical pattern. Finally Tso realized his error and ordered the executions.[92] Most male relatives of Ma were killed, but the Chinese spared his daughter and grandson. The latter, Ma Tsen-wu, was exiled to Yunnan where he stayed for many years before returning to Kansu. Once home Ma Tsen-wu settled near the old Chin-chi-pao headquarters and was recognized by some of the surviving New Teaching members as a pir.[93]

    Ma Hua-lung's daughter also journeyed in exile to Yunnan where she met and married Ma Yuan-chang. This couple spent nearly two decades in Southwest China before returning to Kansu in the late 1880s. There they settled in Chang Chia Ch'uan in Eastern Kansu.[94] Near Chang Chia Ch'uan in a place called Hsuan Hua Kang, the head of Ma Hua-lung was interred; the rest of his body was buried at Wu-chang-pao, the home of Ma Tsen-wu.[95] Like the latter Ma Yuan-chang was recognized as a pir of the New Teaching movement and his power grew spreading to Yunnan, Chinese Turkestan, and other parts of China. Ma was pious, ascetic, and performed kiramat like foretelling the future in the manner of his predecessors.[96] In addition Ma likened himself to a representative of Allah and claimed to be a qutb or axis of the Jahriyya, an eminent position within Islam.[97] Muslims paying respects to him had to kneel in the prescribed manner to show their submissions to his will. Although Chang Chia Ch'uan was described as China's Mecca, Ma's pacific reputation remained untainted by charges of rebelliousness. He worked instead to heal the New-Old Teaching breach. Ma died in late 1920 in an earthquake,[98] and two of his six sons eventually succeeded him, Ma Huei-wu and Ma T'ien-wu. The latter two leaders were still alive in the 1930s.[99] Thus the activist nature of the New Teaching movement seems to have changed in the twentieth century to a more peaceful mode.

    The New Teaching did influence Muslims throughout Chinese Turkestan but was most important in Zungharia. Tariqat-sparked Muslim rebellions against Chinese rule began in 1864 and continued to 1866 with most centers of Chinese power falling under Muslim control. In Zungharia tariqats incited the Tungans to capture Urumchi one of the most important oasis centers in Chinese Turkestan.[100] Ma Hua-lung's strong influence among the Tungans encouraged a local supporter, Su Huan-chang, to invite to Urumchi, T'o-ming, a Muslim leader who recently spent some time in Chin-chi-pao. T'o-ming emerged as the most important leader of the Urumchi Muslim regime and soon brought other oasis centers in Zungharia under his control. In 1869-1870, however, Yakub Beg secured dominance of the Kashgarian rebel forces, expanded toward Zungharia, and engaged the forces loyal to T'o-ming. The latter was defeated and died, severely weakening the Hsin Chiao group's power in that region.[101] After that victory Yakub Beg contented himself with ruling Zungharia through a series of puppet leaders until its reconquest by Tso Tsung-t'ang's forces in 1876.

## Networks and Interest Groups

Our understanding of the New Teaching's rise and fall in Kansu and Zungharia becomes more clear if we apply two analytical tools: the network concept and the interest-group perspective. The latter has been developed in the previous chapter and need not be explored in detail. By networks is meant the interlocking relations between groups, subgroups, and individuals emphasizing their durability, extensiveness, as well as the manner in which they were conceived.[102] Thorough consideration of the network matrices in Kansu and Zungharia is beyond the scope of this study; instead complexes relating to the New Teaching generally and that of Ma Hua-lung specifically will be discussed.

Perhaps the most important method of establishing and maintaining a network of relations in Islam is through traveling. Generally speaking, one of the five major injunctions for the Muslims is that one make a pilgrimage if at all possible at least once in a lifetime. Evidence abounds concerning Muslim pilgrims in and from Central Asia and China. Ma Ming-hsin, for example, traveled in Turkestan and elsewhere in Southwest Asia before returning to China. Ma Hua-lung also traveled to the West while the teacher of his grandfather and father made a pilgrimage to the West.[103] Certain incentives must have encouraged Muslims to travel; generally the pilgrim could expect a welcome, free board, and lodging from Muslim dwellings along the way. In addition on the return trip the Hadji would be especially venerated.[104] The Tungans, Ma Hua-lung was a Tungan, were singled out as sending groups to Mecca on an annual basis.[105] The Salars arrived in Kansu after a long, interrupted journey from Samarkand, probably in the fourteenth century. Robert Shaw, a British merchant and traveler, met a group of Salars in Yarkand in the nineteenth century. They told him much about their brethren in Kansu.[106]

A second dimension to traveling by Muslims included preaching among non-Muslim or Muslim groups. Hazrat Afaq journeyed from Alti Shahr to north-eastern Tibet to proselytize among the peoples there. Ma Ming-hsin went to the Salars in the 1760s and spread his Hsin Chiao among them as well as elsewhere. Once religious communities were established and organized _akhunds_ traveled periodically to strengthen the oft-times fragile ties between the subgroups and the parent order.[107] Evariste Huc came to Kansu in the 1840s and gave a detailed account of a local Muslim community which was visited by an important religious figure. The latter led the local Muslims in a series of prayer sessions lasting for three days then on the final day, a sheep was sacrificed, cooked, and eaten by the gathered worshippers.[108]

The New Teaching seemed to have inherited a traveling tradition which became regularized under Ma Hua-lung. Travel on an annual basis was required of all New Teaching adherents, and Westerners living in Kansu reported meeting many New Teaching disciples on the road.[109]

Journeying was practiced in relation to visiting saints' tombs in China as in Central Asia. Like their Central Asian predecessors, the New Teaching followers also visited the tombs of their eminent saints. Pilgrims traveled from all parts of China to visit the tomb of Ma Ming-hsin.[110] Ma Hua-lung's two tombs also attracted great numbers of pilgrims. This, of course, was natural as his power was quite strong in his own lifetime then continued after his death. Tombs in other parts of China served as frequent meeting places for those who traveled there from afar; Hochow, a center of numerous tombs was an especially venerated spot for pilgrimages.[111] As one early scholar of Islam noted these tomb centers acted as connecting links in a network of ties uniting elements of Chinese Islam. He asserted that knowledge and information moved quite rapidly among the Chinese Muslims.[112] Certainly a religious or any group organized like the Hsin Chiao could provide a ready flow of information and other forms of intelligence for the leadership and membership alike.

What knowledge that exists about the New Teaching's internal religious structure indicates the existence of a network of relationships. Below the pir would be the akhunds and khalifas. These subordinates did most of the traveling to the scattered New Teaching communities, and by the twentieth century could obtain a considerable amount of religious training at schools in Lanchow and other centers.[113]

Economic livelihoods also enabled number of Muslims to travel widely outside Kansu. Muslims worked as merchants, traders, and transporters of goods in most parts of Northwestern China. Just as in Central Asia, merchants played an important role in the spread of Islam as well as maintaining ties between the parent group and the local branches.[114] Other Muslims took jobs as muleteers, cameleers, and traders, occupations necessary for extensive journeying. Some served in the armed forces or were bandits and smugglers. The wool and hide trade from Tibet into Kansu and from there ultimately to the coastal ports of the empire was largely controlled by Muslims in the Western sections then by Chinese merchants farther East.[115] In this context it should be noted that Chin-chi-pao specifically and Ninghsia generally dominated many of the trade routes passing from China Proper into Mongolia. The close proximity of these two places to the Yellow River, itself a major route to other parts of China was another aspect of the Hsin Chiao's economic strength and network interconnection. Certainly Ma Hua-lung at the center of this religious and economic complex could and did tap a significant amount of economic wealth, political prestige, and religious influence. All these elements combined to make him a most formidable figure in Kansu, one who occupied much of Tso Tsung-t'ang's time and attention. Early in the Muslim rebellions of the 1860s the city of Ninghsia fell to the rebels. Ma Hua-lung was called from his headquarters fifty miles away to take charge of the situation. One of Ma's first commands after arriving was that business should be conducted as usual.116

Other evidence concerning the New Teaching network existed. Ma Hua-lung maintained close ties with the Shensi Muslims bordering Eastern Kansu and stationed thousands of them near his command center when they were chased out of their home province.117 On one occasion he offered to mediate between the central government and the Muslims who had captured the important city of Suchow. Even when the government forces under the command closed in on his Chin-chi-pao headquarters, a relief column from Hochow seeking to aid Ma was stopped by the Chinese.118 Ties between Ma and T'o-ming have been considered above as well as his connections with Muslims in other parts of the empire. Much of the New Teaching movement's power in the mid-nineteenth century therefore rested on the personality charisma of Ma Hua-lung and the complex religious, economic, political network which served him.

Despite the appearance of a centralized religious order within Chinese Islam and Kansu; in reality many powerful forces worked against sustained unity and created different interest groups. As noted in the previous chapter geographic, ethnic, and ideological factors played important roles in interest group formation. Within Islam itself religious rivalries developed interest-group characteristics. Both the 1781 and 1895-1896 troubles involving the Muslims erupted from clashes between members of the New and Old Teaching groups.119 In the eighteenth century conflicts of 1781 and 1784, substantial numbers of Old Teaching forces substantially contributed to the government's victories over the New Teaching movement. As a reward for their services the Old Teaching fighters gained land and property confiscated from the Muslim rebels.120 About eighty years later, the Hochow Muslim leader, Ma Chan-ao joined the government's side and with his son, Ma An'liang ably served the Chinese government for decades. Ma Chan-ao's reasons for switching sides will be considered in the next chapter; one stemmed from the fact that he was an Old Teaching leader.121

Within the New Teaching movement itself a split occurred between the grandson of Ma Hua-lung, Ma Huei-wu; and Ma Hua-lung's son-in-law, Ma Yuan-chang. Both men lived at different geographic sites and competed with one another for the loyalty of the remaining New Teaching adherents in the twentieth century.122

Ma Ming-hsin founded the New Teaching movement in the 1760s; it was an Islamic group with Central Asian characteristics. This particular order centered around a series of powerful, charismatic figures who created a relatively centralized network of important religious, economic, and political dimensions. Underlaying this structure were corrosive elements fostering interest groups. Ma Hua-lung, the New Teaching head, joined the Muslim rebellions of the 1860s but kept his role largely secret. Tso Tsung-t'ang, however, uncovered evidence of Ma Hua-lung's activities and laid siege to his Chin-chi-pao headquarters. After capturing it and executing Ma, Tso turned toward other Muslim centers of resistance and the destruction of the remaining New Teaching network.

CHAPTER VI

THE NORTHWEST CAMPAIGNS

When Tso Tsung-t'ang was appointed the governor-general of Shensi and Kansu in September 1866 he faced an extremely difficult situation there. Various Muslim forces defeated or neutralized the Imperial forces sent against them while controlling sizeable parts of the area. Travelers reported much devastation which followed the Muslim conquest of towns and villages or government reprisals. This, of course, severely disrupted the provincial economies. In addition the loss of life was extremely large. Further West in Chinese Turkestan similar conditions prevailed as the Muslims overthrew and annihilated the Ch'ing administrative and military structure there then confined their attention to combating one another for political predominance.

To surmount obstacles like logistic deficiencies, funding, or devising strategies and tactics suited to the hostile terrain and ethnic diversity, Tso drew on his personal geographical and military knowledge as well as that given by Lin Tse-hsü and Hsü Sung. Tso even employed techniques or programs drawn from Chu-ko Liang, Chang Chu-cheng, and Shen Pui-hai.[1] Reconstruction of the war-torn region followed his earlier efforts in Chekiang and Fukien or policies of T'ao Chu and Hu Lin-i. As Tso himself noted he owed much to Wei Yuan and the statecraft group.[2] Thus indirectly as well as directly the Northwestern campaigns reflected the continuing influence of the statecraft way.

In this chapter the central problems Tso Tsung-t'ang faced before campaigning in the Northwest, and the solutions he devised will be considered. Then the main military campaigns in Shensi, Kansu, and Chinese Turkestan will be noted.[3] Finally certain crucial aspects of Tso's reconstruction efforts including the revitalization of its economic structure, programs to solve the Muslim-Han Chinese problem, and the establishment of Chinese Turkestan as a province in the context of China's relations with Great Britain and Russia will be treated.

The Campaigns: Problems

Tso Tsung-t'ang's ability to plan carefully, thoroughly, and devise a viable strategy largely determined the success of his military program. The nearly exact estimate of time necessary to recover Shensi and Kansu certainly reflected his appreciation of the difficult task confronting him as well as his elaborate calculations.[4] As noted earlier Tso Tsung-t'ang's interest in Northwest China began early, and he dreamed not only of reconquering the entire region but also of restoring its former splendor as a sphere of influence for Chinese civilization.[5] In addition, of course, Tso tried to re-establish Northwest China's security in relation to foreign powers on a more permanent basis.

After learning of his appointment as the Shen-Kan Governor-general, Tso began to reflect about the tasks he faced there.[6] Time for thinking, however, must have been severely limited because Tso supervised the building of the Foochow shipyard and acted in the capacity of chief administrator of Chekiang Fukien.[7] Later on route to Shensi via Hankow, early in 1867, Tso Tsung-t'ang outlined his military strategy.[8] He gave much thought to three important issues: securing an adequate yet steady flow of supplies, gathering reliable troops, and developing a workable military program.[9] Tso solved each problem in turn then continued on the way. Although interrupted for nearly one year by an involvement in the final stages of the Nien theater, he resumed his Shensi and Kansu duties in November 1868.[10]

Tso encountered many difficulties when he tried to maintain an adequate and uninterrupted flow of supplies to that distant part of the empire. As noted above Shensi and Kansu depended on annual subsidies from other provinces which stopped during the Taiping rebellion.[11] The new governor-general therefore realized that he must largely rely on his own ability to sustain a constant movement of materials to the battle zones. Tso did manage to persuade colleagues like Chiang I-li, the Kwangtung Governor and Yang Ch'ang-chun, financial commissioner of Chekiang, both of whom controlled substantial monetary resources, to contribute part of the former annual quotas.[12] With the court's permission Tso also tapped some of the empire's customs revenue.[13]

Since the shipment of provisions required meticulous handling procedures, Tso built supply depots and warehouses at key junctures, like Hankow and Sian, along the routes.[14] The entire logistical operation resulted in the creation of several separate ways to serve Shensi and Kansu.[15] One began in Shanghai continued along the Yangtze to Hankow thence to Sian. This journey effected by both land and water surmounted obstacles like adverse river currents, obstructions in the water, and poor roads sometimes located in rugged mountainous territory. Another supply line passed from Hankow through Szechwan to Shensi. A third involved using communication lines from Tientsin via Shansi to Shensi. As bandits threatened the passage of supplies along this latter way Tso provided for armed escorts to accompany shipments.[16] Tso fully utilized his outstanding knowledge of Chinese geography to plan this enormously complex operation.

In keeping with his trait of thorough planning, Tso carefully investigated weather conditions, local prices, and natural obstacles, any of which might possible hinder the movement of supplies. As theft and corruption also had to be considered, Tso strictly forbade his soldiers to handle the provisions. Loading and unloading therefore began with careful checking, periodic reports, and frequent auditing. The curtailment of losses from pilferage correspondingly lessened the burden of the local tax payers who traditionally made up deficiencies so that the soldiers could be adequately clothed, fed, and armed. Tso knew that since the transportation of war materials was important for a successful campaign, he must positively motivate the shippers and establish in their minds a sense of pride in their logistical efforts.[17]

The organization of an army capable of fighting in Shensi and Kansu often taxed the energy of Tso Tsung-t'ang. From the beginning he replaced many old, ailing, or otherwise unreliable troops from his Ch'u-chun. Many of these soldiers nevertheless had fought for many years already. Constant recruiting expeditions to Hunan regularly added manpower.[18] In addition Tso reorganized other units placed under his command. Since strong personal loyalties often characterized these forces he usually preferred to have as his subordinates those whom he personally knew as this would minimize operation-hampering personality clashes. Through his extensive knowledge of Chinese military history and personal experience in Hunan and the Southeast, Tso knew that a well-disciplined force could significantly aid a campaign while a contingent of unprincipled, rampaging troops could often be more harmful to a successful outcome than the enemy. Thus in the Northwestern theater Tso continually exhorted his subordinates to respect the local inhabitants.[19]

Morale, a key factor in building and maintaining the fighting spirit of any outfit, caused Tso much concern. The prospect of serving in lands several hundred miles from home, residing in areas where the staple foods differed from what was normally eaten, and experiencing frequently miserable weather conditions, especially in the winter months discouraged many from enlisting or staying in the army.[20] Liu Sung-shan, for example, one of Tso's ablest commanders experienced much difficulty in moving his troops north of the Yangtze. Liu finally resorted to extreme measures to intimidate the increasingly unruly soldiers. He arrested and finally executed some of the mutinous leaders. After that incident, fear motivated Liu's remaining forces.[21] Later Liu Sung-shan's sudden death during a crucial point in the campaign against the Muslims demoralized a majority of Tso's soldiers on the northern front, and to remedy the rapidly deteriorating situation, Tso selected Liu's nephew, Liu Chin-t'ang who by force of character and skillful leadership reversed the decline and resumed operations.[22] Within a short time the new commander regained the territory lost in the confusion and thus stabilized the government's effort.

Secret societies proved especially troublesome in Tso's Northwestern campaigns. A large number of these elements entered Tso's units despite intensive actions to discover and eliminate them. Liu Sung-shan encountered two revolts led by secret society members who refused to fight in Kansu. As a result, Tso was considerably embarrassed and had to halt his operations in Northern Kansu. Although frequently discovered thereafter and eliminated, secret society members went with Tso's troops into Chinese Turkestan.[23]

In the earlier military actions in Hunan, Chekiang, and Fukien, Tso quickly grasped the importance of employing foreign weaponry. As early as 1854, Tso headed a Hunanese manufacturing bureau which cast scores of cannon, one type which was reportedly developed by Tso himself.[24] Despite the fact that Tso initially purchased most of the arms and ammunition used by troops in the Shen-Kan campaign in Shanghai, he later constructed arsenals in Sian and Lanchow. There he supervised the production of artilliery, rifles, and ammunition needed in every theatre.[25] At that later time Tso patterned his weaponry largely on German models and hired many foreigners to train his troops and technicians.[26] The use of heavy artillery in siege operations like that of Chin-chi-pao and Suchow hastened their successful conclusions.[27]

Planning the general military strategy for the Shen-Kan and Chinese Turkestan expeditions absorbed much of Tso's time and energy. His initial concern involved the prevention of the Nien, Muslim, and local bandits from uniting to form a formidable coalition. He therefore relentlessly pursued the Nien seeking to force them into a decisive encounter. They broke through his defenses, however, crossed the frozen Yellow River immediately threatening Peking itself. Tso frantically pursued them and left his able subordinate, Liu Tien to contain the Muslims and bandit forces remaining in Shensi.[28] When Tso returned to that province one year later in 1868, he found most of it in a relatively tranquil state save for some minor bandit activity in the northeastern area. Most of the Shensi Muslims had earlier been either forced out of their homeland or killed, many by To-lung-a, a fearless but ruthless commander.[29]

Tso Tsung-t'ang's strategy for Kansu focused on conquering the major Muslim strongholds like Chin-chi-pao, Hochow, Sining, and Suchow. An important part of this campaign was Tso's effort to split the Muslims into different interest groups. One of Tso's early proclamations after entering Shensi in 1867 outlined his policy with regard to the Muslims' surrender or pardon. He declared that Muslims who had not joined the rebellion would be given citations by the government testifying to their good behavior. Those who had joined because of religious beliefs would be pardoned if they surrendered. Furthermore if Muslims arrested other rebels, properly guided government forces in battle, or otherwise assisted the regime's armies they would be pardoned and rewarded.30 This program greatly differed from that of the above-mentioned To-lung-a who generally viewed all Muslims as enemies to be crushed.31 Tso argued against that kind of "liquidation policy" as foolish and quite dangerous.32

One important example of Tso Tsung-t'ang's approach to the Muslim question came when the forces of Liu Sung-shan crossed into Northern Shensi to fight against local bandits and Muslims. In this action Liu confronted two bandits, Tung Fu-hsiang and his father, who offered to surrender along with the Muslims who fought in their armies. Liu agreed. The Tung family position was so strong in Shensi that over 40,000 Muslims joined the Ch'ing government's effort. This action not only provided Tso with an important psychological boost in the gloomy Northern Campaign but also with Muslim troops who effectively served him throughout Northwest China for the next decade.33

Tung Fu-hsiang fought very ably for the Manchus, serving with particular distinction in the action surrounding Chin-chi-pao, the New Teaching headquarters of Ma Hua-lung. Despite some serious reverses, two mutinies by the Chinese forces, the death of Liu Sung-shan, and frustrating delays Chin-chi-pao succumbed to a bitter siege.34 After that victory the remaining Muslims were cleared from the Chin-chi-pao area which was given to Tung and his followers for settlement.35

In the months after the victory over Ma Hua-lung some few Muslim groups surrendered to the Chinese forces. A major success came in the Hochow region, however. There the leader, Ma Chan-ao valiantly resisted Tso's forces and inflicted severe losses on them. Despite the reverses Tso doggedly augmented his troops in the region and continued the attack. Ma Chan-ao faced by this kind of determination offered to surrender. After weeks of negotiation Hochow formally surrendered in February 1872. For his part Tso assented to the surrender because he valued the fighting ability of the Hochow Muslims and could split the Muslims by getting Ma Chan-ao's Muslims in his forces.36

Ma Chan-ao's son, Ma An-liang, fought for the Chinese in the campaigns against Sining and Suchow then later in Chinese Turkestan. Ma's forces unlike those of Tung Fu-hsiang were led and composed entirely of Muslims.

Tung also assisted in the Chinese Turkestan campaigns. Using the interest-group policy to advantage Tso facilitated the remaining tasks confronting him in Kansu. Owing to the Ch'ing government's desire to hasten the conclusion of the Shen-Kan campaign so that troops could be sent to Ili which had been occupied by the Russians (1871), Tso moved more quickly to besiege Suchow. After a bitterly brutal struggle and siege lasting two years Suchow's defenses collapsed in November 1873.37

## The Campaigns (II): Chinese Turkestan

Before Tso Tsung-t'ang began the task of reconquering the last major territory left in the Muslims' hands, he first had to convince the Manchu court to reverse their traditional policy of refusing to permit a Han Chinese to handle significant affairs there. In initially adhering to this practice the government appointed two Manchus, Chin-shun and Ching-lien to take charge of military matters in Chinese Turkestan.38 Tso's role encompassed that of supervising the transportation of supplies and funds supporting them.39

The dramatic reversal of the usual exclusionary practice came during a policy debate in the top levels of the bureaucracy during 1874-1875. The debate's central issue was whether funds and energy on a national level should be assigned to coastal rather than frontier defense. Li Hung-chang and other officials argued that an expedition to recover the remaining Muslim-held territory should be postponed because the main threat to the empire came from the sea.40 In addition they argued that since regions controlled by Russia and the United Kingdom surrounded Chinese Turkestan, it was thus an indefensible territory and should be abandoned rather than antagonize those powerful nations. Finally Li asserted that Northwest China possessed little strategic value.41

Tso Tsung-t'ang vehemently opposed this view and in a masterful memorial combining strategic as well as emotional arguments stated that historically-speaking Northwest China constituted China Proper's first line of defense.42 If the position of Chinese Turkestan deteriorated then Inner Mongolia would be threatened and eventually Peking itself would be endangered. Tso also noted that most Westerners desired trade rather than conquest, and that the policy of attributing vital importance to the Turkestan region stemmed from the K'ang-hsi and Ch'ien-lung emperors.43 These forceful arguments persuaded the highly influential official Wen-hsiang not only to assure the frontier region a top priority status, but also that Tso Tsung-t'ang was the person most suited to oversee the recovery task.44 As many problems relating to Chinese Turkestan paralleled those of Shensi and Kansu they will be briefly considered below while the major emphasis will center on aspects unique to Chinese Turkestan.

In his new position Tso faced the old concern of creating a transport network capable of dispensing supplies from Shensi and Kansu hundreds of miles through deserts, mountains, and desolate lands. After tackling that issue with his wealth of information and organizational ability Tso concluded that he must rely heavily on camels for transport because they could carry heavy loads while consuming small quantities of foodstuffs themselves.[45] One major problem with camels was that they perished rather easily in harsh weather conditions.[46] When camels were inconvenient Tso used wagons. They could carry more items and heavier objects but could not negotiate the treacherous route across the T'ien Shan fully loaded. Also a considerable amount of space had to be allocated for the transport workers' and animals' supplies. Tso circumvented his inability to hire sufficient numbers of camels from Mongolia the traditional market area by giving local merchants tax incentives. This method also helped revitalize local markets something which greatly concerned the statecraft group:[47] As before Tso built commissariats at key points along the transportation routes.[48]

Several interesting schemes to alleviate the grain procurement and allocation situation grew out of Tso Tsung-t'ang's meticulous planning. Since his soldiers knew the basic essentials of farming Tso ordered that small contingents should precede the main forces, plant and grow crops in suitable places, then move on; a second detachment would follow to harvest the grain.[49] In this manner the Hunanese soldier-farmers marched steadily across the waste and desolate lands of Zungharia. Excellent growing seasons for 1876-1878, of course greatly aided these efforts, while Tso assisted the effort by contracting with the Russians to provision the Chinese with large supplies of grain.[50] The Russian grain was used as a reserve. In these conditions Tso's Ch'u-chun drove rapidly, rested for a time, harvested then moved anew.

Financial conditions of an unstable nature plagued Tso, and forced him to develop many fund-raising measures.[51] Economy practices within the Ch'u-chun and the other forces under Tso's command consisted of eliminating unnecessary troops as well as those who were ineffective.[52] In Shensi and Kansu Tso also reorganized and improved the land, salt, and likin tax collection procedures much as he had done earlier in Chekiang and Fukien. He relied on previous efforts by T'ao Chu and Hu Lin-i in developing his own programs.[53] From Shanghai, Hu Kuang-yung, a comprador with close ties to Tso from his days in Southeast China raised significant sums through foreign loans.[54] Millions necessary to finance the Northwestern operation flowed to Tso through these actions. Hu later received rewards from the Manchus in appreciation of his many services.[55]

Having created an adequate logistics network, supplied the required funding, and reorganized his military forces, Tso Tsung-t'ang moved his headquarters to Suchow and in April 1876 commenced the attack on Chinese Turkestan. Tso's primary objective was to secure Zungharia then use it as a staging area for the push into Alti Shahr.[56] A six-month encounter with much hard fighting accomplished that task.

Liu Chin-t'ang who commanded the vanguard troops was in charge of military operations in Chinese Turkestan. He rested the armies for the winter then in early 1877 three columns led by Liu, Chang Yueh, and Hsu Chan-piao knifed into Alti Shahr.[57] Two intriguing aspects of this attack was that one column used a little-known route across the mountains showing Tso's effective use of his geographical knowledge, and the skillful employment of interest-group rivalries.[58] The latter occurred when Liu released prisoners native to Alti Shahr and gave them safe conduct passes to return home. These captives had been singled out for special treatment and told by the Chinese that they considered the "foreign" Andijanis under Yakub Beg as the enemy. The natives were known to be friendly and would be favorably treated because they had been "forced" into fighting against the Chinese by Yakub Beg. This tactic which capitalized on the growing restlessness of the people in Alti Shahr proved highly successful. Yakub Beg hearing of the prisoners return and the message which accompanied them ordered that they be killed which further demoralized the defenders.[59] A combination of internal weakness and aggressive campaigning by the Chinese brought about the rapid defeat of the defending forces in Alti Shahr.[60] This military effort greatly impressed many foreign observers including the sceptical British who had previously championed Yakub Beg.[61]

Reconstruction

For Tso Tsung-t'ang reconstruction was at times more difficult than conquest. His major concern, of course, was to create conditions of stability, good government, and a solution to the Muslim question. The latter issue took top priority because of the nature of the Northwest China conflict. Tso decided that the Muslims must surrender on his terms, needed to be completely separated from the Han people whenever possible, and eventually assimilated culturally.[62]

As proof of their sincerity in offering to surrender Tso demanded that the Muslims yield their horses, weapons, grain, leaders, and agree to repair all damaged buildings in their areas.[63] Failure to comply with these tough conditions would mean a resumption of hostilities.[64] The reasons for the harshness of Tso's terms was that the Muslims frequently "surrendered" and then resumed hostilities at a later time when they had recovered their strength or felt that the government was weakened by new losses on the battlefield. Tso reasoned that he must prevent such practices in the future if peace was to be permanent.65 On receiving a surrender offer Tso usually dispatched a subordinate to investigate the situation.66 If the conditions were deemed satisfactory then a period of careful and detailed planning began.67 First a complete census of the Muslims was undertaken to determine not only the number, sex, and ages of each but also the place of origin; the latter statistic became important because the Shensi Muslims often refused to dwell with their co-religionists from Kansu.68 Tso permitted the Kansu Muslims to reside in their native places only if these lay distant from strategically important communication lines.69 Simultaneously with the group survey Tso initiated a policy of determining the proper relocation sites. Each approved center needed to have sufficient arable land to support its community, proper road networks linking with other parts of the province, and an adequate water supply.70 Tso generally adhered to the policy of segregating Muslims and Han Chinese because he strongly felt that they could never again reside with each other peacefully.71 The hatreds and fears generated by the rebellions would further exacerbate the cultural and religious differences which normally caused friction.

When transferred to their new living accommodations, the Muslims received protection from possible harassment by Han Chinese for the entire journey. Upon arrival the Muslims were given land, housing, implements, animals, and money.72 Tso created a pao-chia system of control for each settlement and generally fostered religious toleration except when the New Teaching was involved.73 As noted above Tso considered the New Teaching to be a heterodox movement which fomented rebellion and unrest.74

In a program designed as much to assimilate the Muslims as to reassert ideological primacy, Tso created a separate examination for Kansu with the court's permission.75 He also established free public schools and private academies for all groups. A printing office was built for the publication of the Confucian Classics.76 In this way Tso attempted to create "Confucianized" elites among the Muslims, elites who would serve in a similar way that the Han Chinese elites did in their society. If their allegiance could be assured by the government then Tso hoped that this would reduce the chances of future Muslim disturbances. In this manner a kind of stabilization would evolve.77

Save for the repressive measures against the New Teaching Tso tried to treat the Muslims fairly. He endeavored to give substance to the cliché that a person should be only judged because he was good or bad and not because he was Han or Muslim.78 He in the manner of many statecraft predecessors attempted to apply the law equally to all and gained some respect from various Muslims for his efforts.79 He was often a generous victor and initiated costly programs for the Muslims' benefit. He carefully investigated each case and selected the plans which he thought would provide for a lasting peace. Some authors have noted that some of the Muslims appreciated Tso's policies while others blasted his efforts as brutal and inhumane.[80] An evaluation of these differing assessments will be given in the next chapter.

Two other important problems, the search for talented people to staff the various administrative levels and the fight against corruption and inefficiency perplexed Tso and forced him to reach back into his statecraft heritage.[81] Tso did not develop an elaborate <u>mu-fu</u> structure like Tsen Kuo-fan. One reason stemmed from his lifelong tendency to involve himself personally in all administrative matters rather than delegate much of it to his subordinates like others.[82] This habit came from his activist nature and contradicted the practice of some of his statecraft predecessors.[83] In addition Tso did understand that he needed some assistance for the gigantic tasks in Northwest China but was continually frustrated by his inability to recruit and keep able prople. His often abrasive personality hampered his efforts because though individuals might work with him for a time dispute would frequently arise along with tempers and sharp words. Resignations then usually followed.[84]

Abuse of one's office equally demoralized the lower level of his administration and the populace. Tso Tsungt'ang thoroughly investigated the conduct of subordinates in his administrative area by making reality conform with the norm (<u>tsung-ho ming-shih</u>).[85] His successful actions brought demotions, prison terms, and even capital punishment to the guilty people.[86] At the same time Tso realized that some of the corruption resulted from the bureaucrats' inability to live off their relatively insignificant salaries. Tso therefore encouraged wage increases whenever possible, something difficult when one considers that the first priority was to secure funds for his campaigns. Tso also instituted a system of periodic audits coupled with a relatively tolerant policy toward minor fiscal infractions.[87]

Relief measures employed in the Northwest reflected both Tso's <u>ching-shih</u> tendencies and his earlier experience with such matters in his native place. Upon defeating an enemy in an area Tso began to set up temporary relief programs. Soup kitchens, for example, appeared along with the creation of rehabilitative bureaus. In particularly devastated territories Tso would appeal for the court to grant special dispensations to postpone the land tax collection process. Tso regularly pressured pawn shops to lower interest rates for the destitute peasants.[88] During Tso's campaigns in the Northwestern region natural disasters apart from war also occurred. A great drought, for example, descended on Shensi and Kansu forcing Tso to use energetic relief measures. He purchased rice from elsewhere in the empire, constructed supply depots, and devised new transportation routes for the relief supplies. He urged the gentry to supervise the local relief operations and to be co-operative with the government's efforts. Tools, clothes, draft animals, and medicines were provided to the destitute whenever possible. Tso oversaw the digging of wells and the creation of a public granary system.[89] Many of these programs began or continued while severe fighting raged elsewhere in the provinces.

Tso's troops also participated in land reclamation projects in the Northwest. After the fighting passed out of a region and a measure of stability returned Tso employed his troops as soldier-farmers. Some troops would first be demobilized to save money although the commander took care to avoid demoralizing the soldiers and causing instability.[90] In addition to relieve some of the local people's tax burden as well as provide a fiscal base for local and provincial governments Tso inaugurated a military colonist system.[91] Soldier-farmers tilled reclaimed or deserted lands until harvest time when they returned it to peasants. The condition for this was that the peasants agreed to farm the land in the future.[92] By this means alone eighty thousand mou of badly-needed farm land was recovered.[93] This project was also integrated with the development of a Westernized mechanical irrigation network. The soldiers dug new wells and canals, dredged rivers, rotated topsoils to preserve the earth's moisture as well as practiced reforestation by planting millions of trees.[94] Many travelers in later times commented favorably on the tree-lined roads which stretched for hundreds of miles in the Northwest.[95] In addition to the above measures Tso strongly promoted the development of trade with other parts of China as well as with other countries like Russia.[96] Most of these activities paralleled those of earlier statecraft adherents.[97]

Two goals underlay Tso Tsung-t'ang's economic policies; financial stabilization and self-sufficiency. One vital means of monetary support for the government was the salt monopoly. Kansu's Kokonor region was an important salt production region. Since the collection of salt taxes had dwindled away in the fighting of the 1860s and 1870s Tso asked that the remaining uncollected duties be cancelled as a measure to revive salt production. He carefully investigated all aspects of the monopoly and based his reforms on his accumulated experience concerning the salt monopolies in Hunan, Chekiang, and Fukien as well as the practices of T'ao Chu and Wei Yuan in the 1830s. The key element in all these programs was the implementation of a salt ticket system.[98] One other important Kansu income source was the tea tax. Revenue from this item stemmed largely from trade with Chinese Turkestan and Russia. Again after investigating the old system of handling tea production and trade Tso adopted a two-fold policy. He tried measures to expand what little trade still existed and instituted a ticket program much like that of the salt monopoly.[99] Other reforms included a revitalization of the government's coinage production for the Northwest and a revision of the likin tax.[100]

As part of a larger economic scheme Tso introduced many new products and practices into the region. His men cultivated cotton and practiced sericulture on a limited scale with the aid of experts transferred from silk producing centers in the Southeast. Tso reintroduced and promoted sheep herding in areas of the Northwest to supply material for a planned woolen industry there. He was in the process of constructing and then operating a Western-style factory in Lanchow, Kansu's provincial capital.[101] The latter enterprise, the first of such magnitude for a long time would bring jobs, diversification of the economy, and a sizeable step toward restoring provincial self-sufficiency.[102] Machines for the woolen mill were purchased from Germany, transported across the extremely difficult route from Shanghai to Hankow then to Lanchow. Mountains had to be crossed and obstacles surmounted; finally the machinery began to arrive in the late 1870s and was repaired then installed.[103]

As in Shensi and Kansu Tso rebuilt the devastated areas in Chinese Turkestan,[104] and provided the local inhabitants with seeds, agricultural implements and animals wherever possible.[105] Generally he promoted agricultural development as a top priority enterprise there.[106] To spur overall economic growth for Chinese Turkestan he revived gold and jade mining while casting coins. He even built a banking system there.[107] All these activities blended to stabilize the region's currency and economy.[108]

In the political realm although reinstituting the practice of allowing Muslim officials to rule their own peoples, the governor-general realized that these local intermediaries often oppressed the natives.[109] To forestall the reappearance of these oppressive practices which often led to unrest Tso again made reality conform with the norm in evaluating these officials. The worst offenders were punished.[110] He delegated sufficient authority to his trusted lieutenants, Liu Chin-t'ang and Chang Yueh, to rule the conquered territory and did not himself enter Chinese Turkestan until the Sino-Russian crisis of 1880-1881.[111] Tso Tsung-t'ang's conquest also opened Chinese Turkestan to colonization by Han Chinese settlers who began to penetrate the region with the cessation of hostilities. This settlement process sometimes encouraged by the central government has continued to the present.[112]

The successful promotion of Chinese Turkestan to be a province constituted one of Tso's most significant political achievements. In a series of memorials over a five year period Tso repeatedly urged that the frontier region be fully incorporated into the Chinese empire.[113] The Ch'ing court finally implemented his suggestion in 1884 when it created the province, Sinkiang, a few months before Tso died.[114] In addition they appointed Liu Chint'ang as the first governor-general of that new dominion.[115] Tso's accomplishment in that regard fulfilled the vision of earlier statecraft adherents, especially Wei Yüan. Tso spoke of the importance of Wei Yüan as a statecraft thinker and noted that he (Tso) had followed the statecraft way for his adult life.[116]

## International Questions

International problems related to Northwest China deeply concerned both Tso Tsung-t'ang and the Ch'ing government. Since Yakub Beg the ruler of Alti Shahr had obtained diplomatic relations with Britain and Russia in the early 1870s Tso's campaigns against him meant the possibility of antagonizing both those powers. Similarly although the Russians occupied the Ili Valley in 1871 they promised to return it to the Chinese when the latter restored stable rule in Chinese Turkestan, something the Russians conceived as difficult if not impossible in the early 1870s.[117] Tso's solutions to the problems will be briefly considered below.

As seen elsewhere Yakub Beg seized control of the Muslim rebellions in Alti Shahr and created his own kingdom there in the mid 1860s.[118] Anglo-Russian rivalry in Central Asia then led to much diplomatic maneuvering with Yakub Beg's regime which culminated in their recognition on his rule in 1873 and after.[119] The British not only wished to establish trade relations but also to fill the vacuum created by the collapse of Ch'ing power in Eastern Turkestan and thus forestall a Russian advance through that region toward India.[120] Later British subjects like Douglas Forsyth tried to persuade the Chinese to recognize Yakub Beg as the de facto ruler of Alti Shahr provided that he would agree to recognize China's ultimate authority there. The Chinese seemed to be flexible in that matter but were strongly influenced by the implications of Tso Tsung-t'ang's military activities there because success by the Chinese could end the diplomatic entanglements and Tso had committed his prestige to its reconquest.[121] The unsettled state of affairs continued until late 1876 when Yakub Beg troubled by Tso's swift taking of Zungharia dispatched an emissary to London in an attempt to pressure the British to mediate between the Chinese and himself. The United Kingdom agreed to his proposal and a complicated process of maneuver began.[122] Initially Kuo Sung-t'ao the Chinese minister in London seemed somewhat receptive to the idea of holding discussions about Alti Shahr and even met with Yakub Beg's emissary. Kuo became much more cautious, however, when he learned of the astonishing Chinese victories there as well as reports of Yakub Beg's death in mid 1877.[123] Talks were finally broken off when the reports were confirmed shortly thereafter.

At the time when Yakub Beg consolidated his control over Alti Shahr and began pushing north toward Zungharia and the Ili Valley the Russians were extending their influence in that part of Central Asia. Soon on the pretext of saving lives and preventing total chaos from engulfing Ili which was ravaged by killing and destruction as the Muslim interest groups fought with each other for control there, the Russians sent a force under the command of General G.A. Kolpakovsky who drove into and occupied that region. The Russians were also anxious to secure the remaining trade routes between Russia and China.[124] This action followed a traditional pattern of Tsarist conquest because the Russian government refused to offer Kolpakovsky's mission direct support but did accept its results.[125] Instead St. Petersburg tried to soften the action's impact on the Ch'ing government by promising to return the valley later. Tso's reconquest of Chinese Turkestan by 1878 thus placed the Russians in an awkward position. The Ili territory enticed those who might hope to dominate Central Asia and Eastern Turkestan.[126] Ili possessed large amounts of very fertile and rich mineral resources thus Ili had the potential to support a relatively large population and could provide much revenue for the controlling state. In addition the major trade and communication routes from Russia and China passed through Ili as well.[127] The country controlling Ili would therefore dominate the entire Turkestan region and could seriously threaten China Proper.[128]

The position of the Russians and the British in relation to the Chinese over the Ili dispute reversed that of the Yakub Beg crisis. In the latter situation the Russians aided the Chinese by providing grain because the Russians feared the establishment of a powerful Muslim state bordering their own recently-conquered Muslim territories.[129] The British on the other hand offered the Ch'ing regime moral support and advice on the Ili question which helped the Chinese obtain a favorable diplomatic settlement.[130] The British knew that it was in their interests to support the Chinese as a replacement to Yakub Beg as a buffer force between India and Russia.[131] In addition the British tried to prevent conflict between Russia and China because a defeat of the latter by the Russians might seriously interfere with Britain's trading prospects or even bring Russian domination of China.[132]

Immediately after retaking Chinese Turkestan the Chinese government asked that the Russians return the Ili Valley. They later sought and gained negotiations on the matter. The Russians then managed to outmaneuver Chunghou, China's emissary and gained a settlement highly favorable to themselves. The accord was angrily denounced by Tso Tsung-t'ang and other top officials so that relations between Russia and China became quite strained. The tense political situation prompted Tso to shift his headquarters to Hami in Northern Chinese Turkestan so that he could personally direct an invasion of Ili or repel any Russian thrust against his area of responsibility.[133] Tso's military preparations also strengthened the new Chinese emissary's bargaining position in the renewed negotiations. Despite additional crafty maneuvering and skillful delaying tactics the Russians could not blunt Tso's threat.[134] They ultimately returned most of the disputed land and provided China with one of her few diplomatic triumphs in the nineteenth century. Tso's aggressive actions in Chinese Turkestan therefore greatly assisted his government in obtaining a favorable outcome from the dispute.[135] At the height of the Ili crisis in late 1880 Tso was recalled to Peking to assist in preparing for the overall defense of the empire. He left Northwest China in December 1880 for the first time in more than a dozen years. His service was completed but his influence remained long after.

CHAPTER VII

EVALUATION

During his long period of service in Northwest China Tso Tsung-t'ang defeated the various rebel forces there, reconstructed many devastated towns, began revitalizing the war-ravaged economy, and re-established an administrative structure. He acted in these endeavors not only as an individual carrying out personal ambitions for Shensi, Kansu, and Chinese Turkestan but also as a member of the Hunanese statecraft group. That particular group as a whole implemented a program of dynastic restoration which followed a theme of a bureaucratic-led reform movement originating with Shen Pu-hai in the Chou period.

The focus of concern in this chapter centers on certain aspects of Tso's military, administrative, and economic activities not covered earlier. Questions such as reasons for the immense loss of life in his campaigning, the famine which struck China in 1877-1878, the opium problem which perplexed him, the treatment of the Muslims, and his economic programs will be considered. These issues will be explored in a Chinese and comparative process. The latter is intended not to sound apologetic on Tso Tsung-t'ang's behalf but rather to indicate that things he dealt with also confronted the British in India and the Russians in Central Asia.

Military Aspects

The striking military successes of Tso Tsung-t'ang in the Northwest has been appreciated by a variety of Chinese and Western sources including some of the most sceptical nineteenth century European critics.[1] The heavy burden that these campaigns placed on the Chinese people is another side of the Northwestern question needing to be considered here. One issue was raised in the policy debate of 1874-1875 on whether funds should be assigned first to frontier or coastal defense. Some scholars have tended to stress the interpretation that in essence the debate reflected a power struggle between Li Hung-chang and Tso Tsung-t'ang.[2] Although elements of a sharp rivalry concerning these two officials certainly did exist the debate's implications went far beyond personal disputation. Tso knew of the importance for China to maintain a strong maritime defense from his days as a governor-general of Fukien and Chekiang, and he initiated the building of the Foochow shipyard and arsenal. Later in the 1880s during the Sino-French conflict he once again became intensely involved in naval matters. In the 1870s, however, he viewed the most deadly threat to the empire as coming from Tsarist Russia in Central Asia. Here Tso echoed an earlier concern of Lin Tse-hsü when the latter was exiled there in the 1840s.[3] The Russians' occupation of the Ili Valley gave them a commanding position which overlooked and threatened Chinese Turkestan. The vital importance of Ili may be seen when reading the writings of F.C.H. Clarke and other military-minded travelers of the period.[4]

Even with the possession of the Ili Valley after 1881, the Chinese barely avoided losing Chinese Turkestan to the Russians prior to 1949. Chinese Communist writers who bitterly attacked Tso Tsung-t'ang for his campaigns against the Taiping rebels, the Nien, and the Muslims in Shensi and Kansu; laud his accomplishments in Eastern Turkestan because he managed to prevent the British and Russians from turning it into a colony.[5] Nevertheless the immense financial burden of the Northwestern campaigns meant that funds were diverted from other parts of the empire where they might have been used. More and better ships or weapons might have been built as Li Hung-chang wished. At times in the 1880s, however, money earmarked for shipbuilding was shifted to less strategic items like palaces.[6] A related financial question is the trend of growing Chinese indebtedness to Western countries in the late nineteenth century. Although the loans which Tso contracted with the British to underwrite his Northwestern campaigns may not have initiated China's economic problems the high interest rates he agreed to pay on his loans did surprise some Western observers.[7] The costly loans led to prolonged economic weakness which brought new loans and an increasing dependence on foreign money. Perhaps the most accurate assessment of the financial problems may be summed up by the words of one scholar who noted that the recovery of Chinese Turkestan was good for China but bad for the Ch'ing government.[8]

As students of Chinese history sometimes confront the staggering loss of life in Chinese military expeditions they need to probe the complex reasons for an army's or outfit's behavior in combat.[9] Although heavy wartime casualties are not unique to the Chinese one must seek answers here as elsewhere. In this section therefore the immense loss of life associated with Tso Tsung-t'ang's Northwestern campaigns will be examined. Westerners in China during this time period expressed feeling of shock when learning that the Chinese capture of Suchow, Manas, and Urumchi in the 1870s was accompanied by heavy casualties.[10] Furthermore Russian and British newspapers charged that Tso's forces at Suchow and later in Hami committed acts which "made the blood run cold."[11] The Chinese Communist armies after their conquest of the Northwest denounced Tso as a "Butcher" of the Muslims.[12] Frequently most if not all the adult male inhabitants of these cities were killed. Women, aged men, and children might be spared although adult females did at times become the property of Tso's officers.[13] Such a thorough liquidation of the enemy although disgusting from a humanist perspective did reflect expected or accepted wartime practices. It also revealed a certain toughness about Tso Tsung-t'ang's character.[14] When some Russian travelers met Tso in Lanchow and had spent some time with him they asked him on one occasion what his response would be to the receipt of a blow from an enemy. He answered that he would return it with equal or greater force.[15] This "eye for an eye" philosophy which characterized Tso's reply is not unknown in other parts of the world. In addition Tso sought to impress the Russians that he and China were not weak and incapable of fighting back if challenged. Combat with foreign states was something to be contemplated if the conditions warranted it. Still Li Hung-chang once remarked that Tso Tsung-t'ang was inclined towards violence.[16]

Tso Tsung-t'ang's personality aside there is some evidence in the writings of the Confucian thinker, Hsun Tzu supportative of a tough policy against rebels on the battlefield:

> Hsun Tzu replied: <u>The king's army does not kill the enemy's old men and boys</u>, it does not destroy crops. It does not seize those who retire without a fight, <u>but it does not forgive those who resist.</u> It does not make prisoners of those who surrender and seek asylum. In carrying out punitive expeditions, it does not punish the common people, <u>it punishes those who lead the common people astray</u>. <u>But if any of the common people fight with the enemy, they become enemies as well</u>. Thus those who flee from the enemy forces and come in and surrender shall be left to go free.[17] (Underlining is my own.)

A bit later in this same essay Hsun Tzu noted that:

> A true king carries out punitive expeditions but he does not make war....He does not massacre the defenders of a city.[18]

Still later he stated that:

> The righteous man...takes up arms to put an end to violence and...the soldiers of the benevolent man...are like the seasonal rain in whose falling all men rejoice.[19]

There is no evidence available that Tso took these passages as a guide. He did study military history extensively and may have known of Hsun Tzu's views on warfare. If Tso did not learn of that aspect of Hsun Tzu's writings, he may have read the Confucian thinker's other works, which enjoyed considerable popularity in the Ch'ing period.[20]

Tso's military policies often adhered to the injunctions of Hsun Tzu. Tso did not permit the killing of old men and boys in combat. He clearly did not forgive those who fought against him except those like Ma Chan-ao who could render powerful assistance to him. He punished Muslim leaders rather than the common people. After carefully investigating those cases of captured Muslims he ordered the release of innocent parties then resettled them. He did follow a strict policy with regard to those Muslims who offered to surrender but only because he had been fooled by insincere Muslims in the past. Tso whenever possible did not permit the massacre of a city's defenders but rather tried to employ his forces in a constructive manner. They undertook extensive rehabilitative measures because Tso aimed to make Northwest China permanently free from strife.[21]

Interest group hatreds is another dimension to the battlefield losses that must be considered. Hatreds between the Han Chinese and Muslims generated by cultural, social, and religious rivalry frequently led to incidents resulting in injury and death in peacetime. Political discrimination by Han Chinese officials against the Muslims compounded the situation. The loss of life during the Muslim uprisings in the eighteenth and nineteenth centuries not only brought general desires for revenge but also the families who suffered personal losses harbored long term vengeful ambitions. Fighting had engulfed Shensi and Kansu for years before Tso's arrival there and the loss of life there was quite sizeable.

A personal view of interest group animosities was given by H.W. Bellew who traveled with T.D. Forsyth to Yakub Beg's area in the 1870s. Bellew once encountered a young Muslim man who spoke at length about the Chinese as rulers. This person recounted how the Chinese after crushing a Muslim rebellion led by his relatives, took the leaders ripped open their chests cut out their hearts then threw them to the street dogs. An astonished Bellew then queried the young Muslim about his feelings concerning the described incident. The latter replied that this was an expected result of warfare which the Muslims also applied to the Chinese.[22] Atrocities on both sides dehumanized all concerned and led to retaliations and counter-measures which greatly increased the loss of life.[23]

A contributing factor to the Muslim deaths at Chin-chi-pao, Suchow, Hami, and Urumchi was Tso's hatred of the New Teaching which he regarded as a movement needing thorough eradication. Like T'ao Chu earlier at Nanking Tso vigorously suppressed heterodox religious groups.[24] Tso therefore sought to destroy Ma Hua-lung's headquarters and permanently eradicate his influence there and elsewhere.

He ordered the killing or exile of the surviving males there.25

When campaigning against the Muslim (Dungan) regimes in Zungharia Tso's forces dealt very harshly with the enemy killing large numbers of them.26 Owen Lattimore once surmised that the central reason for this behavior was Tso's hatred of the Dungans whom he regarded as Han Chinese who converted to Islam thus betraying their traditional culture.27 On at least one occasion Tso did verbally vent his anger against Chinese who had converted to Christianity.28 Another factor was revenge for numerous Chinese who lost their lives in the initial stages of the Muslim rebellions.29 Although these above-mentioned elements are worthy of consideration it must also be recalled that the Dungans originally migrated to Zungharia from Kansu in the mid eighteenth century. They had close ties to the same Muslims who had been influenced by Ma Ming-hsin and later Ma Hua-lung. T'o-ming an important leader of the Muslims in Northern Chinese Turkestan came to that region from Ma Hua-lung's Chin-chi-pao headquarters.30 Tso therefore viewed these Muslims as identical with those of the New Teaching and treated them accordingly.

Siege warfare like that at Chin-chi-pao, Sining, and Suchow is an especially devastating form of combat for both sides. The besiegers often spend months if not years in trenches or tunnels without achieving much visible success. Casualties may seem to mount hourly. The frustrated troops may grow demoralized and difficult to control. Hatred for the enemy builds as does the tension then when the city finally falls soldiers often rampage with brutal behavior. Adult males able to fight are killed and the women given to the soldiers for their pleasure.31 In a prolonged siege many of the defenders perish long before the city itself falls. They may die of starvation, disease, or wounds. Sometimes eighty per cent of the population may be eliminated thereby.32

A final consideration is the extent to which Tso was able to control the behavior of his troops owing to the fact that they campaigned in areas hundreds of miles distant with roads which inhibited rapid communication. Tso did not personally assume command of the Chin-chi-pao, Hami, or Urumchi operations.33 In the distant actions in Alti Shahr Tso's troops killed relatively few of the enemy unlike in the earlier battles.34 This policy was part of the overall strategy to isolate Yakub Beg and the Central Asians from the natives of Alti Shahr. This playing off of interest groups against one another continued to be successful for the Chinese months later when remnants of Yakub Beg's army crossed from their sanctuary in Russian-held Turkestan into Alti Shahr then tried to incite the local Muslims against the Chinese. The attempt collapsed from a lack of support and strong Chinese resistance.35

Nevertheless foreigners who traveled in the Northwest during this time noted that some of the troops under Tso's command but distant from his person occasionally displayed a lack of discipline and even terrorized local peoples. Mandl, a young German hired by Tso witnessed that kind of situation. Soldiers sent from Kansu to reinforce the main Ch'u-chün contingent stationed in Chinese Turkestan during the Ili crisis of 1880 created many incidents of intimidation and destruction then were calmed only after smoking opium.[36] Piassetsky reported that elements of the Ch'u-chün far from Tso's attention smoked opium.[37] A contributing factor in the troops' unruly behavior may have stemmed from the fact that they went without pay for months at a time.[38] Certainly battlefield excesses must have come from troops of this type. The irony was that Tso paid much attention to selecting able troops by weeding out poor ones on a regular basis.

One of Tso's most vocal accusers for permitting brutal actions against the Muslims was Tsarist Russia's main Central Asian commander, General Konstantin von Kaufman. This leader's charges against Tso and his Chinese troops circulated in the Russian capital and reached the Chinese in the form of an open letter to Tso later printed in the North China Herald.[39] An underlying motive behind publicizing this action was the desire to discredit the Chinese reconquest because the return of Russian-held Ili depended from the Russians point of view on the resumption of order and stability in Chinese Turkestan. The Russians by sensationalizing the battlefield losses could argue that the Chinese should not be permitted control of Ili if they were unable to stabilize their reconquered lands. Perhaps another element was to magnify the chaos in Turkestan so that if conditions similar to those in Ili in 1871 developed then they would be justified in taking control of the Chinese-held region. This, of course, is open to question. After initially joining in the condemnation of the Chinese for the killings in Zungharia the British pointed out that the Russians had acted in a similarly brutal fashion while fighting in Central Asia. General von Kaufman himself was quoted by them as saying that his troops should kill all those who resisted the Russians sparing none.[40]

Several sources report atrocities by the Russians during their Central Asian campaigns. Eugene Schuyler, an American diplomat in Russia in the 1870s, was one of the first to describe acts of brutality committed during the conquest of Tashkent and Aulie Ata.[41] Variations of this account appear in Demetrius C. Boulger's Central Asian Portraits and in David Mackenzie's recent monograph about General M. G. Cherniaev. The slaughter inflicted by troops under General Skobelev in taking the Turkmen fort of Geok-Tepe in 1881 was notorious. Accounts of the Muslim revolt in Western Turkestan in 1916 reveal atrocities by both the Muslims and the Russians.[42] As these and many other examples involving the troops of various countries would show brutality in war is a universal phenomenon.

One final aspect of the Northwestern campaigns is their influence on Tso Tsung-t'ang himself. The impressive victories which he claimed rivaled earlier ones of the Ch'in and Han periods two thousand years ago seemed to reinforce his commitment to traditional values and ideas.[43] He also became more rigid in opposing foreign ideas and inventions like the telegraph or railroad. Thus anti-Western Chinese saw him as a spokesman-symbol for their perspective.[44] The successes in the Ili Crisis supported his view that aggressiveness in the face of foreign pressure would ultimately strengthen China. The Sino-French War erupted partly as a result of such attitudes within the court and bureaucracy.

Political Concerns

As has been seen above Tso's successes in the Northwest caused some Western powers to desire alliances with what they felt to be a revitalized China. Rather than address that aspect however, elements of Tso's domestic policies will be examined. A great famine observed and chronicled by Chinese and Westerners alike struck Northwest China during Tso's tenure of office there. The loss of life was especially great in 1877-1878. A contributing factor came from the years of destructive warfare which destroyed villages and left fields untilled sometimes for many years. As noted previously Kansu's economy was weak so that the warring intensified the fiscal crisis especially in the agricultural sector. Travelers to Kansu in the 1870s reported in extensive detail the utter devastation of the countryside and the desperate living conditions for the inhabitants.[45] Tso's vigorous recovery operations alleviated part of the suffering but could not reverse the situation in a few years.

The weather also played an important part in the 1877-1878 catastrophe. According to S.W. Williams an able historian of the day the famine-plagued region which stretched across most of North China resulted from a four-year period of declining rainfall.[46] As R.B. Ekvall later pointed out the loess if properly watered could support a rich harvest. On the other hand a lack of sufficient rainfall quickly led to drought and famine.[47]

Tso Tsung-t'ang's vigorous program to combat the famine described above reflected his previous experience in Hunan and elsewhere. His letters to his family also show him to be a man who took personal responsibility for those who might possibly starve to death in areas under his administration.[48] This perspective and activity renders certain British observations and charges about the famine and relief operations most interesting. Writers in the North China Herald repeatedly scored the Chinese government and Tso for the pursuit of the goal of reconquering Chinese Turkestan while millions suffered and died in China Proper.[49] This theme appeared in the House of Commons Sessional Papers which asserted that the famine situation was worsened owing to the depletion of rice within the empire. Tso's campaigns had indeed proved costly.[50] In addition the North China Herald attacked the general famine relief effort of the Chinese as being inefficient and insensitive.[51]

Certainly it must be admitted that Tso's costly campaigns did divert money to military concerns in the Northwest. Such funds might have been employed to aid the famine victims but they might have also been spent elsewhere. One must not forget that at a time when the North China Herald editorial critical of the Chinese appeared Britain vigorously supported Yakub Beg's regime and sought to undermine the Chinese military effort against him. They failed. Their criticism of the general relief program is inaccurate where it concerned Tso because the latter acted energetically and conscientiously in aiding the sufferers. Problems and mistakes undoubtedly did occur but once again an examination of a similar situation elsewhere in the world shows that the Chinese government responded better than most foreigners realized. An article in the June 16, 1879 issue of Friend of India reported that a serious famine struck Kashmir with indications that perhaps one third to one half of the local population in certain regions perished. Furthermore local officials did little to combat the problem while failing to inform the Indian government of the extent of the situation. It was further noted that in many provinces large numbers of people experienced chronic hunger and that the British must bear the blame for that tragedy.[52] Even in the twentieth century with better communications and transportation facilities famine continues to plague peoples and governments.

Another problem that Tso Tsung-t'ang grappled with, one related to the food shortage discussed above, was the production and consumption of opium. Tso's hatred of that substance and of the British for their importation of it arose in the 1830s. He knew of and admired the strenuous efforts of Lin Tse-hsu to eradicate "the poisonous weed."[53] He saw what opium smoking did to people, especially the troops under his command and made vigorous efforts to stop it.[54] After the fall of Suchow, the last Muslim center in Kansu, Tso initiated a complex opium eradication scheme. To check the enforcement of his stern laws he sent out members of his staff. Crops found were ploughed under or otherwise destroyed. When opium poppies were found mixed with other crops for concealment then only they would be destroyed. Adhering to an important statecraft tradition which stressed that an official should seek as many different sources of information as possible, Tso dispatched additional but "secret" investigators to check on the inspectors. Thus he caught many officials, officers in the army, and local elite members; they were vigorously punished despite their rank and position. The law should apply to all. Recruits for the army were supposedly screened to eliminate opium consumers although the effectiveness of these procedures must be suspect because of the eye-witness accounts of opium consumption mentioned elsewhere.[55]

Tso's eradication program extended beyond the destruction of crops, he similarly attempted to disrupt the transportation of it through or within Shensi and Kansu. He established checking points along the highways to seek out, seize, then destroy it. He forbade the Russians from carrying it as well. Those who grew or shipped opium were flogged and had to wear the cangue. Addicts were given medicine to help break their dependence, and Tso encouraged the local elites to mobilize social pressure so that potential users would be intimidated and those already addicted could be helped.[56]

Despite these vigorous measures production and consumption of the substance continued in Northwest China, especially in areas relatively distant from Tso's headquarters.[57] Travelers in the 1860s and 1870s like N.M. Prjevalsky and Freiherr Ferdinand von Richthofen reported that opium fields dotted the countryside while users included soldiers as well as officials.[58] A few years later after the beginning of Tso's more comprehensive program Pavel Piassetsky, an astute Russian who came to Kansu, noted on several occasions the existence of opium fields. He too reported that soldiers and officers alike smoked that toxic substance.[59] As indicated above Mandl, a German employee of Tso's, reported the continuing existence of opium use despite the presence of Tso's tough laws against it.[60] The British eager to justify their continued importation of opium into China seized on reports like these to discredit Tso's claim that he had stopped its production and consumption. Generally Tso's program proved so successful that the conventional opium trade patterns shifted with the Szechwan-grown opium replacing that from the Northwest.[61]

Tso himself gradually realized that his programs were ineffective and that when he left the Northwest whatever reduction in the opium trade he had caused might evaporate. On one occasion, in the 1880's, he proposed to the British that heavy import duties be levied on opium so that only the rich could afford to buy it. The British then pressured the Chinese to reduce their proposed rate and the latter, specifically Li Hung-chang, agreed.[62] The opium question continued to plague the Chinese into the twentieth century. Renewed efforts to effect an eradication of its production, consumption, and importation brought temporary results only. During the years of the

Peoples Republic of China the combination of a strong government with a thoroughly mobilized people led to the elimination of "that poisonous weed." Clearly the statecraft group alone could not rectify this basic socio-economic problem.

Since Tso Tsung-t'ang's treatment of the Muslims is a difficult question it needs careful consideration here. His ultimate goal was to create the conditions for a lasting peace in Northwest China, and his various programs aimed at accomplishing that task. As indicated above Tso viewed the New Teaching of Ma Hua-lung as a secret society organization and dealt with it in a brutal manner. Despite its revival under Ma Yuan-chang and others the New Teaching did generally adopt a pacific posture with respect to the central government.[63] The rehabilitative measures relating to the Muslims taken by Tso were quite detailed and aimed at providing security for Muslims and government alike. Muslims often segregated themselves from non-Muslim groups through China and other parts of Asia for hundreds of years. Some sources indicated that at least certain groups of Muslims did appreciate Tso's program.[64] Twentieth century writers, however, point to the other side of the Muslim question. In many cases the resettled Muslims did not receive adequate funds for survival and continued to suffer discrimination at the hands of Han Chinese officials.[65] Dislocation and the forced movement from one's native place must have caused terrible psychological and personal hardships on the Muslims many of whom had just lost loved ones or friends in the previous fighting. Peasants generally have extremely close ties to their home villages and are quite reluctant to leave them. Tso tried to develop conditions where local officials would not intimidate of otherwise harm the Muslims but as with the opium question Tso's control over officials far distant from his headquarters was reduced so that oppressive acts could certainly have gone unpunished.

Tso's own memorials from his later years in Northwest China also show that several post-surrender rebellions by Muslims occurred indicating much dissatisfaction with their situations.[66] The vigorous program of sinifying the Muslims through publication and distribution of Confucian works, the creation of many shu-yuan (academies), and the building of free schools was criticized as unnecessarily harsh and insensitive to the Muslims desire to retain their own religious or ethnic identities.[67] Russia's handling of her Muslim minorities vacillated between the promotion of Russification and allowing the Muslims to retain their native cultural practices.[68] Both the Chinese and Russians in the past and even today have made many mistakes in dealing with their minority peoples showing that it is quite difficult to create a viable administrative program for properly governing ethnic minorities.[69]

Another dimension of the impact of Tso Tsung-t'ang's campaigns in Northwest China is reflected in a connection between the 1862-1873 rebellions and one in 1895-1896. When Liu Chin-t'ang's troops conquered Sining they killed many Muslim leaders. The wife of one of these figures was "given" to a secretary of Liu to be used as he wished. The woman, however, also had an infant son by her Muslim husband but managed to keep his existence hidden. Two decades later when the 1895-1896 rebellion began the child now an adult became a leader of the anti-governmental forces. He naturally desired to revenge the misfortunes which had befallen his family.[70]

Finally as indicated above Tso Tsung-t'ang successfully exploited the differing interests of various Muslim groups by persuading powerful leaders like Ma Chan-ao to fight for the government. Ma and his son, Ma An-liang continued to support the political status quo be it Manchu or Han Chinese because they themselves benefited thereby.[71] Their successors in Hochow also managed to increase the Muslims' political influence in Northwest China, and by the late 1930s and early 1940s the Muslims largely dominated the administrations of Kansu and Ch'inghai at the provincial as well as the local levels.[72] This is of course an indirect legacy of Tso's campaigns there.

Economic Programs

The primary economic focus of the ching-shih group like that of many Chinese elites was agriculture. Certainly several of Tso's most striking accomplishments came in that sector. His soldiers tilled abandoned farm land reclaimed other land, used soil rotation methods to improve yields per land unit, and generally improved harvests by 1880. They dug canals and constructed irrigation systems in P'ing-lian , Hochow, Ninghsia, and Sining. Similar efforts in Chinese Turkestan followed closely earlier efforts of Lin Tse-hsü in the late 1840s.[73] One author stated that Tso's achievements in agriculture outshone his many other accomplishments in the Northwest.[74]

Tso demonstrated his flexible use of the statecraft perspective in that he employed Western machinery in place of traditional Chinese practices.[75] As a pragmatic person Tso followed the methods which he felt would bring the best results.[76] Probably his greatest attempt to use Western machinery and technology concerned the establishment of a woolen mill in Lanchow. This elaborate scheme prompted him to buy, transport, and install the latest equipment so that local wool could be processed into clothes and blankets. This operation was to be the cornerstone of his effort to revitalize the Northwest's economy because Tso believed that the woolen mill would tap and thereby stimulate wool production by the region's monadic peoples. Then the Chinese could process the wool for his troops and the population so that the importation of Western goods might be lessened. Eventually these goods might be produced and sold at prices cheaper than equivalent foreign products.[77] If cotton could be developed into an important cash crop as well through the creation of a cotton-processing factory then people might more readily abandon the opium planting. Both these programs received praise from foreign observers in China.[78]

Tso implemented his economic program by purchasing most of the wool-processing machinery from Germany and the cotton machinery from the United Kingdom.[79] He hired experts to accompany the purchases on the long, arduous journey to Lanchow.[80] The energy and expenditure behind this endeavor rivaled some of his most impressive military achievements in Shensi, Kansu, and Chinese Turkestan. The German experts, of course, not only helped built the mill, they trained Chinese to operate the spinning, dyeing, and weaving machinery.[81]

William Mesny, an American who spent many years in China training Chinese troops, toured the woolen mill in February 1881. He later wrote an account of his observations for publication in the North China Herald. Mesny was highly critical of the way the local officials implemented Tso's plan because much wastage resulted from the way that the mill was being run. Mesny felt that the wool was too coarse, the native apprentices too ignorant, and the management too incompetent. He generally felt that Tso's effort manifested laudable goals but foundered through poor implementation.[82]

Several months later the German directors of the woolen mill replied to Mesny's charges. They noted that Mesny's should not be considered as a competent judge of whether the mill was functioning properly because he lacked expertise to evaluate it. Furthermore he stayed there for a few days only a time span inadequate to formulate sound conclusions. Problems which did exist at the time of his visit had since been corrected, and the machines were functioning more efficiently. They also pointed out that many machines arrived in Lanchow but a year or so previously and had not been made operational until some months later. They asserted that local Chinese officials remained very cooperative and not obstructionist as Mesny claimed. The Chinese apprentices performed well at tasks which took Europeans years to master.[83] Although understandably somewhat defensive in their reply the German directors did present their case in a more effective way than Mesny. Certainly his lack of expertise in such a technical process must undercut some of his criticism. As they also indicated his letter may have reflected his anger at not being treated in a regal fashion by the woolen mill's staff.[84] Certainly when reviewing the woolen mill's case at a later date William Mesny did not repeat his earlier criticism.[85]

Ultimately, however, the mill ceased its operation because W.W. Rockhill and Colonel Mark Bell found it closed when they traveled to Lanchow in the late 1880s.[86] Later the mill was reopened but used as a school of telegraphy.[87] Bell surmised that the termination of the mill's activities reflected its close connection with the military needs of the 1870s. By the mid 1880s the need for large numbers of troops stationed in the Northwest declined and with it smaller quantities of uniforms or bedding for the soldiers.[88] A contributing factor may have been an inability to get replacement parts easily and with a minimum of expense.[89] Furthermore in an agrarian-oriented bureaucracy an industrial enterprise would certainly find few enthusiastic or sympathetic supporters. When Tso Tsung-t'ang left the Northwest in the early 1880s and especially after he died in 1885, an imaginative scheme like the woolen mill would be hard to support particularly if it lost money. Either overt opposition or indifference could have shelved the project. Thus although a noble effort the North China Herald's sceptical view that the great capital expenditure might be irretrievably lost seems warranted.[90] Once again a comparative process may prove enlightening. The Russian governor-general von Kaufman created cotton and silk processing plants to develop West Turkestan's economy. For a time though his successor abandoned or reversed many of the efforts because they were too "modern." Ultimately von Kaufman's schemes were revived.[91] Opposition to far-reaching plans existed therefore not only within the Chinese empire but equally in the Russian empire of the same period.

## CONCLUSION

Tso Tsung-t'ang remained in Northwest China from 1867 to 1880 without once returning home; his successful career there came with much personal sacrifice. Sickness plagued him, and family members like Tso Tsung-chih, Chou I-tuan, Tso Hsiao-wei, and the latter's wife all died during his tenure of office there. Of course, like Chu-ko Liang and Chang Chu-cheng, two statecraft adherents as well as others, Tso placed service to the state above conflicting personal interests. Throughout his long career Tso adhered to his statecraft heritage and acted as a reformer in that tradition. The Hunanese <u>ching-shih</u> group, unlike that group studied by James Polachek, was sober, relatively honest, and service oriented.

Tso's most impressive political achievements were the reconquest of Shensi, Kansu, and Chinese Turkestan from the various Muslim rebel groups. Not only did he attain military success but through a vigorous reform program he re-established a great measure of stability, political and economic. The fulfillment of his actions came in 1884 when Chinese Turkestan became Sinkiang, a province. This was a personal as well as a statecraft achievement.

The creation of the new province meant several things for China. Future rulers and regimes would not only have strong emotional ties there but also administrative ones as well. Unlike Vietnam, Korea, or even Outer Mongolia, Sinkiang became an integral part of China one which should be and was retained. Communist writers like Tsui Chi-en certainly appreciated that fact. Provincial status meant increasing sinification in that Han Chinese administrators would be sent there replacing Manchus, Mongols, and local <u>begs</u>. Han Chinese colonists also received encouragement to migrate there so as to strengthen central control in the frontier territory. In addition the immense mineral wealth eventually came to be exploited by and for the Chinese alone.

One should remember that Tso Tsung-t'ang's political and economic accomplishments were achieved through an immense cost in human terms. At times his handling of the Muslims though not motivated by racial bias did reflect a harsh side of Tso's character and resulted in considerable suffering. The energetic and comprehensive opium eradication scheme although flawed in part was generally successful as long as he personally oversaw the implementation of his program. The long term failure reflects the vast extent of the problem and the necessity for political and social control to a degree found only in the post

1949 era. Indeed the use of a comparative perspective shows that his deficiencies were not unique in the "civilized" world.

Tso and the Hunanese ching-shih adherents struggled against great obstacles to implement their reform programs because corruption and inertia permeated the court and bureaucracy. Imaginative schemes like the woolen mill were criticized and withered from neglect. Tso understood that in these conditions within the dynastic cycle perspective any restoration be it imperially or bureaucratically inspired could last but a few decades at best. The essential thing, however, in the manner of his statecraft predecessors was to serve ably and loyally even if you failed. Tso in his particular statecraft perspective not only searched out the past for traditional/modern techniques like ming-shih, he used Western machinery and weaponry to strengthen China. Like his brother Tsung-chih who combined elements of Western and Chinese astronomy, Tsung-t'ang meshed Western and Chinese practice to revitalize Northwest China.

Too often the nineteenth century reformer's efforts have been examined through a Western bias and found deficient. From this perspective the T'ung-chih Restoration failed ultimately because Chinese who insisted on rooting their programs in the past could not effectively cope with the "modern age." A different viewpoint such as presented in this work suggests that the ching-shih group drew upon a rich and non-stagnant tradition. Political techniques like the ming-shih were based on a solidly rational foundation centuries before British and Western bureaucracy knew of them. In combination with other things like the ch'u-t'ien method, irrigation techniques, or military procedures such as thoroughly studying the climate, terrain, and peoples of an area where one is sent to head a campaign; impressive results could be achieved. Great rebellions unprecedented in scope and ferocity in world history raged for a time in the Ch'ing empire. They were all quelled and a striking degree of stability was restored. Thus in the domestic realm Tso Tsung-t'ang and the Hunan ching-shih group succeeded in their restoration efforts.

Considering Northwest China, Tso Tsung-t'ang defeated the Muslim rebellions there, outmaneuvered the Russians concerning Ili, and returned Ch'ing control to Shensi, Kansu, and Sinkiang. Not only did he accomplish those things but within a few years Chinese administrative control of the new province, Sinkiang was stronger than ever before. Therefore one could argue that considering these achievements there was indeed a T'ung-chih Restoration. In that and other regions the Hunan statecraft group spearheaded the government's efforts. Tso Tsung-t'ang left a legacy inherited by the Peoples Republic of China which posits Chinese dominion of and within Northwest China.

NOTES

CHAPTER I

¹Hui-chen Wang Lu, "An Analysis of Chinese Clan Rules: Confucian Theories in Action," in Arthur F. Wright, ed., Confucianism and Chinese Civilization (Stanford, 1965), Albert E. Dien, "Yen Chih-t'ui," in Arthur F. Wright and Denis Twitchett, eds., Confucian Personalities (Stanford, 1962), 44. These are but two among many studies of clan rules and traditions.

²Lo Cheng-chun, Tso Wen-hsiang-kung nien-n'u (The chronological biography of Tso Tsung-t'ang hereafter TWHKNP) in Tso Tsung-t'ang, Tso Wen-hsiang-kung ch'uan-chi (The collected works of Tso Tsung-t'ang, hereafter TWHKCC) (Taipei, 1964 reprint), I, 2-3. Arthur Hummel, ed., Eminent Chinese of the Ch'ing Period (hereafter ECCP) (Washington, D.C., 1943-1944), 762.

³Kuo Sung-t'ao, ed., Hsiang-yin hsien t'u-chih (Illustrated gazetteer if the Hsiang-yin district, hereafter YHYTC) (N.P., 1880), XVIII, 21-24. Wu Ju-lun, T'ung-cheng Wu hsien-sheng ch'uan-shu (Wu Ju-lun's collected literary works) (Taipei, 1964 reprint), II, 68.

⁴Kuo, HYHTC, XIII, 28-29. Lo, TWHKNP, I, 3.

⁵Ch'ing-shih lieh-chuan (Bibliographies of the Ch'ing period, hereafter CSLC) (Shanghai, 1928), LI, 35. Kuo, HYHTC, XVIII, 22-23; XXX, 19,27; XXXIII, 25.

⁶Tso Tsung-chih, Shen-an shih wen ch'ao (Writings and poetry from the Shen studio) (N.P., 1875), Tso Tsung-t'ang's preface, 1-2.

⁷W.L. Bales, Tso Tsung-t'ang: Soldier and Statesman of Old China (Shanghai, 1937), 58-59. Chu Wen-djang, The Moslem Rebellion in Northwest China (The Hague, 1966), 89. Ch'in Han-ts'ai, Tso Wen-hsiang-kung ts'ai Hsi-pei (Tso Tsung-t'ang in the Northwest, hereafter TWHKTHP) (Shanghai, 1946), 1-14. Kao Ch'u, Tso Tsung-t'ang chuan (Biography of Tso Tsung-t'ang) (Taipei, 1962), 5. Wu, T'ung-cheng, II, 68.

⁸Ch'in, TWHKTHP, 13-14.

[9] Tso Tsung-t'ang, Tso Wen-hsiang-kung chia-shu (Tso Tsung-t'ang's letters written home, hereafter chia-shu (Shanghai, 1920), Tso Hsiao-t'ung, ed., II, 16-18. J.O.P. Bland, "Manchu Miscellaneous," in the Bland Papers, Boxes 26-28, folder 27. The latter source details an anecdote related to Tso's reputation for refusing to sponsor people for jobs.

[10] Kao, Tso Tsung-t'ang, 5.

[11] Chu K'ung-chang, Chung-hsing chiang-shuai pieh-chuan (A collection of biographies of the T'ung-chih era generals) (Nanking, 1897), V.1. Tso Tsung-t'ang Tun-pi yü-shen (Knowledge acquited after military life, hereafter TPYS) (Changsha, 1881), 17. Tso Tsung-chih, Shen-an, II, 18. James Polachek, "Gentry Hegemony: Soochow in the T'ung-chih Restoration," in Frederick Wakeman, Jr. and Carolyn Grant, eds., Conflict and Control in Late Imperial China (Berkeley, 1975), 237-238. The latter source notes that Kuo Sung-t'ao asked and got a memorial in defense of Tso from P'an Tsu-in, an influential official and others. Tso was on Lo Ping-chang's staff not that of Hu Lin-i.

[12] Ch'in, TWHKTHP, 13-15.

[13] Tseng Kuo-ch'uan and Li Han-chang, eds., Hunan t'ung-chih (Gazetteer of Hunan province, hereafter HNTC) (N.P., 1885), CLXXVI, 21. Tso's paternal grandfather also asked members of the clan to contribute a portion of their grain harvests annually to a clan granary from which supplies might be drawn in times of famine. Thus the Tso clan usually avoided serious suffering in those times. See also Kuo, HYHTC, XXXIII, 24-25.

[14] Tseng and Li, HNTC, CLXXX, 45-46. Tso, chia-shu II, 16-18. Ch'u T'ung-ts'u, Local Government in China Under the Ch'ing (Cambridge, 1962), 175, 182; and Hsiao Kung-ch'uan, Rural China: Imperial Control in the Nineteenth Century (Seattle, 1960), 316 ff. One way to encourage this pattern of behavior among the elites was, of course, to note such examples in the local histories. There also may have been a degree of enlightened self-interest behind these measures because by alleviating the miseries of the masses then outbreaks of peasant discontent focused against the local elites might be avoided or lessened. Certainly as Ch'u and others have stated the inculcated attitudes of aiding people in distress similarly played an important role.

[15] Tso, chia-shu, II, 16-18. Tso, TPYS, 17. In the letter cited here Tso not only recalls the 1848-1849 experience with some pride but uses it to instruct his sons

about the importance of aiding destitute people whether at home or in government. In the latter capacity Tso stated that an official could save thousands of lives. During the late 1870s a severe drought and famine did strike Northwest China and many people died despite vigorous organized efforts by Tso. The negative side of elite control characterized by inhumane money-grabbing measures in post-bellum Soochow is viewed in Potacheck, "Gentry hegemony," 216.

[16] Tseng and Li, HNTC, 21.

[17] Tso, chia-shu, II, 18-22. In this letter Tso cautioned his family to act properly in mourning and burying their deceased mother. He urged them to study the Ch'ieh-wen chai wen-ch'ao and the Huang-ch'ao ching-shih wen-pien as guides for accepted heavior. These works were important for the late Ch'ing statecraft movement and will be considered below.

[18] Lo, TWHKNP, I, 6-7.

[19] Kuo, HYHTC, XVI, 36. The wife of Tso Tsung-chih's son was a daughter of Kuo Sung-t'ao. This relationship will be explored below.

[20] Tso, TPYS, 18, 44. Kuo, HYHTC, XI, 18. The North China Herald (hereafter NCH), XXVII (1881), 378, 430. This action by Kuo's daughter drew much unfavorable comment from the North China Herald's editors.

[21] Kuo, HYHTC, 46-47. Tseng and Li, HNTC, CLXXVL, 15-16.

[22] Kao, Tso Tsung-t'ang, 5. Tso, chia-shu, I, 40. Ch'in, TWHKTHP, 5. Ts'ui Chi-en, "Tso Tsung-t'ang shu-p'ing (A critical narrative of Tso Tsung-t'ang), Shih-hsüeh yueh-k'an, (July 1957), 9.

[23] Tso, chia-shu, I, 55. Ch'in, TWHKTHP, 47.

[24] Kao, Tso Tsung-t'ang, 5. Tso was ill much of the time he campaigned in Northwest China as his chia-shu of 1868-1880 clearly show.

[25] Tso, TPYS, 16-17. Lo, TWHKTHP, I, 10, 21-22. The tone of and commentary in the TPYS writing vividly indicate Tso's humiliation in this situation of being unable to provide a suitable home for his family.

[26] Bland, "Manchu Miscellaneous," in the Bland Papers, Boxes 26-28, folder 27. NCH, XXVII (1881), 230-231.

[27] Tso TPYS, 18. Wu, T'ung-cheng, II, 69-70. Chang Ch'i-yun, et al., Ch'ing-shih (History of the Ch'ing dynasty, hereafter CS) (Taipei, 1961), 4766. Tso Tsung-t'ang, Tso Wen-hsiang-kung shu-tu (Letters of Tso Tsung-t'ang) in Tso, TWHKCC, I, 1. Robert Crawford, "Chang Chu-cheng's Confucian Legalism," in William T. deBary, et al., Self and Society in Ming Thought (New York, 1970), 368-370. Wu and Chang in their writings cited here indicate that Tso cared little for his family. A reading of Tso's many letters and other writings shows that he loved them deeply. He rather in the manner of Chu-ko Liang and Chang Chu-cheng, two great statesmen, placed consideration of the state before himself and his family.

[28] NCH, XXXIV (1885), 479, 535; XXXV (1885), 294-295, 440. The latter report was by an eyewitness of the receipt of the news of Tso's death by the citizens of Foochow. Tso's reputation for honesty and his able feats as an administrator and warrior made him a person idolized by the people.

[29] Tso, TPYS, 16-17. Tso, chia-shu, I, 40. Hummel, ECCP, 763. Ch'in, TWHKTHP, 18.

[30] Tai Mu-chen, Tso Tsung-t'ang p'ing-chuan (A critical biography of Tso Tsung-t'ang) (Sian, 1943), Nien-p'u section, 4.

[31] Tso, TPYS, 16.

[32] Kao, Tso Tsung-t'ang, 7-8.

[33] Tso, TPYS, 18. NCH, XXXIII (1884), 531. The latter source gives a lengthy "account" of a dream Tso supposedly had concerning his first wife. She told him that after her death she entered the ranks of the immortals. Now she appeared to congratulate him on his many honors in the past several years and on his appointment as commander of the government's forces in Fukien. Chou then predicted that although the French would be somewhat troublesome in their war with China they would do little serious harm to the empire. She also said that the two of them would be reunited in about six years. Tso awoke considerably refreshed. I see no compelling reason to doubt the account and feel that it does show Tso's deep feelings for Chou.

Notes to pages 6-7

³⁴Wang Hsien=ch'ien, Hsu-shou-t'ang wen-chi (Collected writings of the Hsu-shou hall) (Taipei, 1966 reprint), X, 7-8. Tso, TPYS, 16. Tso Tsung-t'ang had eight children; four daughters: Hsiao-yu (b.1833), Hsiao-chi (b. 1834), Hsiao-lin (b. 1837), and Hsiao-pin (b.1837); and four sons: Hsiao-wei (1946-1873), Hsiao-k'uan (b.1847), Hsiao-hsün (b.1853), and Hsiao-t'ung (1857-1924).

³⁵Paul Cohen, China and Christianity: The Missionary Movement and the Growth of Anti-Foreignism, 1860-1870 (Cambridge, 1963), 122. C. John Stanley, Late Ch'ing Finance: Hu Kuang-yung as an Innovator (Cambridge, 1961), 10-12, Tso, TPYS, 35-36.

³⁶H.G. Creel, Shen Pu-hai (Chicago, 1974), 47.

³⁷E.V.G. Kiernan, British Diplomacy in China, 1880-1885 (Cambridge, 1939), 242. Gideon Ch'en, Tso Tsung-t'ang, Pioneer Promoter of the Modern Dockyard and the Woolen Mill in China (Peking, 1938), 1. Mary C. Wright, The Last Stand of Chinese Conservatism: The T'ung-chih Restoration, 1862-1874 (Stanford, 1957), 216. Stanley, Late Ch'ing Finance, 17-18.

³⁸Lloyd E. Eastman, Throne and Mandarins: China's Search for a Policy During the Sino-French Controversy, 1880-1885 (Cambridge, 1967), 107. J.O.P. Bland and E. Backhouse, China Under the Empress Dowager: Being a History of the Life and Times of Tz'u-hsi (London, 1910), 510. Bland, "Manchu Miscellany," in the Bland Papers, Boxes 26-28, folder 33.

³⁹Lo, TWHKNP, IV, 19.

⁴⁰Bales, Tso Tsung-t'ang, 57-59. Lo, TWHKNP, I, 4.

⁴¹Tso Tsung-chih, Shen-an, Tso Tsung-t'ang's preface, 1-2.

⁴²Ibid.

⁴³Lo, TWHKNP, I, 7; I, 8. These are two examples.

⁴⁴Ho T'ien-chu, San-ming-chen shu-tu (Letters of three famous statesmen) (Shanghai, 1908), Hu section, 29.

⁴⁵The Analects, trans., Arthur Waley, II, 12. This passage quotes Confucius as saying that a scholar is not an implement. This has been interpreted as meaning that

the scholar should not be a narrow-minded specialist but rather a person who possessed a broad, generalized body of information particularly about ethics. The educational training of the scholar and the content on which he was to be tested in the examination system has been a subject of great controversy for hundreds of years in China.

[46] The Analects, trans., Waley, V, 13; VII, 27; XI, 21; XII, 1; XII, 2; XII, 14; XIII, 5.

[47] Tseng and Li, HNTC, CLXXVI, 16. Dorothy Borci, "Eccentricity and Dissent: The Case of Kung Tzu-chen," Ching-shih wen-ti, III #4 (December 1975), 54.

[48] Lo, TWHKNP, I, 8.

[49] Tso, TPYS, Borci, "Eccentricity and Dissent," 51-58.

[50] Lo, TWHKNP, I, 7-8.

[51] Tseng and Li, HNTC, CLXXVL, 16.

[52] Lo, TWHKNP, I, 7.

[53] Ibid.

[54] Ch'in, TWHKTHP, 7.

[55] Ho, San-ming-chen, Tseng section, 64-65.

[56] Ho Hsi-ling, Ch'ung-ssu-hsiang hsien-lu (Virtuous record of the Ch'ung-ssu-hsiang) in Ho Hsi-ling, Han-hsiang-kuan shih-ch'ao (Works from the Han-hsiang-kuan) (N.P., 1848), 12-13.

[57] Lo, TWHKNP, I, 7. Tso displayed this organizational ability throughout his life particularly when serving as a staff member and an official.

[58] Ho, Han-hsiang-kuan, book III, chuan I, 11-12.

[59] Gideon Ch'en, "Tso Tsung-t'ang, the Farmer of Hsianshang," Yenching Journal of Social Studies, I (1939), 213. Ch'in, TWHKTHP, 7.

[60] Lin Tse-hsü, Lin Wen-chung-kung ch'ian-chi (The collected works of Lin Tse-shu) (Taipei, 1963 reprint), II, 13.

Notes to pages 9-10

⁶¹Ch'in, TWHKTHP, 7.

⁶²Tso Tsung-t'ang, Tso Wen-hsiang-kung wen-chi (The writings of Tso Tsung-t'ang) in Tso, TWHKCC, I, 1-5.

⁶³Ch'in, TWHKTHP, 193-195.

⁶⁴Tso, TPYS, 16-17. Lo, TWHKNP, I, 21-22. Ch'en, "Tso Tsung-t'ang, the Farmer," 213-214. Tso carefully saved his teaching salary, and both wives worked outside the home to raise additional money. The Tso farm occupied about 70 mou of land.

⁶⁵Tso, chia-shu, I, 1. Lo, TWHKNP, I, 22.

⁶⁶Ch'in, TWHKTHP, 12.

⁶⁷Lo, TWHKNP, I, 17.

⁶⁸Ch'en, "Tso Tsung-t'ang, The Farmer," 214. Hummel, ECCP, 763.

⁶⁹Ho, San-ming-chen. Hu section. 24-26. Edward L. Buote, Chu-ko Liang and the Kingdom of Shu-Han (University of Chicago Ph.D. thesis, 1968), 48-49. The former source, a letter from Hu Lin-i to Tso combined flattery, pleading, and logic to try and convince him to emerge from seclusion and join the staff of Chang Liang-chi. Hu argued that the empire not to say his district needed Tso who had been called by Lin Tse-hsu as a great genius, to fight the Taipings. Chang twice sent emissaries to Tso but the latter did not budge. Buote's work indicates that Chu-ko Liang, a man whom Tso deeply admired also followed a rustic life. Chu-ko twice refused to see Liu Pei, an important military figure who later became the ruler of the Shu-Han kingdom. Chu-ko's earlier actions might be considered as a factor in Tso's own actions.

⁷⁰Ch'in, TWHKTHP, 12.

⁷¹Kao, Tso Tsung-t'ang, 7-8.

⁷²Pavel, I. Piassetsky, Russian Travelers in Mongolia and China, trans., J. Gordon-Cumming, (London, 1884), II, 166.

⁷³Lo, TWHKNP, I, 7-8. Tso especially liked Ku Yen-wu's writings on strategy. Both these early Ch'ing scholars had several works in the statecraft manual, the Huang-ch'ao ching-shih wen-pien.

[74] Hummel, ECCP, 420, 422-424.

[75] Tai, Tso Tsung-t'ang, nien-piao section, 4.

[76] Ch'in, TWHKTHP, 11-12. Tai, Tso Tsung-t'ang, p'ing-chuan section, 3.

[77] Tso, chia-shu, II, 14-15, 16-18.

[78] F.O. 17/825, British Foreign Office Correspondence Respecting China, 12/29/1877, Fraser to Derby. Fraser said, "...if the Chinese forces have indeed accomplished a march of 1000 miles in 30 days they have reason to be proud of their achievement." F.O. 17/825, 3/7/1878, Fraser to Derby. Fraser noted that "Tso Tsung-t'ang carried out his plan with perfect success."

[79] "The Chinese Reconquest of Eastern Turkistan," The Spectator, LI #1 (1878), 466. Demetrius C. Boulger, "Three Chinese Generals," Calcutta Review, LXXI (1880), 307, 310. Herbert A. Giles, A Chinese Biographical Dictionary (London, 1898), 771. Piassetsky, Russian Travelers, II, 118.

[80] Tso, shu-tu, I, 1. Tso said, "Chia I, Chu-ko Liang, and Ch'en Liang, they are very rare people so much so that they may be counted on one's fingers...."

[81] Buote, Chu-ko Liang, 1-2, 16, 56-61, 69-71, 75, 131-137.

[82] Tso, chia-shu, II, 14-15.

[83] Yang Kung-t'ao, Tso Tsung-t'ang i-shih (Anecdotes about Tso Tsung-t'ang (N.P., 1919), 16-17.

[84] Ho, San-ming-chen, Tso section, 58.

[85] Kao, Tso Tsung-t'ang, 5. There was a revival of interest in Sun Teu in the late Ch'ing period, see Susan Mann Jones, " Scholasticism and Politics in Late Eighteen Century," Ch'ing shih wen-fi, III #4 (December 1975) 37-38.

[86] Yang, Tso Tsung-t'ang, 69-70. This anecdote closely approximates the instructions outlined for the use of spies in Sun Tzu, Ping-fa (Methods of warfare), XIII, 18-20.

[87] Yang, Tso Tsung-t'ang, 1.

[88] Philip Kuhn, <u>Rebellion and Its Enemies in Late Imperial China: Militarization and Social Structure, 1796-1864</u> (Cambridge, 1970), 53, 134.

[89] Bales, <u>Tso Tsung-t'ang</u>, vide supra. Chu, <u>The Moslem Rebellion</u>, Chapters IV and V. Immanuel C.Y. Hsü, "The Late Ch'ing Reconquest of Sinkiang: A reappraisal of Tso Tsung-t'ang's Role," <u>Central Asiatic Journal</u>, XII (1968), 50-63.

[90] Hsu I'shih, "Tso Tsung-t'ang yu Liang Ch'i-ch'ao (Tso Tsung-t'ang and Liang Ch'i-ch'ao)," <u>Ku-chin pan yueh kan</u>, #32, 1197. In Tso's case one might argue that less attention to unconventional subjects and more interest in the eight legged essay might have resulted in the attainment of the chin-shih degree. Although Tso quit the examination route in disgust in 1838, he temporarily resumed it two decades later in 1860.

[91] Tso, shu-tu, XXXIV, 18. Lo, <u>TWHKNP</u>, I, 7, 10.

[92] Tso Tsung-chih, <u>Shen-an</u>, Tso Tsung-t'ang's preface, 1-2; II, 12-13.

[93] Buote, <u>Chu-ko Liang</u>, 48-49.

[94] Tso, <u>chia-shu</u>, II, 16-18. Bland, "Manchu Miscellaneous," in the <u>Bland</u> Papers, Boxes 26-28, folder 27.

[95] Ch'in, <u>TWHKTHP</u>, 12-13.

Notes to pages 14-15

## CHAPTER II

[1] The Analects, trans., Waley, I, 1. The Book of Rites (Li Chi), trans., James Legge, (New York, 1967 reprint), II, 13.

[2] The Doctrine of the Mean (Chung, Yung) in the Four Books (Sau Shu) trans., James Legge (New York, 1966 reprint), XX, 8.

[3] The Book of Rites. trans., James Legge, II, 14. This selection provides an interesting model: "The scholar when he hears what is good, tells it to (his friends), and when he sees what is good, shows it to them; in view of rank and position, he gives the precedence to them over himself; if they encounter calamities and hardships, he is prepared to die with them; if they are long (in getting advancement), he waits for them; if they are far off, he brings them together with himself:- such is he in the employment and promotion of his friends."

[4] L.S. Yang, "Great Families of Eastern Han," in E-tu Zen Sun and John de Francis, eds., Chinese Social History (New York, 1956), 103-133.

[5] Ho Ping-ti, The Ladder of Success in Imperial China (New York, 1962), 127-167. Ho discusses the factors operating against success by one family for several successive generations in the examination system.

[6] Here I wish to distinguish between the earlier form of power based largely on economic factors and the later more fragile structure dominated more by social connections. Such groupings like the latter seldom lasted beyond two generations.

[7] Factionalism, a debilitating consequence in this period, became extreme in the eleventh and seventeenth centuries.

[8] Johnathan Porter, Tseng Kuo-fan's Private Bureaucracy (Berkeley, 1972), 116. In the Taiping period the Manchus feared a concentration of power by the Han Chinese generals who began to dominate the military forces. One example of this concern was their comparison of Tseng

Kuo-fan with Wu San-kuei, a Chinese warrior who surrendered to the Manchus but later rebelled against their Ch'ing state.

[9] See figure #1.

[10] T'ao was the Liang Kiang Governor-general (1830-1839), Lin Tse-hsü was the Hu-kuang Governor-general (1837-1838), and Ho Ch'ang-ling was the Kweichow Governor (1836-1845). A previous example of a statecraft reform group with strong kinship connections came from the Tung-lin group of the seventeenth century; see Jerry Dennerline, "Fiscal Reform and Local Control: The Gentry-Bureaucratic Alliance Survives the Conquest," in Wakeman and Grant, eds., Conflict and Control, 109, 115, 118.

[11] Roger V. DesForges, Hsi-liang and the Chinese National Revolution (New Haven, 1973), 55,189. Their influence extended beyond the 1880s as well. One example is Hsi-liang's rather fruitful combination of elements from China's past with new techniques brought by the West. In the first decade of the twentieth century he established a school for officials in Szechwan. This institution took as its basis for instruction the philosophy and methods of statecraft.

[12] Tseng and Li, HNTC, CLXXVL, 14-16.

[13] Chang Hsien-Lun, comp., Shan-hua hsien-chih (Changsha, 1877), XI, 40-80. Most of the Hunan statecraft members attended one of the two schools.

[14] Up to about 1850, Tso wrote twenty-eight letters to Ho Hsi-ling, more than to any other person. They contain much information about his thoughts, activities, and practices especially relating to statecraft pursuits.

[15] Lo, TWHKNP, I, 23.

[16] Momose Hiromu, "Shimmatsu no keiseibumpen ni tsuite (On the Ching-shih wen-pien)," in Ikeuchi hakushi kanreki kinen Toyoshi ronso (Essays on Oriental History collected to commemorate the 60th birthday of Dr. Ikeuchi) (Tokyo, 1940), 891. Tseng and Li, HNTC, CLXXVI, 14. Lo, TWHKNP, I, 7. The latter source shows Tso's early familiarity with the statecraft manual.

[17] Hummel, ECCP, 282

[18] Peter M. Mitchell, Wei Yüan (1794-1857) and the Early Modernization Movement in China and Japan, (Indiana

Notes to pages 16-17

University Ph.D. thesis, 1970), 25-26. Liang Ch'i-ch'ao, Intellectual Trends in the Ch'ing Period, trans., Immanuel C.Y. Hsü, (Cambridge, 1959), 73. Wei also benefitted from Ho Ch'ang-ling's interest and assistance. This type of sponsorship was rather commonplace in Ch'ing China as the latter source indicates.

[19] Hummel, ECCP, 282, 710.

[20] Ch'in, TWHKTHP, 7-8.

[21] CSLC, XXXVII, 31-36. Thomas Metzger, "The Organizational Capabilities of the Ch'ing State in the Field of Commerce," in W.E. Willmott, ed., Economic Organization in Chinese Society (Stanford, 1972), 9-45. Thomas Metzger, "T'ao Chu's Reform of the Huai-pei Salt Monopoly (1831-1833)," Papers on China, XVI (1962), 1-47. The latter two accounts are the fullest and most clearly presented.

[22] Chu, Chung-gsing chiang-shuai, V, 1. Chu-ko similarly impressed those whom he met. Liu Pei made him an important political aide after their first meeting.

[23] Lo, TWHKNP, I, 15-16. Ch'in, TWHKTHP, 7-8.

[24] Kao, Tso Tsung-t'ang, 8.

[25] Tso Tsung-chih, Shen-an, II, 39. Wu, "T'ao-wen-i-kung," 32-33. Hummel, ECCP, 540. Buote, Chu-ko Liang, 48. Many statecraft members came from families which experienced serious economic difficulties. These conditions may have fostered a more serious, pragmatic orientation upon them.

[26] Yen Shu-shen, Hu Lin-i nien-p'u (Chronological biography of Hy Lin-i) Shanghai, 1933), I, 12-13. Lo, TWHKNP, 14-15, 18. Tso, TPYS, 19. CSLC, XXXVII, 36. This son received many honors from the emperor in memory of his father's great service record. Tso learned of T'ao's "will" from Ho Hsi-ling.

[27] Tso, TPYS, 19.

[28] Lo, TWHKNP, I, 21. Tso, TPYS, 16-17.

[29] Chang, et al., CS, 4593. Li Shao-ling, Tseng, Tso, Hu (Tseng Kuo-fan, Tso Tsung-t'ang, and Hu Lin-i) (Kaohsiung, 1962), Hu section, 75. Hummel, ECCP, 334, 763. Hu married the seventh daughter.

Notes to pages 17-18

[30] Ho Ch'ang-ling, Wei Yüan, and Pao Shih-chen were all in T'ao's mu-fu.

[31] See Chapter III and Note #21 of this section.

[32] Lin Chung-yung, Lin Tse-hsü chuan (A biography of Lin Tse-hsü) (Taipei, 1968), 8, 704. T'ao and Lin first became friends when they served together in the Han-lin Academy.

[33] Ibid., 108.

[34] Ch'in, TWHKTHP, 8.

[35] Ho, San-ming-chen, Hu section, 25.

[36] Lo, TWHKNP, I, 24. Hummel, ECCP, 763. Tso made excuses such as he had to make the arrangements for his nephew's marriage and must continue teaching T'ao Chu's son. He may also have been emulating Chu-ko Liang which has been discussed above.

[37] Lo, TWHKNP, I, 25-26. Ho, San-ming-chen, Hu section, 25-26. Lin, Lin Tse-hsü, 612-613. All sources agree that Lin was greatly impressed by Tso Tsung-t'ang's intellect and said that he was a rare genius.

[38] Tso, Chia-shu, II, 37-38. Ch'in, TWHKTHP, 191-192. The former source noted that although Lin used troops to fight the Moslems in Shensi and Kansu, he failed to give a long range solution to the problem. In the latter source Ch'in says that Tso's water control efforts, especially those in Chinese Turkestan, owed much to Lin's earlier efforts.

[39] Bales, Tso Tsung-t'ang, 200. Ch'in, TWHKTHP, 32. Hummel, ECCP, 68-69. Interest in Northwest China was relatively strong among students who lived in Peking in the 1820s and 1830s. Although Ch'ien-lung's great campaigns in that region occurred decades earlier, the histories concerning them had appeared only quite recently. In addition Chinese Turkestan frequently suffered from Moslem uprisings and invasions from Central Asian khanates in the 1830s.

[40] Ho, San-ming-chan, Hu section, 2-3.

[41] Lin, Lin Tse-hsü, 612-613, 616, 620, 623-625.

[42] Ch'in, TWHKTHP, 8-9. Lin worked on this problem while Governor-general of Hunan and Hupeh as well as later in Canton.

[43] Hummel, ECCP, 513.

[44] Ch'en, Tso Tsung-t'ang, Pioneer, 2-4.

[45] Li, Tseng, Tso, Hu, Tso section, 68-69. Ho, San-ming-chen, Tso section 81. In the latter source Tso noted that T'ao and Lin were great friends, they were both fair-minded, and no one "today" approached them. He added that had they lived ten years longer then the foreign and Taiping problems would not have become serious. The latter assertion is more interesting for its indication of Tso's regard for them than the questionable speculation about the Taiping and foreign crises.

[46] Wang Chia-chien, Wei Yüan nien-p'u (Chronological biography of Wei Yüan) (Taipei, 1967), 25, 60-61, 63, 67-68.

[47] Mitchell, Wei Yüan, 23-24.

[48] Ibid., 71. Wang, Wei Yüan, 32.

[49] Mitchell, Wei Yüan, 69, 91-96.

[50] Ch'in TWHKTHP, 9.

[51] Mitchell, Wei Yüan, 26-27, 127-132.

[52] Tso, TPYS, 30-33. Tso, Shu-tu, I, 35, 39. Ch'in TWHKTHP, 10. The latter source indicates that Tso and Wei were good friends. Tso's brother, Tsung-chih, also may have known him as the two of them were regarded as two of Hunan's four best poets of that time. Wei Kuang-t'ao, a relative of Wei Yüan, became an important advisor to Tso in Northwest China.

[53] Much material from this work later appeared in the collected works pertaining to the Moslem rebellions in Tso's period, the Hui-min ch'i-i.

[54] Tso, Shu-tu, XXIV, 18. Lo, TWHKNP, I, 10. In the letter noted here, Tso comments that while in the Northwest as well as earlier, he followed the ching-shih way for over fifty years. He noted that Wei's precise and profound knowledge made him an important statecraft thinker. Tso said that Wei's view that Chinese Turkestan should be

Notes to pages 20-22

made a province must be adhered to because that was the only way to give the region an effective administration.

[55] Ta-ch'ing li-ch'ao shih-lu (Veritable records of the Ch'ing dynasty hereafter Ch'ing shih-lu (Chung-chun, Manchuria. 1935-1940), Te-tsung section, CXCIV, 27-28. Chinese Turkestan became the province Sinkiang in November 1884.

[56] Tseng and Li, HNTC, 45-46.

[57] Tso, TPYS, 3.

[58] Li Huan, Kuo-ch'ao chi-hsien lei-cheng ch'u-pien (Classified collections of eminent Chinese of the Ch'ing period, first series) (Changsha, 1884-1890), CXXXII, 61. Tso, TPYS, 5. Tso, Chia-shu, I, 4.

[59] Yen, Hu Lin-i, 6. Lo, TWHKNP, I, 6-7.

[60] Tso, TPYS, 3, 5. Lo, TWHKNP, I, 21, Li, Tseng, Tso, Hu, Hu section, 24-25.

[61] Hummel, ECCP, 711.

[62] Lo, TWHKNP, I, 21. At the occasion of this meeting Hu had returned home to mourn his father.

[63] Tso, TPYS, 6. Ch'in, TWHKTHP, 10.

[64] Kao, Tso Tsung-t'ang, 7.

[65] Buote, Chu-ko Liang, 48-49.

[66] Lo, TWHKNP, I, 29. Li, Tseng, Tso, Hu, Tso section, 15. Hummel, ECCP, 763. Yang, Tso Tsung-t'ang, 4. According to the latter, unverified account Lo "tricked" Tso into coming out of seclusion by pretending to arrest T'ao Chu's son. When Tso appeared before Lo to seek T'ao's release Lo explained his plot which gave the two men a hearty laugh and Tso a job.

[67] Hummel, ECCP, 763.

[68] Wu, T'ung-cheng, 69.

[69] Tso, TPYS, 6, 18. Li, Tseng, Tso, Hu, Tso section, 15. Lo, TWHKNP, II, 32.

[70] Lo, TWHKNP, II, 31-32. Tso, TPYS, 5. Li, Tseng, Tso, Hu, Hu section, 76.

[71] Tso, TPYS, 5.

[72] Wu, T'ung-cheng, 69-70. Tso, Shu-tu, I, 1.

[73] Tso TPYS, 5. This work is a warm tribute to Hu whom Tso greatly admired and relied on.

[74] Tseng Kuo-fan, Tseng Wen-chung-kung nien-p'u (Chronological biography of Tseng Kuo-fan) in Tseng Kup-fan, Tseng Wen-chung-kung ch'uan-chi (Collected works of Tseng Kuo-fan) (Peking, 1876), I, 9. Tseng Kuo-fan, Shu-ch'a (Letters of Tseng Kuo-fan) in Tseng, ch'uan-chi, 1-2.

[75] Ibid. As will be seen in Chapter III, this concept was crucial to the statecraft movement and provides a link going back to the statecraft wing of the Fa-chia.

[76] Tseng Kuo-fan, Tseng Wen-chung-kung tsou-kao (Memorials of Tseng Kuo-fan) in Tseng, ch'uan-chi, XI, 49-51; XII, 55-58; XX, 1-4; XXI, 35-39.

[77] Hu Ch'ang-tu, "The Yellow River Administration in the Ch'ing Dynasty," Far Eastern Quarterly, XIV (1954-1955), 505-514. Han-yin Chen Shen, "Tseng Kuo-fan in Peking, 1840-1852: His Ideas on Statecraft and Reform," The Journal of Asian Studies, XXVII (1967-1968), 75.

[78] Hsueh Fu-cheng, "Tso Wen-hsiang-kung wan-nien i-chi(Tso Tsung-t'ang's bearings in his later years," in Tso Shun-sheng, ed., Chung-kuo chin-pai-nien shih tzu-liao ch'u-pien, (source materials of Chinese history during the last one hundred years, first series) (Taipei, 1958 reprint), 185-187. Ho, San-ming-chen, Tso section, 58. S.Y. Teng, "Some New Light on the Nien Movement and Its Effect on the Fall of the Manchu Dynasty," Symposium on Chinese Studies Commemorating the Golden Jubilee of the University of Hong Kong, III (1968), 50-69. Lu Hsi-ta, "Tseng-Tso chiao-o ch'i-t'a (The bad relations between Tseng and Tso and other things)," Ku-chin p'an yueh kan, #32, 28-32. Luo An, "Tseng Kuo-fan yu Tso Tsung-t'ang (Tseng Kuo-fan and Tso Tsung-t'ang)," Ku-chin yueh-kan #4, 135-141.

[79] Li, Tseng, Tso, Hu, Tso section, 24-25.

[80] Tso, shu-tu, VIII-XXV, passim.

[81] Tso, chia-shu, II, 29,34. These two citations

show that Tso felt a great respect for Tseng and the honors he received after his death.

[82] Tseng, tsou-kao, XXVII, 13; XXVIII, 8.

[83] Ch'in, TWHKTHP, 174. Li, Tseng, Tso, Hu, Tso section, 71.

[84] Lu, "Tseng-Tso," 1214-1215. Wu, T'ung-cheng, II, 68, 73. Tso, chia-shu, II, 23.

[85] Ho, San-ming-chen, Tso section, 58. Yang, Tso Tsung-t'ang, 60-61. Tso and Tseng deeply respected each other but always seemed to argue heatedly about many things.

[86] Ho, San-ming-chen, Tso section, 58. Lu, "Tseng-Tso," 1215. Tso claimed that the argument stemmed from a misunderstanding of the tone of his memorial refuting Tseng's report of the Taiping crown prince's death in 1864. Tso stated as late as 1878 that he was just reporting the situation and not ridiculing Tseng.

[87] Wu, T'ung-cheng, II, 69. Lo, TWHKNP, I, 27-29.

[88] Kuo, HYHTC, XVI, 36.

[89] Hummel, ECCP, 755.

[90] Ch'in, TWHKTHP, 14.

[91] Hummel, ECCP, 438.

[92] Kuo, HYHTC, XXIV, 9; XXXIII, 32.

[93] Lo, TWHKNP, I, 7.

[94] Hummel, ECCP, 540.

[95] Ho, San-ming-chen, Tseng section, 63. Chang Hao, "On the Ching-shih Ideal in Neo-Confucianism," Ch'ing-shih wen-t'i, III #1 (November 1974), 26-58. The latter author in this cited article and a personal letter argue that Lo Tse-nan and Tseng Kuo-fan should be differentiated from Tso, Wei, and Ho Ch'ang-l'ing in that the former were more strongly anchored in the idealistic tradition of Ch'ing shih while the latter group were more pragmatic institutionalists. Certainly more united these reformers than divided them, however, Lo and Tseng do seem

to give greater stress to self cultivation as the primary means to establish or re-establish order than do statists like Tso, Wei, and Ho.

[96] Kuo Sung-t'ai, ed., Lo Tse-nan nien-p'u (Chronological biography of Lo Tse-nan) (Taipei, 1967 reprint), I, 11.

[97] Ibid., I, 10-11. Hummel, ECCP, 755.

[98] Ibid, 541.

[99] Wu, T'ung-cheng, II, 69-70.

[100] Ch'in, TWHKTHP, 40.

[101] All of the above-mentioned officials had articles in the Huang-ch'ao ching-shih wen-pien or its various successors. Tseng, Tso, and Hu usually had the most essays in the later collections.

[102] Miu Ch'uan-sun, I-feng-t'ang wen-chi (Writings from the I-feng hall) (N.P., 1901, I, 47). Hummel, ECCP, 322, 692.

[103] Miu, I'feng-t'ang, I, 44, 47.

[104] Mitchell, Wei Yüan, 21. Wang, Wei Yüan, 21, Ch'in, TWHKTHP, 33.

[105] Lo, TWHKNP, I, 35; IV, 23. Ch'in, TWHKTHP, 10.

[106] Lo, TWHKNP, IV, 22-23. Chu, The Moslem Rebellion, 91-92.

[107] Lo, TWHKNP, I, 28.

[108] Hummel, ECCP, 707. Chu, The Moslem Rebellion, 44, 76-77.

[109] Ibid, 91-92.

[110] See Chapter VI.

[111] S.Y. Teng and John K. Fairbank, China's Response to the West: A Documentary Survey, 1839-1923 (Cambridge, 1954), 80.

CHAPTER III

[1] Thomas Metzger, The Internal Organization of Ch'ing Bureaucracy (Cambridge, 1973), 25-27.

[2] Metzger, "The Organizational Capabilities," 9, 44-45.

[3] Wright, The Last Stand, 50-56. She emphasizes the importance of the imperial role.

[4] This tendency is particularly characteristic of the first generation statecraft group and is reflected in the Huang-ch'ao ching-shih wen-pien. The second generation adherents looked farther back into the past as well for their models of statecraft reform. There were other statecraft groups in the late Ch'ing period. One centering around Li Hung-chang and Fen Guei-fen seemed more concerned with enhancing gentry hegemony in the Lian Chiang region than restoring effective, corruption-free, government. The Li-Feng group has been studied by James Polarchek in his work cited above and shows the complexity of the measures and attitudes involved in the T'ung-chih Restoration.

[5] The very appearance of the Huang-ch'ao ching-shih wen-pien, of course, reflects a view by its editors that many Ch'ing bureaucrats would profit from the information and techniques found in their work.

[6] Lo, TWHKNP, I, 7.

[7] Certainly since the Huang-ch'ao ching-shih wen-pien was organized and edited by two scholars it did reflect their own subjective biases. They attempted, however, to provide the broadest possible perspective and contrary opinions. Many differing schools of thought were represented. This same "open-minded" tendency also made it possible for the statecraft members to consider techniques associated with the Fa-chia as well.

[8] The second generation members lived during the great mid-nineteenth century crises and stressed things like military history more than their forerunners. Nevertheless the striking similarity of both generations' outlooks concerning domestic problems is interesting.

[9] H.G. Creel, *The Origins of Statecraft in China* (Chicago, 1970), 69-80. 101-103, 388-416, for example.

[10] Creel, *Shen-Pu-hai*, 54.

[11] *Ibid.*, 75-76.

[12] *Ibid.*, 136-162.

[13] *Ching-shih* was used in the Chou period but in a generalized fashion with little meaning to the scholar. Other references appear in the *Hou Han Shu*, for example. *Hsing-ming* and *ming-shih*, two fundamental concepts of the statecraft wing may be found in the writings of Shen and later people as H.G. Creel, "The Meaning of Hsing Ming," in Soren Egerod, *Studia Serica: Bernhard Karlgren Dedicata* (Copenhagen, 1959), 199-211, shows.

[14] Creel, *Shen Pu-hai*, 47,53,57,52-63,130. The British civil service standardized the merit rating system only after World War I.

[15] Ch'in, *TWHKTHP*, 174-175. Creel, *Shen Pu-hai*, 121-123. The former source states that Hu Lin-i, Tseng Kuo-fan, and Tso Tsung-t'ang all knew of and used *ming-shih*. They probably got their inspiration from Chang Chu-cheng who followed Shen's direction. Tseng once wrote that the essence of statecraft was the comparison of name and reality (*tsung-ho ming-shih*). See also Note #1. of Introduction above.)

[16] Yang Sung-kuo, *Chung-kuo ku-tai ssu-hsiang-shih* (An intellectual history of China's ancient period) (Peking, 1954), 405-406. Crawford, "Chang Chu-cheng's Confucian Legalism," 393. Chang said that the "means by which to ensure a reliable and consistent application of rewards and punishments is by checking names against realities. If the emperor does this he will be assured that the talented men of his day who do not differ in kind or number from ancient times will clamor to serve him and will do so effectively and efficiently."

[17] Creel, *Shen Pu-hai*, 51-53, 113-114.

[18] Ho, *San-ming-chen*, Hu section, 37-38. In this letter Hu told Tso that he (Tso) spent too much time considering matters of minor importance and should hire specialists to take charge of those things. Then he could more effectively deal with critical affairs.

[19] Creel, *Shen Pu-hai*, 103. Crawford, "Chang Chu-

cheng's Confucian Legalism," 392.

[20] Creel, Shen Pu-hai, 63,98,134. Ho, San-ming-chen, Tso section, 21. In the latter source Tso criticized Hu for becoming too familiar with his subordinates, later in the Northwest, however, adopted a sympathetic manner with his own men.

[21] Creel, Shen Pu-hai, 259-270, 273-274.

[22] Crawford, "Chang Chu-cheng's Confucian Legalism," 379. Tso, Shu-tu, I, 1. Creel, Shen Pu-hai, 256-257. Both Chang and Tso greatly admired Chia I.

[23] Creel, "The meaning of hsing-ming," 207.

[24] Creel, Shen Pu-hai, 277-278. Tso Shu-tu, I, 1. As seen elsewhere Tso patterned his life on that of Chu-ko Liang at times.

[25] Buote, Chu-ko Liang, 85.

[26] Robert B. Crawford, The Life and Thought of Chang Chu-cheng (University of Washington, Ph.D. thesis, 1961), 245, 257. Crawford, "Chang Chu-cheng's Confucian Legalism," 367-379.

[27] Chang Chu-cheng, Chang Wen-chung-kung ch'üan-chi (The collected works of Chang Chu-cheng) (Peking, 1935), I, 4-5. Creel, Shen Pu-hai, 280-284.

[28] Crawford, "Chang Chu-cheng's Confucian Legalism," 386-392.

[29] Chang, Tsou-shu, I, 4-5. Crawford, "Chang Chu-cheng's Confucian Legalism," 371, 393-394, 397-399.

[30] Ibid., 368, 390, 394.

[31] Creel, Shen Pu-hai, 284.

[32] Ch'in, TWHKTHP, 174-175. Ho, San-ming-chen, Tseng section, 65.

[33] Hellmut Wilhelm, "The Heresies of Ch'en Liang," Asiatische Studien, XI (1957), 102, 106. Tso, Shu-tu. I, 1. Hso, "On the Ch'ing-shih Ideal," 47-50.

[34] Ch'en Liang, Ch'en-T'ung-fu wen-chi (The writings of Ch'en Liang) (Ch'ing era), VII, 1-5; XII, 3-4, 11-12. John W. Dardess, Conquerors and Confucians (New York, 1973), 79. Wilhelm, "The Heresies," 106.

[35] Wright, The Last Stand, 46-48.

[36] Ibid., 50.

[37] Ibid.

[38] Tso, Shu-tu, I, 1. Ho, San-ming-chen, Hu section, 28-30; Tseng section, 63, for example.

[39] Porter, Tseng-Kuo-fan's, 85, for example.

[40] Ho, San-ming-chen, Tseng section, 63.

[41] E.G. Pulleyblank, "Chinese Historical Criticism: Liu Chih-chi and Ssu-ma Kuang," in W.G. Beaslet and E.G. Pulleyblank, Historians of China and Japan (London, 1961), 153-158.

[42] Ibid., 156-157.

[43] Hummel, ECCP, 102.

[44] Ko Shih-chun, ed., Huang-ch'ao ching-shih wen-hsü-pien (Continued collection of works relating to statecraft in the present dynasty) (Shanghai, 1888), 1. Momose, "Shimmatsu no keiseibumpen," 885.

[45] Dennesline, "Fiscal Reform and Local Control," 99; Hummel, ECCP, 102, 282.

[46] Many reasons may be offered for the appearance of the Huang-ch'ao ching-shih wen-pien at that time, the major one being that the meeting and close association of a group of like-minded people under the leadership of T'ao Chu provided its stimulus. They also struggled together to overcome the problems and corruption facing them in the Kiangsu area and felt that other bureaucrats might profit from their knowledge and experience.

[47] T'ang Shou-ch'ien, ed., Min-kuo ching-shih wen-pien (Collected works relating to statecraft in the Republican period) (Shanghai, 1914), preface, 1-2. I do not intend to present an exhaustive analysis of the Huang-ch'ao

Notes to pages 35-36

ching-shih wen-pien because that task would be difficult if not impossible considering the diverse nature of the hundreds of essays therein.

[48] Momose, "Shimmatsu no keiseibumpen," 877-878.

[49] Ibid. Ch'in TWHKTHP, 160-175.

[50] Ho, San-ming-chen, Tseng section, 65.

[51] Ho and Wei, eds., Huang-ch'ao, preface, 1. Momose, "Shimmatsu no keiseibumpen," 884. Tso, Shu-tu, I, 1. Conrad M. Shirokauer, "Chu Hsi's Political Career: A Study in Ambivalence," in Arthur F. Wright and Denis Twitchett, eds., Confucian Personalities (Stanford, 1961), 187. Ch'en Liang, a statecraft thinker of the Sung era argued against Chu Hsi and said that the Sung differed by little from the Golden Age of the past. Ch'en felt that reforms must be realized through up-to-date methods.

[52] Ho and Wei, eds., Huang-ch'ao, vide supra.

[53] Metzger, The Internal Organization, Chapter I.

[54] Tso, Chia-shu, II, 18-22. Tso urged his family to consult the statecraft manual for learning the proper ways to conduct themselves at a parent's funeral. This, of course, was an important reason for the writing of Ssu-ma Kuang's great historical work.

[55] Ho and Wei, eds., Huang-ch'ao, XI, 26-28.

[56] Ibid., XLVII, 15-19.

[57] Tso, Shu-tu, II, 10; XXIV, 18. Tso, Chia-shu, II, 16. Lo, TWHKNP, I, 7.

[58] Keiseibumpen no moku-roku (General index to the editions of the writings on statecraft), comp., Kindai Chugoki Kenkyu Iinkai (Committee on the research into modern China) (Tokyo, 1956), I, table of contents. Momose, "Shimmatsu no keiseibumpen," 878-884. Depending on the method of inclusion and counting the various successors, at least twelve appeared in the century after.

[59] Ko, ed., Huang-ch'ao, 555-556.

[60] Momose, "Shimmatsu no keiseibumpen," 879.

[61] *Ibid*.

[62] See note #47 above.

[63] T'ang, ed., *Min-kuo*, preface, 1-2.

[64] Teng and Fairbank, *China's Response*.

[65] Apart from making a few observations the statecraft group's relations with the West will not be considered here but perhaps at a later time.

[66] Piassetsky, *Russian Travelers*, II, 151-156, 172-174. Tso once told the Russians that he continually discovered fresh things in China's past. Certainly Shen's administrative techniques would be one such example.

[67] Shirokauer, "Chu Hsi's Political Career," 163. Hso, "On the *Ch'ing-shih* Ideal," 36-59. Cheng Hso persuasively argues that the *ch'ing-shih* ideal existed within the Confucian revival in the Sung era. Ch'en Liang, Yeh-shih, and others although critical of aspects in Neo-Confucianism should be considered as Confucianists. The main difference between Ch'en Liang and Chu Hei was that Ch'en took a stronger statist or institutional approach to government while Chu emphasized the vital nature of the moralist statesman. In this work the compatibility of the Fa-chia and Confucian traditions by Sung times meant that bureaucrats could use *ch'ing-shih* methods for Confucian ends.

[68] Tso, *Shu-tu*, I, 1. Tso thought Ch'en to be a great person of the stature of Chu-ko Liang and Chia I.

[69] William T. deBary, "Introduction," in William T. deBary, ed., *Self and Society in Ming Thought* (New York, 1970), 23.

[70] Ray Huang, "Ni Yuan-lu: 'Realism' in a Neo-Confucian Scholar-Statesmen," in deBary, ed., *Self and Society in Ming Thought* (New York, 1970), 421-425.

[71] *Ibid*.

[72] Ho, *San-ming-chen*, Tseng section, 63. Lo, *TWHKNP*, I, 7-8. Dennesline, "Fiscal Reform and Local Control," 86-119.

[73] Porter, *Tseng Kuo-fan's*, 16-17.

[74] Buote, *Chu-ko Liang*, 48-49.

[75] Hellmut Wilhelm, "From Myth to Myth: The Case of Yüeh Fei's Biography," in Arthur F. Wright and Denis Twitchett, *Confucian Personalities* (Stanford, 1961), 154.

[76] Ho and Wei, ed., *Huang-ch'ao*, XI, 26-28; XXV, 1-22.

[77] Creel, "The Meaning of Hsing-ming," 200.

[78] Porter, *Tseng Kuo-fan's*, 40.

[79] *Ibid.*, 36-40.

[80] Ch'in, *TWHKTHP*, 174-175.

[81] Porter, *Tseng Kuo-fan's* 85-86.

[82] *Ibid.*, 16-17.

[83] Ho, *San-ming-chen*, Tseng section, 65. Self-cultivation is another aspect of *ming-shih* not considered here.

[84] This illustrates the vitality of Chinese thought because the Chinese can effectively combine aspects of different schools such as the *Fa-chia* and *Ju-chia* to produce positive results.

[85] Ho, *San-ming-chen*, Hu section, 30; Tseng section, 63. Ch'in, *TWHKTHP*, 174-175. Tseng and Li, eds., *HNTO*, CLXXVI, 15-16.

[86] Ho Ch'ang-ling and Kuo Sung-t'ao were particularly admired for their economic achievements. Hu Lin-i and Tso Tsung-t'ang also used budgeting procedures, accounting method, and statistics in their administrations.

[87] Mitchell, *Wei Yüan*, 100

[88] *Ibid*.

[89] Benjamin Schwartz, "Some Polarities in Confucian Thought," in Arthur F. Wright, ed., *Confucianism and Chinese Civilization* (Stanford, 1964), 3-15.

[90] Porter, *Tseng Kuo-fan's*, 92-93.

Notes to pages 40-41

[91] Metzger, "T'ao Chu's Reform," 1-35. Ho Ping-ti, "The Salt Merchants of Yangchow: A Study of Commercial Capitalism in Eighteenth Century China," Harvard Journal of Asiatic Studies, XVII (1950), 145-148. Harold Hinton, The Grain Tribute System of China: 1845-1911 (Cambridge, 1956), 4. Hu Ch'ang-tu, "The Yellow River Administration in the Ch'ing Dynasty," Far Eastern Quarterly XIV (1954-1955), 510.

[92] Hu Lin-i, Hu Wen-chung-kung i chi (The posthumously collected works of Hu Lin-i) Taipei reprint, 1967), XXXIII, 11-14. Ch'in, TWHKTHP, 8.

[93] Creel, Shen Pu-hai, 38-39.

[94] John K. Fairbank, The Chinese World Order (Cambridge, 1968), vide supra.

[95] Buote, Chu-ko Liang, 71, 132-137.

[96] Tso, Chia-shu, II, 8.

[97] Creel, Shen Pu-hai, 284. Crawford, The Life and Thought, 38-39.

[98] Kuhn, Rebellion and Its Enemies, 47-49, 186.

[99] CSLC, LXXV, 45. Chang, et al., CS, 4502.

[100] Ibid., 4502-4503.

[101] Buote, Chu-ko Liang, 16-17, 27, 75. Crawford, The Life and Thought, 38-39. The t'un-t'ien and related settlements of military colonists have long been used in Chinese history. Chu-ko, Chang, and Tso, all effectively employed the t'un-t'ien when they were in power.

[102] Chang, et al., 4502-4503.

[103] Ho and Wei, eds., Huang-ch'ao, LXXXII, 1-7; LXXXIII, 7-8; LXXXIX, 7-8. CSLC, LXXV, 45-46. Yen's rehabilitative methods also included ch'u-t'ien (soil rotation) methods. The soldiers should concentrate on agricultural activities, irrigation, and land reclamation problems. Through these measures the soldier-colonists would have a more self-sufficient life.

[104] Ho and Wei, eds., Huang-ch'ao, LII, 53-55; LXXXVI, 1-3; LXXXVIII, 7-9.

Notes to pages 41-43

[105] Tso Tsung-t'ang, Lo Wen-chung tsou-kao (Memorials written for Lo Ping-chang) in Tso, TWHKCC, V, 44-52; VI, 13-14; VII, 19-24. Tseng and Li, eds., HNTC, CLXXVI, 16. Tso's writings show a familiarity with Yen's earlier writings and a knowledge of the t'un-t'ien system.

[106] Tso, Chia-shu, II, 36. Imanaga Seiji, "Rin Soku-jo no kaimin seisaku ni tsuite (Lin Tse-hsü's Moslem policy)," Shigaku kenkyu #69 (May 1958), 1-18.

[107] Ch'in, TWHKTHP, 160-175. Tso, Shu-tu, XXIV, 18. Tso's experiences in the mu-fu of the two governors, Chang Liang-chi and Lo Ping-chang, proved quite negative at times, and he often wrote disparagingly about it. He did have several advisers in Northwest China but did most work personally.

[108] Lo, TWHKNP, I, 28-30. CSLC, LI, 35.

[109] Tso, Tsung-t'ang, Chang Ta-assu-ma tsou-kao (Memorials for Chang Liang-chi) in Tso, TWHKCC, I-II, especially.

[110] Ch'en, Tso Tsung-t'ang, 4-5.

[111] Tso, Chang Ta-ssu-ma, III, 3-5; IV, 37-40, 54-57. Lo, TWHKNP, I, 35.

[112] Ch'en, Tso Tsung-t'ang, 6. Lo, TWHKNP, II, 3-6, 26.

[113] Ibid., II, 27. Ch'en, Tso Tsung-t'ang, 6-18.

[114] Ibid. Tso, Shu-tu, III, 3, 19. Lo, TWHKNP, II, 27.

[115] Tso, Lo Wen-chung-kung, III, 30-34.

[116] Ibid., V, 28-29.

[117] Lo, TWHKNP, II, 19. Tso, Lo Wen-chung-kung, VIII, 9-11.

[118] Ibid., V, 44-52; VI, 13-14; VII, 19-24.

[119] Ibid., V, 45-46.

[120] Lo, TWHKNP, II, 34.

Notes to pages 43-44

[121] Tso, *Chia-shu*, I, 1. 7-10.

[122] Bales, *Tso Tsung-t'ang*, 135.

[123] Lo, *TWHKNP*, II, 34.

[124] *Ibid.*, III, 3.

[125] Tso, *Tsou-kao*, VIII, 60-62.

[126] *Ibid.*, V, 18-19, 38-40; VI, 12-13, 31-33; XIV, 42-43.

[127] *Ibid.*, XIV, 24-27.

[128] Lo, *TWHKNP*, III, 29.

## CHAPTER IV

[1] Wei Yuan, *Sheng-wu chi* (Record of imperial military exploits) (Taipei, 1962 reprint), III, 28-63; IV, 1-24. Northern Chinese Turkestan is also known as Zungharia while Southern Chinese Turkestan has been alternately called Kashgaria and Alti Shahr.

[2] Tso, *Chia-shu*, II, 36.

[3] Pai Shou-i, *Hui-hui min-tsu ti hsin-sheng* (The new life of the Muslim peoples) (Shanghai, 1951), 44, 48.

[4] Religious aspects in the interest group perspective within Islam will be considered in the next chapter.

[5] C.Y. Chen, "A Review of the *Hsien-T'ung Yun-nan Hui-min Shih-pien*," Journal of Asian Studies, XXX (1970), 177-178. The idea of using an interest-group perspective came in this review relating to the Muslim rebellions in Yunnan.

[6] Chu Wen-djang titled his thesis and monograph on the Muslim rebellions as *The Moslem Rebellion*.

[7] Jonathan N. Lipman, "Patchwork Society, Network Society: A Study of Sino-Muslim Communities," Paper presented at International Conference on Islam in Asia, Jerusalem, Israel (April 1977), Conference Volume in preparation, 3-4, 10-11; and a personal communication from Jonathan Lipman.

[8] Tso, *Tsou-kao*, XLVI, 36-38. F.C.H. Clarke, "Kuldja," Proceedings of the Geographic Society of London, N.S.II (August 1880), 489-492.

[9] L.F. Kostenko, *The Turkistan Region: Being a Military Statistical Review of the Turkistan Military District or Russian Turkistan Gazetteer* (Simla, 1882-1884), I, 61.

[10] G. Kreitner, "Die Wege von Ansifan durch die Wuste Gobi nach Hami," *Petermann's Mittheilungen*, XXVIII (1882), 419-422.

[11] Ch'in, TWHKTHP, 35-36, 90-92. Kreitner, "Die Wege," 420. Kostenko, The Turkistan Region, II, 15. The middle source noted the many camel carcasses on the Ansi-fan-Hami route. The Russians also used the camel as a beast of burden in Western Turkestan.

[12] S.W. Williams, The Middle Kingdom: A Survey of the Geography, Government, Literature, Social Life, Arts, and History of the Chinese Empire and Its Inhabitants (New York, 1883), II, 731. Henry Lansdell, Chinese Central Asia: A Ride to Little Tibet (London, 1893), I, 334. "The Chinese Reconquest of Eastern Turkistan," The Spectator, LI (1878). 466.

[13] Bales, Tso Tsung-t'ang, 320, 350-357.

[14] NCH, XXII (1879), 237-238. British Foreign Office (hereafter F.O.) 17/825, 12/29/1877, Fraser to Derby. F.O. 17/824, 3/7/1878, Fraser to Derby. The latter two sources said that "the Chinese have every reason to be proud of their achievement" and that "Tso carried out his plan with perfect success."

[15] Mary G. Taylor, The Call of China's Great Northwest: Kansu and Beyond (London, N.D.), 3. This author referred to the rugged lonely distances in Northwest China.

[16] F.O. 17/826, "An Account of the Capture of Kashgaria by the Chinese," 156-157. G. Macartney, "Eastern Turkestan: The Chinese as Rulers Over an Alien Race," Proceedings of the Royal Central Asian Society, VI (March 1909), 12.

[17] Chu, The Moslem Rebellion, 96.

[18] Chen Keng-ya, "How the Benefits of Irrigation are Nullified in Ninghsia," in Agrarian China: Selected Source Materials from Chinese Authors (Chicago, 1938), 131.

[19] Bales, Tso Tsung-t'ang, 273-275. Tso, Tsou-kao, XXXIX, 17.

[20] Tso, Chia-shu, II, 80-83. Ch'in, TWHKTHP, 103-106.

[21] Mark Bell, "The Country of the Dungan Rebellions of 1861 and 1895-1896," Asian Review, 3rd series, II (1896), 26-29.

Notes to pages 48-49

[22] Tso, Chia-shu, II, 78-80. Kreitner, "Die Wege," 416-422.

[23] Mildred Cable and Francesca French, Dispatches From Northwest Kansu (London, 1925), 2-5, 69.

[24] N.M. Prjevalsky, Mongolia, the Tangu Country, and the Solitudes of Northern Tibet, Being a Narrative of Three Years Travel in Eastern High Asia (London, 1878), E.D. Morgan, trans., I, 20, 199. Piassetsky, Russian Travelers, II, 186, 232. Eleanor H. Lattimore, Turkestan Reunion (New York, 1934), 254.

[25] Tso, Chia-shu, II, 78-79. Ch'in, TWHKTHP, 60-61.

[26] Tso, Chia-shu, II, 79-80, 80-82.

[27] "Letters from Colonel N.M. Prjevalsky," Proceedings of the Royal Geographic Society, VII (1885), 67.

[28] Ibid. Cable and French, Dispatches, 5. Prjevalsky, Mongolia, I, 20.

[29] Tso, Chia-shu, II, 80-83. Cable and French, Dispatches, 31.

[30] Kreitner, "Die Wege," 420.

[31] Lattimore, Turkestan, 257. Tso, Chia-shu, II, 79-80. Kreitner, "Die Wege," 420.

[32] "Gregor N. Potanin's Journey Through the Altai Mountains," The Geographical Magazine, IV (May 1, 1877), 118-119. Prjevalsky, Mongolia, I, 215. Lattimore, Turkestan, 254.

[33] Tso, Chia-shu, II, 80-81, 82-83, 84-85.

[34] Kreitner, "Die Wege," 421-422.

[35] Ho, San-ming-chen, Tso section, 96.

[36] Ashton W. Dilke, "On the Valley of the Ili and the Water System of Russian Turkestan," Proceedings of the Royal Geographical Society, XVIII (April 13, 1874), 249. Demetrius C. Boulger, Central Asian Portraits: Celebrities of the Khanates and the Neighboring States (London, 1880), 90.

³⁷Tso, Tsou-kao, L, 75-77.

³⁸M. Abel-Remusat, Histoire de la Ville de Khotan: Tires des Annals et Traduite du Chinois (Paris, 1820), 3-103. Macartney, Eastern Turkistan, 6.

³⁹Ethel Forsyth, ed., Autobiography and Reminiscences of Sir Douglas Forsyth (London, 1887), 67.

⁴⁰E.H. Parker, "Manchu Relations with Turkestan," The China Review, XVI (1888), 321-326.

⁴¹Wei, Sheng-wu chi, IV, 13-15.

⁴²Hu, Tsou-kao, XV, 20; XX, 25. Tseng, Tsou-kao, III, 76. Ch'in, TWHKTHP, 35-38, 56.

⁴³Chen, "How the Benefits," 126-127, 131.

⁴⁴Huang Pei, A Study of the Yung-cheng Period, 1723-1735: The Political Phase (Indiana University, Ph. D. thesis, 1963), 316-317. M. Huc, Travels in Tartary, Thibet and China During the Years, 1844-1846 (Chicago, 1898), W. Hazlitt, trans., I.

⁴⁵Tso, Tsou-kao, XXVII, 48-49. I'hsin, et al. Ch'ing-ting p'ing-ting Shen, Kan, Sinkiang Hui-fei fang-lueh (Account of the suppression and pacification of the Muslim rebels in Shensi, Kansu, and Sinkiang, hereafter CTPTSKSHFFI) (Taipei, 1968 reprint), CI, 17-20. M. Sushanlo, "The Migration of the Dungans, 1877-1882," Central Asian Review, VI (1958), 266.

⁴⁶Wang Hung-chih, Tso Tsung-t'ang p'ing Hsi-pei Hui-luan liang-hsiang chih ch'ou-hua yu chuan-yun (A study of the logistics and supplies in Tso Tsung-t'ang's pacification of the Muslim rebellions in the Northwest) (Taipei, 1972), 4-20. Chu, The Moslem Rebellion, 98-102.

⁴⁷Saguchi Toru, "The Revival of the White Mountain Khwajas, 1760-1820," Acta Asiatica, XIV (1968), 7-14. Parker, "Manchu Relations," 331. "The Late Yakoob Beg of Kashgar," Westminster Review, N.S. V (July 1878), 40. Bales, Tso Tsung-t'ang, 295-300. Herold Wiens, "Change in the Ethnography and Land Use of the Ili Valley and Region. Chinese Turkestan," Annals of the Association of American Geographers, LIX (1969), 753-775. V.V. Barthold, "Kuldja," Encyclopaedia of Islam, II (1927), 1113.

⁴⁸Saguchi, "The Revival," 12-18. Parker, "Manchu Relations," 331-335. Saguchi Toru, "The Eastern Trade

Relations," 331-335. Saguchi Toru, "The Eastern Trade of the Koqand Khanate," Memoirs of the Research Branch of the Toyo Bunko, XXIV (1965), 50-54, 85-110.

[49] Schuyler, Turkistan, II, 174. Saguchi, "The Eastern," 50-110.

[50] Ch'ing shih-lu (Veritable record of the Ch'ing) (Sheng-tsu section), CCXLIX, 14-16. The rate was based on the 1711 return.

[51] Frederick Wakeman, "High Sh'ing," in James B. Browley, ed., Modern East Asia: Essays in Interpretation (New York, 1970), 4-27.

[52] Ho Ping-ti, Studies on the Population of China, 1368-1953 (Cambridge, 1959), 36-67, 101-123.

[53] S.Y. Teng, The Taiping Rebellion and the Western Powers (Oxford, 1971), 27.

[54] Robert Ekvall, Cultural Relations on the Kansu-Tibetan Border (Chicago, 1939), 20-26. Lipman, "Patchwork Society," 9. Lipman indicated that the Muslims sometimes were victorious in legal disputes and that at times they were seen by local officials as "being fond of litigation."

[55] Ho and Wei, eds., Huang-ch'ao, XXXIX, 1-19.

[56] Kao Teng-chih, "Ch'ing-tai T'ung-chih nien-chien Shen-Kan Hui-min ch'i-i (The Shensi and Kansu Muslim Uprisings during the T'ung-chih era of the Ch'ing dynasty," Jen-wen k'o-hsueh ts'a-chih, #6 (1969), 37-38.

[57] Ho and Wei, eds., Huang-ch'ao, XXXIX, 1-18.

[58] Imanaga Seiji, "Shindai Chugoku Kaimin shakai kenkyu (A study of the Chinese Muslim community in the Ch'ing period)," Tohogaku, #24 (1962), 54-55. Ch'in, TWHKTHP, 24-26.

[59] Chu, The Moslem Rebellion, 11-14.

[60] Ibid.

[61] Joseph Fletcher, "China and Central Asia, 1368-1884," in John K. Fairbank, ed., The Chinese World Order (Cambridge, 1968), 213-224.

[62] Wei, ed., Sheng-wu chi, III, 28-63; IV, 1-24.

[63] Ibid. Saguchi, "The Revival," 7-18. Fletcher, "China," 219.

[64] Hummel, ECCP, 73.

[65] V.V. Barthold, "Khokand," Encyclopaedia of Islam, II (1927), 963-965. Seymour Becker, Russia's Protectorates in Central Asia: Bukhara and Khiva, 1865-1924 (Cambridge, 1968), 3-23 and passim. E. Allworth, Central Asia: A Century of Russian Rule (New York 1967), 2-59. Travel by merchants and Muslim pilgrims seemed to have increased in the eighteenth and nineteenth centuries. As will be seen in the next chapter such journeying had important results in Northwest China.

[66] Saguchi, "The Eastern Trade," 50, 53-55.

[67] Ibid., 50

[68] Mary Holdsworth, Turkestan in the Nineteenth Century: A Brief History of the Khanates of Bukhara, Kokand, and Khiva (Oxford 1959), 5-6. Hummel, ECCP, 67-69. Saguchi, "The Eastern Trade," 54-55.

[69] Hummel, ECCP, 68.

[70] Fletcher, "China," 223.

[71] Ibid., 222-223. Saguchi, "The Eastern Trade," 85-110.

[72] Jack A. Dabbs, History of the Discovery and Exploration of Chinese Turkestan (The Hague, 1963), passim.

[73] V.S. Kuznetsov, "British and Russian Trade Relations in Sinkiang, 1819-1851," Central Asian Review, XIII (1965), 151. Dabbs, History, 31.

[74] Ibid., 34.

[75] G.A. Mikhaleva, "Diplomatic Relations Between Russia and Bukhara at the Turn of the Eighteenth Century," Central Asian Review, XI (1963), 268. Yuan Tsing, "Yakub Beg (1820-1877) and the Moslem Rebellion in Chinese Turkestan," Central Asiatic Journal, VI (1961), 140. Kuznetsov, "British," 156. The Ch'ing regime appeared shrewd in this settlement because they not only controlled the numbers of caravans and thereby minimized international incidents but they could also monitor the Russian intelli-

gence agents who accompanied such ventures.

[76] Dabbs, History, 36.

[77] Ahmed Shah Nakshabandi, "Route from Kashmir via Ladakh to Yarkand," The Journal of the Royal Asiatic Society of Great Britain and Ireland, XII (1849), 372-383. "Narrative of the Travels of Ahmed Shah," The Journal of the Royal Asiatic Society of Bengal, #4 (1856), 344-358. Dabbs, History, 46-47.

[78] Pai, Hui-hui, 44,48. Ma Hsiao-shih, Hsi-pei hui-tsu ko-ming chien-shih (A short history of the revolution of the Muslim peoples in the Northwest) (Shanghai, 1951), 81-82.

[79] Chu, The Moslem Rebellion, 20-22.

[80] Tso, Tsou-kao, XL, 66-67; LI, 68; LIV, 66.

[81] Pai Shou-i, ed., Hui-min ch'i-i (The Muslim uprising) (Shanghai, 1952), IV, 308-310.

[82] A.K. Wu, Turkistan Tumult (London, 1940), 55 ff.

[83] F.O. 17/826, 11/6/1879, "Ney Elias' Report on His Mission to Yarkand," 289. Macartney, "Eastern Turkestan," 12.

[84] Chen, "How the Benefits," 126.

[85] Lawrence Krader, Social Organization of the Mongol-Turkic Pastoral Nomads (The Hague, 1963), 19-27.

[86] S.I. Bruk, "The Ethnography of Sinkiang and Tibet," Central Asian Review, VII (1959), 85. Lawrence Krader, Peoples of Central Asia (Bloomington, 1963), 63.

[87] Prjevalsky, Mongolia, II, 8-9, 125.

[88] Krader, Social Organization, 190. Edward Dennis Sokol, "The Revolt of 1916 in Russian Central Asia," The Johns Hopkins University Studies in Historical and Political Science, LXXI (1953), 135.

[89] Prjevalsky, Mongolia, II, 125.

[90] Tso, Chia-shu, II, 12-14. This letter shows that

Tso Tsung-t'ang received some important evidence from the Alashan Mongols about the rebellious intentions of Ma Hua-lung, head of the New Teaching (Hsin chiao) group.

[91] Lipman, "Patchwork Society," 11.

[92] Krader, Social Organization, 10, 287, 290. Louis M.J. Schram, The Monguors of the Kansu-Tibetan Border, Part II: Their Religious Life," Transactions of the American Philosophical Society, new series, XLVII (1957), 1-164.

[93] Louis M.J. Schram, "Records of the Monguor Clans: History of the Monguors in Huangchung and the Chronicles of the Lu Family," Transactions of the American Philosophical Society, new series, LI (1961), 63-68. Bruk, "The Ethnography," 85.

[94] S.I. Bruk, "Sinkiang," Central Asian Review, IV (1956), 433-434. Wiens, "Change," 764. Chu, The Moslem Rebellion, 163.

[95] G.F. Andrew, The Crescent in Northwest China (London, 1921), 65, 68. Yuan, "Yakub Beg," 149. Wendjang Chu, The Policy of the Manchu Government in the Suppression of the Moslem Rebellion in Shensi, Kansu, and Sinkiang from 1862-1878 (University of Washington, Ph.D. thesis, 1955), 392, note #7.

[96] Ibid. Imanaga, "Sindai Chugoku," 53.

[97] Ekvall, Cultural Relations, 5-87.

[98] Ma, Hsi-pei, 81.

[99] Pai Jui-ch'ang, Hui-chiao shih-chieh (Islamic world) (Taipei, 1959), 150. Nishida Tamotsu, Sa so-to to Shinkyo mondai (Tso tsung-t'ang and the Northwest) (Tokyo, 1941), 146. Pai Shou-i, Hsueh-pu chi (learning steps) (Peking, 1962), 21-24. S.M. Zwemer, "The Fourth Religion in China," The Moslem World, XXIV (1934), 3.

[100] Pai, Hui-hui, 12.

[101] Pai Shou-i, Chung-kuo hui-chiao hsiao-shih (A brief history of Islam in China) (Chungking, 1944), 1-4. Pai, Hui-hui, 13.

[102] Pai, Chung-kuo, 7-8.

[103] Morris Rossabi, "The Muslims in the Early Yuan Dynasty," Paper presented at International Conference on Islam in Asia, Jerusalem, Israel (April 1977), Conference Volume in preparation, 1-2.

[104] V.V. Barthold, "Kansu," Encyclopaedia of Islam, II (1927), 719.

[105] Rossabi, "The Muslims," 28-31. Iwamura Shinobu, "The Structure of Moslem Society in Inner Mongolia," Far Eastern Quarterly, VIII (1948-1949), 37. M. L'Abbe Grosier, De La Chine ou Description Generale De Cet Empire (Paris, 1819), IV, 507-508. John Anderson, "Chinese Mohammedans," Royal Anthropological Institute of Great Britain and Ireland, I (1872), 149-150. W.G. Walshe, "Religious Toleration in China, Mohammedanism," Contemporary Review, LXXXVI (July 1904), 128. Ekvall, Cultural Relations, 26-27. According to Anderson and Grosier the Muslims accelerated their efforts at converting people in the seventeenth and eighteenth centuries. No convincing reasons are given for this although Anderson links it to a Muslim reaction to growing Chinese oppression. Walshe and others have stressed the Ch'ing hostility to missionary efforts by the Muslims.

[106] Lipman, "Patchwork Society," 3, 11.

[107] Ibn Battuta, Travels of Ibn Battuta (New York, 1958-1962), trans., H.A.R. Gibb, II, 290-300. Isaac Mason, "How Islam Entered China," The Moslem World, XIX (1929), 259.

[108] Rossabi, "The Muslims," 33.

[109] Mason, "How Islam," 260. Pai, Chung-kuo, 15-26.

[110] Pai Shou-i, "Hui-hui min-tsu ti hsin-ch'eng ho ch'u-pu fa-chan (The formation and early development of the Muslims)," Hsin chien-she, #110 (November 1957), 38. Imanaga, "Shindai Chugiku," 51-54.

[111] Pai, Chung-kuo, 27.

[112] Ahmed Ali, Muslim China (Karachi, 1949), 32-33. Canon Sell, Muslims in China (London, 1905), 21.

[113] Tso, Tsou-kao, XLI, 60-62. Andrew, The Crescent, 73, F.O. 17/826, "Ney Elias' Mission," 289.

Notes to pages 59-60

114 Imanaga, "Shindai Chugoku," 54-55.

115 Ibid., 55-57. Gunnar Jarring, "Materials to the Knowledge of Eastern Turki: Tales, Poetry, Proverbs, Riddles, Ethnological and Historical Texts from the Southern Parts of Eastern Turkestan," Lunds Universitets Arsskrift IV (1951), 117. Saguchi Toru, "The Community and Religious Life of the Chinese Moslems," Minzokugaku kenkyu, XIII (1949), 21-29.

116 Harold D. Hayward, "The Kansu Moslems," The Moslem World, XXIV (1934), 74-65. Iwamura, "The Structure," 37, 40.

117 Imanaga, Shindai Chugoku," 57.

118 F.O. 17/826, "Ney Elias' Mission," 289-290. Jarring, "Materials," II (1948), 130, 163.

119 This is characteristic of the Muslim centers which erupted in rebellion in the 1860s against the Chinese. Each major oasis town had its individual leader. Yakub Beg was finally able through warfare to provide a kind of unity to the Islamic risings.

120 Demetrius C. Boulger, The Life of Yakub Beg: Athalik Ghazi and Badaulet Ameer of Kashgar (London, 1878), 144-149, Yuan, "Yakub Beg," 138-147. D. Tikhonov, "The Internal Policies of Yakub Beg of Kashgar," Central Asian Review, VII (1959), 404. William Samolin, The Turkisation of the Tarim Basin up to the Qara-Qytay: A Preliminary Survey of the Problems Involved (Columbia University Ph.D. thesis, 1954), 114. The practice of using intermediaries to rule subject peoples was used by the Chinese from the earliest times of their political penetration into Chinese Turkestan as the latter source indicates.

121 Tso, Shu-tu, XXI, 8-11.

122 Ibn Battuta, Travels, II, 283-299. Richard Pipes, "Muslims of Central Asia," Middle East Journal, IX (1955), 299. This practice of segregation existed for centuries in China and Central Asia.

123 Andrew, The Crescent, 21, 34, 68.

124 Ibid., 73. Tso, Tsou-kao, XLI, 60-62.

125 Fletcher, "China," 364, note 97.

[126] Nicholas Poppe, "Remarks on the Salar Language," *Harvard Journal of Asiatic Studies*, XVI (1953), 477. Lipman, "Patchwork Society," 10.

[127] Schram, "History," 63-69. Andrew, *The Crescent*, 11-17. C.E. Bonin, "The Kansu Mohammedans and Their Last Revolt," *Revue de Monde Musulman*, X (1915), 210-216. United States Government, Office of Strategic Services (hereafter, O.S.S.), Research and Analysis Branch, "Peoples and Politics of China's Northwest," #1921 (1945), 13-14. F. Grenard, "Note sur les Musulmans Solar du Kansou," *Journal Asiatique*, series IX (1898), 546-551.

[128] "Kirgizia," *Asian Review* (January 1955), 70-74. Bruk, "The Ethnography," 85. M. Sushanlo, "The Dungans in China," *Central Asian Review*, IX (1961), 201-205. A.K. Wu, "The Fourteen Peoples of Chinese Turkestan," *West China Border Research Society*, (1944), 91. Armin Vambery, *Travels in Central Asia* (New York, 1970 reprint), 402-403. Eugene Schuyler, *Turkistan: Notes of a Journey in Russian Turkistan, Bukhara, Kuldja* (New York, 1876), II, 175. Wilhelm Filchner, *Hui Hui: Asiens Islam Kämpfe* (Berlin, 1928), 85. Kostenko, *The Turkistan Region*, I, 270.

[129] Wu, "The Fourteen Peoples," 91.

[130] *Ibid.*

[131] Jarring, "Materials," II (1948), 130. "Kirgizia," 74. Chu, *The Moslem Rebellion*, 2. Schuyler, *Turkistan*, II, 169-170.

[132] Wu, "The Fourteen Peoples," 91. Jarring, "Materials," II (1948), 130.

[133] O.S.S. Research and Analysis #1921, 4-8. Prjevalsky, *Mongolia*, II, 125.

CHAPTER V

[1] Ira M. Lapidus, "Hierarchies and Networks: A Comparison of Chinese and Islamic Societies," in Frederick Wakeman, Jr., and Carolyn Grant, eds., Conflict and Control in Late Imperial China (Berkeley, 1975), 26-42. Lipman, "Patchwork Society," 1-32. Lanny Bruce Fields, "Ethnicity in Tso Tsung-t'ang's Armies, 1867-1880: The Interest Group Perspective," Journal of Asian Affairs, (Spring 1978).

[2] J. Spencer Trimingham, The Sufi Orders in Islam (Oxford, 1971), 59.

[3] T'ang Chen-yu, "The Four Men Huan," Friends of Moslems, XVI (January 1942), 6-7.

[4] H.A.R. Gibb, "The Structure of Religious Thought in Islam (IV), Sufism," Moslem World, XXXVIII (1948), 287-288. Arthur F. Wright, Buddhism in Chinese History (New York, 1965), 56. The latter reference noted that the Buddhists also employed magic to awe and convert nomadic peoples.

[5] John A. Subhan, Sufism: Its Saints and Shrines, An Introduction to the Study of Sufism with Special Reference to India (Lucknow, 1938), 110-111.

[6] Michael Gilsenan, Saint and Sufi in Modern Egypt: An Essay in the Sociology of Religion (Oxford, 1973), 43.

[7] Alexander Bennigson, "Traditional Islam in the Customs of the Turkic Peoples of Central Asia," Middle East Journal, XII, (1958), 230.

[8] Joseph Castagne, "Le Culte des Lieux Saints de L'Islam au Turkestan," Societe d'Ethnographie de Paris, XLVI (1951), 70, 80-81.

[9] Gilsenan, Saint and Sufi, 3-4

[10] William Bateson. Letters From the Steppe Written in the Years 1886-1887 (London, 1928), 178. "A Chinese

Muslim Has Recently Returned From a Pilgrimage to Mecca," Chinese Repository, II (1833), 96, Vambery, Travels, 48-49.

[11] Trimingham, The Sufi, 59.

[12] V.V. Barthold, "Bukhara," Encyclopaedia of Islam, I, 782. Serge A. Zenkovsky, Pan-Turkism and Islam in Russia (Cambridge, 1960), 77. "Chu-A Kaikyo no tokyshusei ni tsuite (The special characteristics of Central Asian Islam)," Kaikyo Jijo, IV (1941), 56.

[13] Gilsenan, Saint and Sufi, 44.

[14] Vambery, Travels, 177, 402-403, 409. Schuyler, Turkistan, I, 72.

[15] Krader, Peoples, 126. On certain occasions a pilgrimage to an especially-venerated holy place would replace one to Mecca.

[16] G.W. Hunter, "Islam in Central Asia," Moslem World, XX (1930, 21. H.W. Bellew, Kashmir and Kashgar: A Narrative of a Journey of the Embassy to Kashgar in 1873-1874. (London, 1875), x, 337.

[17] Castagne, "Le Culte," 72-74.

[18] Ibid.

[19] Ibid., 103.

[20] Jarring, "Materials," IV (1951), 174. Trimingham, The Sufi, 232. Castagne, "Le Culte," Jarring noted that women journeyed to the Sut Padishahim mazar in Yarkand to ask for male children as their next born.

[21] Ibid., 62, 76.

[22] Ibid., 53-54, 104. The Mazar Zengui Ata's saint was the guardian of the horned animals.

[23] "Khotan to Kashgar," Friends of Moslems, V (1931), 2-3.

[24] Gibb, "The Structure," 289-290. Castagne, "Le Culte," 48. Subhan, Sufism, 110-111. T'ang, "The Four Men Huan," 5.

$^{25}$Gilsenan, *Saint and Sufi*, 15.

$^{26}$Trimingham, *The Sufi*, 233-239.

$^{27}$Castagne, "Le Culte," 58-60. Bellew, *Kashmir*, 309, 321-327, 378. Schuyler, *Turkistan*, I, 70-72. Ahmed Shah Nakshabandi, "Route to Kashmir Via Ladakh to Yarkand," *Journal of the Royal Society of Great Britain and Ireland*, XII (1849), 348-349.

$^{28}$Vambery, *Travels*, 304. Irving I. Markovitz, "Traditional Social Structure, The Islamic Brotherhoods and Political Development in Senegal," *Journal of Modern African Studies*, VIII (1970), 84.

$^{29}$Ch'en Ch'ing-lung, "Lun Pai Shan (Aktaglik) yu Hei Shan Tang (Karataglik) (The White and Black Mountain Factions)," *Pien-cheng Nien-piao*, #2 (July 1971), 231.

$^{30}$Robert B. Shaw, "The History of the Khojas of Eastern Turkestan Summarized from the *Tazkira-i Khwajagan* of Muhammad Sadiq Kashgari," *Journal of the Asiatic Society of Bengal*, IXVI, Part I (1897), 20-32. Bellew, *Kashmir*, 321-327, 333-344, 366-367. Ch'en, "Lun Pai Shan Tang," 212.

$^{31}$Shaw, "The History," 3. Morris Rossabi, "Muslim and Central Asian Revolts in Late Ming and Early Ch'ing," unpublished paper, 3-5.

$^{32}$Ibid. "Chu-A kaikyo no tokushusei ni tsuite (The special characteristics of Central Asian Islam), *Kaikyo Jijo*, IV (1941), 62. Joseph Fletcher, personal communication.

$^{33}$Bellew, Kashmir, 321. Vambery, *Travels*, 406.

$^{34}$Joseph Fletcher, "The Naqshbandiyya and the Dhikr-i Arra," *Journal of Turkish Studies*, I (1977), 113.

$^{35}$Shaw, "The History," 6. Bellew, *Kashmir*, 321.

$^{36}$Ch'en, "Lun Pai Shan Tang," 223-224. Shaw, "The History," 9-11, 33-35. Like Afaq, Ishaw Vali "raised a person from the dead."

$^{37}$Ibid.

$^{38}$Rossabi, "Muslim and Central Asian," 4.

[39] Ibid., 33-34.

[40] Saguchi Toru, "The Revival of the White Mountain Khwajas, 1760-1820 (from Sarimsaq to Jihangir," Acta Asiatica, #14 (1968), 7.

[41] Morris Rossabi, "The Muslims in the Early Yuan Dynasty," Unpublished paper, 18, 28-31. H.M.G. D'Ollone, Recherches sur les Kusulmans Chinois (Paris 1911), 201-215. "A Biography of Sayyid Edjell," Friends of Moslems, X (January 1936), 10. Tomb veneration came at least as early as the thirteenth century when the tomb of Saiyid Ajall, a Prince of Bukhara and a descendant of Muhammed as well as an able ruler of Yunnan became an object of veneration. Ibn Battuta, the great Muslim traveler reported the existence of two orders in China, see Ibn Battuta, Travels of Ibn Battuta, trans., H.A.R. Gibb, (Cambridge, 1958-1962), II, 248-249. Vincent Monteil, "The Introduction to the Voyages of Ibn Battutah." The Islamic Review, LVIII (March 1970), 35. Other accounts of tomb veneration may be found in D'Ollone, Recherches, 264, 316. Martin Hartmann, "China," Encyclopaedia of Islam, II, 852-853. W.B. Pettus "Chinese Mohammedanism," The Chinese Recorder and Missionary Journal, XLIV (February 1913), 92.

[42] H.D. Hayward, "The Kansu Moslems," Moslem World, XXXIV (1944), 75.

[43] There is some disagreement about Ma Ming-hain's birthplace. Most sources state that he came from Anting but two noted that he came from Hochow. Although a final determination of this question does not seem possible at this time, the earliest references in the eighteenth century seem to be the most accurate in calling Anting his home.

[44] Tso, Tsou-kao, XXXVII, 62-65. Pai, Hui-min, III, 4.

[45] T'ang, "The Four Men Huan," 5. Chin Ch'i-t'ang, "The Rebellion of Ma Ming-hsin," Friends of Moslems, XVII (April 1943), 33.

[46] Baruddin Wee-liang Hai, The Muslim Minority in China (Columbia University M.A. Thesis, 1955), 50-51.

[47] Saguchi Toru, "Chugoku Isuram no Shimpishugi (A Study of Islamic Mysticism in China)," Tohogaku, (October 1954), 76-78.

[48] Yi K'ung-chao, et al., P'ing-ting huan-lung chi-

lueh (Account of the pacification of Shensi and Kansu) (Peking, 1877), I, 1.  Pai, Hui-min, III, 3-4.  Tso, Tsou-kao, XXXVII, 62-63.  Pai Shou-i, Hui-hui min-tzu ti hsin-sheng (The new life of the Muslim peoples) (Shanghai, 1951), 45.  If Ma Ming-hsin was seven when he journeyed to Bukhara, he must have gone in the 1740s or the early 1750s at the latest.  He spent some years at Bukhara and in traveling elsewhere then returned home.  Presumably when called to teach in 1761 he was an adult with an established reputation.  This would seem to indicate that he traveled to Bukhara at least 10-20 years before he was invited to Hsun-hua; therefore he must have traveled there at least in the 1740-1750 period if not earlier.  If this is correct then the transmission of the New Teaching to China Proper was unrelated to the opening of Chinese relations with Central Asia in the 1750s as some scholars have suggested.

[49] Tso, Tsou-kao, XXXVII, 62-64.  Ta-Ch'ing kao-tsung shih-lu (Veritable records of Ch'ing Ch'ien-lung) (Chungchun, Manchuria: 1935-1940), MCXXX, 11; MCXXXVI, 28.

[50] Saguchi Toru, Juhachi to Jukyuseki Higashi Torukisutan shakai shi kenRyu (The social history of Eastern Turkestan in the eighteenth and nineteenth centuries) (Tokyo, 1963), 560-568.  Hartmann, "China," II, 852-853.

[51] Pai, Hui-min, IV, 311.

[52] G. Findlay Andrew, "Islam in Northwest China Today," Journal of the Royal Central Asian Society, XIX (1932), 93.

[53] L. Gardet, "Dhikr," Encyclopaedia of Islam, New Edition, II, 224.

[54] Frederick C. Conybeare, Russian Dissenters (New York, 1962), 27-39.

[55] Nakada Yoshinobu, "Dochi nenkan no San-Kan no Kairan ni tsuite (Muslim uprisings in Shensi and Kansu during the T'ung-chih era)," Kindai chu-goku kenkyu, #3 (1959), 158-159.  Schuyler, Turkistan, I, 158-160.  In addition to the same name Schuyler who attended a dhikr ceremony of the Jahriyya noted that the participants used the "saw dhikr" technique characteristic of the Yasawiyya as well as the moving of the participant's head from side to side during the ceremony.  Schuyler also identified the Jahriyya and Naqshbandiyya as two different groups. Fletcher, "The Naqshbandiyya," 115-119, noted that the Naqshbandiyya also had a group which practiced the vocal dhikr.

[56] T'ang, "The Four Men Huan," 5, note 2.

[57] Fletcher, "The Naqshbandiyya," 115-119. In a personal communication Joseph Fletcher stated that he found new evidence in Yemen indicating that Ma Ming-hsin's New Teaching was a Naqshbandi tariqat, and that Ma was initiated into the order in Yemen. This evidence will be soon forthcoming.

[58] Filchner, Hui Hui, 114, J.J.M. de Groot, Sectarianism and Religious Persecution in China: A Page in the History of Religions (Taipei, 1963 reprint), II, 314. Schram, "History," 63.

[59] W.A. Saunders, "Hsuan Hua Kang," Friends of Moslems, VIII (October 1934), 69.

[60] Pai, Hui-min, III, 9-10. Saguchi, "Chugoku Isuram," 79-83.

[61] Schuyler, Turkistan, I, 158-161.

[62] Pai, Hui-min, IV, 309-311. Pai, Hui-hui, 45-46. Saguchi, Juhachi, 560. Chu, The Policy, 352.

[63] Joseph Fletcher, "Central Asian Sufism and Ma Ming-hsin's New Teaching," in Ch'en Chieh-hsien, ed., Proceedings of the Fourth East Asian Altaistic Conference (Tainan, 1975), 79. L. Massignon, "Tariqat," Encyclopaedia of Islam, IV, 670. Hartman, "China," II, 283.

[64] Fletcher, "Central Asian Sufism," 79.

[65] Pai, Hui-min, III, 4-5. Tso, Tsou-kao, XXXVII, 62-65. Tso commented that Ma Ming-hsin was illegally executed.

[66] Pai, Hui-min, III, 4-5. Tso, Tsou-kao, XXXVII, 62-65.

[67] Yi, et al., P'ing-ting, I, 1. Chin, "The Rebellion," 33. Pai, Hui-min, III, 5.

[68] Saguchi, Juhachi, 569. Pai, Hui-min, III, 6. Tso, Tsou-kao, XXXVII, 65-66.

[69] Fletcher, "Central Asian Sufism," 76.

⁷⁰Edward Sell, The Religious Orders of Islam (London, 1908), 5. A full-scale comparative treatment of the New Teaching and other secret societies is beyond the scope of this study.

⁷¹Trimingham, The Sufi, 233-239.

⁷²Tso, Tsou-kao, XXXVIII, 63.

⁷³Chu, The Moslem Rebellion, 159.

⁷⁴Tso, Tsou-kao, XXXVII, 62-63. Saguchi, Juhachi, 570-571. Pai, Hui-min, IV, 311. Schram, "History," 65. The latter source also indicates that there was a New Teaching disturbance in 1789.

⁷⁵Pai, Hui-min, IV, 310-311.

⁷⁶Po Ching-wei, Feng-hsi ts-ao-t'ang chi (Collection from the grass hut West of the Feng river) (Nanking 1924), III, 7. Fletcher, "The Naqshbandiyya," 114.

⁷⁷C.L. Pickens, "News from the Field, Hung-lo, Ninghsia," Friends of Moslems, XVII (October 1943), 52. Fletcher, "The Naqshbandiyya," 114.

⁷⁸Po, Feng-hsi, III, 7-8.

⁷⁹T'ang, "The Four Men Huan," 5.

⁸⁰Po, Feng-hsi, III, 7. Lipman, "Patchwork Society," 31

⁸¹Schram, "History," 66. One possible practice that Ma Hua-lung might have discovered in Western Turkestan was the use of whips on the errant faithful. Ma used whips as punishment to eradicate sins from the sinners, and they were used by akhunds in Tashkent to enforce proper conduct by the faithful; see Schuyler, Turkestan, I, 159, and Saguchi, "Chugoku Isuram," 83.

⁸²T'ang, "The Four Men Huan," 5. Pai, Hui-min, IV, 311.

⁸³Saunders, "Hsuan Hua Kang," 69-70. Pickens, "News from the Field," 52. Leonard Street, "Islam in Lanchow," Friends of Moslems, XX (October 1946), 34-37. The latter source suggested that Ma Ming-hsin was buried in a tomb outside Lanchow.

[84]T'ang, "The Four Men Huan," 5.

[85]Tso, Tsou-kao, XXXVIII, 62-65. Saguchi, Juhachi, 571-572. T'ang, "The Four Men Huan," 5.

[86]Tso, Tsou-kao, XXXVIII, 63-65.

[87]Po, Feng-hsi, III, 7-8. D'Ollone, Recherches, 263. "Ma Hua-lung," Friends of Moslems, IX (January 1935), 30.

[88]Chu, The Policy, 350-351.

[89]Robert B. Ekvall, "Revolt of the Crescent in Western China," Asia, XXXIX (1929), 946, 1006.

[90]Robert B. Ekvall, Gateway to Tibet: The Kansu-Tibetan Border (Harrisburg, 1938), 137-139. C.E. Bonin, "The Kansu Moslems and their Last Revolt," Revue de Monde Musulman, X (1915), 212. Chu, The Moslem Rebellion, 23-28. Rossabi, "Muslim and Central Asian," 24-29, 34-35.

[91]Piassetsky, Russian Travelers, I, 197-198. Taylor, The Call, 162.

[92]I-hsin, et al., Ch'in-ting p'ing-ting Shen-Kan Sinkiang Hui-fel fang-luch (Account of the suppression and pacification of the Muslim rebels in Shensi, Kansu, and Chinese Turkestan) (Taipei, 1968 reprint), CCXXXVIII, 11-13; CCXXXV, 18.

[93]Pickens, "News from the Field," 52. Hartman, "China," II, 853.

[94]"Ma Yuan-chang," Friends of Moslems, XX (1946), 204. Taylor, The Call, 172. Saguchi, "Chugoku Isuram," 85.

[95]Saunders, "Hsuan Hua Kang," 69-70.

[96]Olive Botham, "The Djahariyeh and Godeemi in Kansu," Friends of Moslems, V (April 1931), 16. T'ang, "The Four Men Huan," 5. "Ma Yuan-chang," 204.

[97]Saguchi, "Chugoku Isuram," 86. "Ma Yuan-chang," 204. H.A.R. Gibb, Mohammedanism: An Historical Survey (New York, 1960), 107. The latter source noted that the Qutb was the highest saint in Islam.

[98] C.L. Pickens, "A Trek Through the Tangut Country," Moslem World, XXXIII (1943), 11. Taylor, The Call, 172. Hayward, "The Kansu Moslems," 76-77. Saunders, "Hsuan Hua Kang," 70. "Ma Yuan-chang," 204.

[99] Saunders, "Huan Hua Kang," 69-71.

[100] Joseph Fletcher, "Central Asian Islam," Unpublished paper, 120-124.

[101] Hai, The Muslim Minority, 59-63. A.K. Wu, Turkistan Tumult (London 1940), 55. Chu, The Moslem Rebellion, 163. Fletcher, "The Naqshbandiyya," 114.

[102] Lapidus, "Hierarchies and Networks," 34-37. Lipman, "Patchwork Society," 21-22.

[103] Pai, Hui-min, IV, 310-311.

[104] Mark Botham, "Chinese Islam as an Organism," Moslem World, XIV (1924), 264. Rossabi, "Muslim and Central Asian," 20.

[105] Vambery, Travels, 403. Filchner, Hui Hui, 130.

[106] Bonin, "The Kansu Moslems," 210. R.B. Shaw, "On the Hill Canton of Salar the Most Easterly Settlement of the Turk Race," Royal Asiatic Society of Great Britain and Ireland, Journal, New Series, X (July 1878), 305.

[107] Botham, "Chinese Islam," 264-265. Huc, Travels in Tatary, II, 16-17.

[108] Ibid.

[109] T'ang, "The Four Men Huan," 5-6. Botham, "The Djahariyeh," 16.

[110] Street, "Islam in Lanchow," 35.

[111] Pickens, "News from the Field," 52. Saunders, Hsuan Hua Kang," 69-70. Mark Botham, Islam in Kansu," Moslen World, X (1920), 377-378, 381, 386, 390.

[112] Botham, "Chinese Islam," 266.

[113] Saguchi, "Chugoku Isuram," 83. Andrew, The Crescent, 42-43. T'ang, "The Four Men Huan," 5-6. Street

"Islam in Lanchow," 35-37.

[114] Imanaga Seiji, "Shindai Chugoku Kaimin shakai kenkyu (A Study of the Chinese Muslim community in the Ch'ing period)," Tohogaku, #24 (1962), 60-65. Botham, "Chinese Islam," 264-265. Andrew, The Crescent, 42.

[115] Lipman, "Patchwork Society," 22-23. Andrew, The Crescent, 42-43.

[116] Po, Feng-hsi, III, 7. Tso, Shu-tu, X, 36-37.

[117] Po, Feng-hsi, III, 8-11.

[118] Tso, Tsou-kao, XXXVII, 48-51.

[119] Lipman, "Patchwork," 12. Schram, "History," 63,68.

[120] Pai, Hui-min, III, 4-5.

[121] T'ang, "The Four Men Huan," 5. T.M. Chu, "Mohammedan Factions in Northwest China," The China Recorder, LXV (1934), 602-604. Andrew, The Crescent, 51.

[122] Saunders, "Hsuan Hua Kang," 69-71. Botham, "The Djahariyeh," 16-17. Pickens, "News from the Field," 52. Saguchi, "Chugoku," 85-93.

## CHAPTER VI

[1] See Chapter III for their influence. The hsing-ming/ming-shih bureaucratic technique is important for Tso Tsung-t'ang in his Northwestern campaigns as Ch'in, TWHKTHP, 174-175, and Shen Yun-lung, Tso Wen-hsiang-kung cheng hsi shih lüeh (History of Tso Tsung-t'ang's Western campaign) (Taipei, 19 reprint), 206-207, indicate.

[2] Tso, Shu-tu, XXIV, 18.

[3] Since W.L. Bales, Ch'in Han-ts'ai, Chu Wen-djang, Nakada Yoshinobu, and others have detailed Tso's military exploits in Northwest China elsewhere, this aspect will be briefly considered below.

[4] Tso told the Empress Dowager, Tz'u-hsi, in an interview in 1868 that it would take him five years to complete the reconquest of Shensi and Kansu. This goal was accomplished in November 1873, as Lo, TWHKNP, IV, 48-49, and Teng and Fairbank, China's Response, 80, indicate.

[5] Ch'in, TWHKTHP, 33-38.

[6] Prosper Giquel, The Foochow Arsenal and Its Results: From Commencement in 1867, to the End of the Foreign Directorate, on the 16th February, 1874, trans., H. Lang, (Shanghai, 1874), 1-2.

[7] Chang, et al., CS, 4763-4764. Tso spent most of his first year in Northwest China fighting the Nien rebels. I will not consider that aspect of his campaigns there as I prefer to concentrate on the Moslem rebellions.

[8] Chu, The Moslem Rebellion, 91-93. Ch'in, TWHKTHP, 48 ff. Bales. Tso Tsung-t'ang, 198-204. Chu argues that Tso devised his plan for fighting the Moslems only after consulting with Wang Po-hsin in Hupeg. Tso's key memorial (Tso, Tsou-kao, XXI, 18-21), was written, however, before he talked with Wang.

[9] Tso, Tsou-kao, XXI, 19-22. Immanuel C.Y. Hsü, "The Late Ch'ing Reconquest of Sinkiang: A reappraisal of Tso Tsung-t'ang's Role," Central Asiatic Journal, XII

(1968), 53. Tso asked to have Liu Tien, an able Hunan general as his subordinate, and the court readily agreed. In military matters Tso considered the Nien as the most dangerous threat and stated that following their defeat, bandits should be quieted, then Shensi consolidated; Kansu would be the next and could later be used as a base for the recovery of Chinese Turkestan.

[10] Hummel, ECCP, 764.

[11] Wang, Tso Tsung-t'ang, 4-20.

[12] Tso, Tsou-kao, XXI, 20. Tso, Shu-tu, VIII, 53, 57. Chu, The Moslem Rebellion, 93. Crawford, The Life and Thought, 38-39. Buote, Chu-ko Liang, 16-27. To help alleviate the logistics problems and the burden on the state and the people. Tso proposed and implemented a military colonist system. This was an important institution used by Chu-ko Liang, Chang Chu-cheng, and Yen Ju-i. Lin Tse-hsü also favored the use of the t'un-t'ien when he was in Chinese Turkestan.

[13] Ch'in, TWHKTHP, 57. Chu, The Moslem Rebellion, 93.

[14] Tso, Tsou-kao, XXI, 19.

[15] Stanley, Late Ch'iang Finance, 16.

[16] Ch'in, TWHKTHP, 59-60. Chu-ko Liang also spent much time and care in ensuring an adequate base of supplies for his military campaigns as it would lessen the burden on the people.

[17] Hu, Tsou-kao, XXXIII, 11-14, Ch'in, TWHKTHP, 61-64. Hu also used an auditing system in Hupeh. Tso's great care as evidenced by the above went far beyond the earlier efforts of Chu-ko Liang and others.

[18] Tso, Tsou-kao, XXXIX, 40-42; XLI, 77-79,

[19] Prjevalsky, Mongolia, II, 11. Krader, "Die Wege," 419-422. Troops could cause great suffering for the people and Tso's army had severe morale problems and became unruly at times as these and other foreigners as well as Tso's own memorials indicate.

[20] Tso, Tsou-kao, XVIII, 8.

[21] Ch'in, TWHKTHP, 48. Both Tso and Tseng greatly

valued Liu Sung-shan's services and reported so to the throne.

[22] Yi, et al., P'ing-ting, VIII, 38-45. The fact that he was related to Liu Sung-shan, of course, helped too.

[23] Ch'in, TWHKTHP, 41, 75-76. Chu, The Moslem Rebellion, 133-134. Richard Yang, "Sinkiang under the Administration of Yang Tseng-hsin, 1911-1928," Central Asiatic Journal, VI (1961), 273.

[24] Lo, TWHKNP, II, 4. Ch'en, Tso Tsung-t'ang, Pioneer, 1-5.

[25] Piassetsky, Russian Travelers, II, 144, 156-157. Bell, "The Country," 28-29. Ch'in, TWHKTHP, 53.

[26] Ch'en, Tso Tsung-t'ang, Pioneer, 53-56.

[27] I'hsin, et al., CTPTSKSKHFFL, CCVVXII, 2; CCXX, 13. Pai, Hui-min, III, 166. Bales, Tso Tsung-t'ang, 291-292. Chang Sen-dou, "Some Observations on the Morphology of Chinese Walled Cities," Annals of the Association of American Geographers, LX (1970), 63-75.

[28] S.Y. Teng, The Nien Army and Their Guerilla Warfare, 1851-1868 (Paris, 1961), 164.

[29] Ch'in, TWHKTHP, 67. Chu, The Muslim Rebellion, 49.

[30] Chu, The Moslem Rebellion, 126. Tso, Kao-shih, 4-7. Nakada, "Dochi nenkan," 145.

[31] Ibid.

[32] Tso, Shu-tu, XXI, 38-39. Chu, The Moslem Rebellion, 128.

[33] Nakada, "Dochi nenkan," 127-128.

[34] Lo, TWHKMP, V, 42. Chang, et al., CS, 4763-4764.

[35] Wright, The Last Stand, 111.

[36] Tso, Tsou-kao, XLI, 36-39, 61-66. Pai, Hui-min, IV, 308-311. Nakada, "Dochi nenkan," 108. Wright, The Last Stand, 112.

37 Tso, Tsou-kai, XLIII, 28-30. Pai, Hui-min, III, 191-193. Ch'in, TWHKTHP, 69-71.

38 I-hsin, et al., CTPTSKSKHFFI, CCLXXXIX, 1.

39 Ibid., CCLXXXIX, 24-25. Hsu, "The Ch'ing Reconquest," 51.

40 Kenneth E. Folsom, Friends, Guests, and Colleagues: The Mu-fu System in the Late Ch'ing Period (Berkeley, 1968), 189.

41 Immanuel C.Y. Hsü, "The Great Policy Debate in China, 1874: Maritime Defense vs. Frontier Defense," Harvard Journal of Asiatic Studies, XXV (1964-1965), 215-218. The actual debate spanned 1874-1875.

42 Ibid., 220. Chu, The Moslem Rebellion, 172-175. Chu has translated Tso's important memorial in this matter.

43 Pai, Hui-min, III, 55-56. Hsu, "The Great Policy Debate," 221. Appeals to illustrious ancestors must have charmed the sinified Manchu. For the treasures of Chinese Turkestan see Chapter IV above.

44 Huang Ping-k'un, et al., K'an-ling Hsin-chiang chi (Account of the suppression of the (rebellion) in Sinkiang) (Taipei, 1963 reprint), II, 1-5.

45 Emeroy Upton, Armies of Asia and Europe: Embassy Official Reports on the Armies of Japan, China, India, Persia, Italy, Russia, Austria, Germany, France and England (New York, 1928 reprint), 25. Tso, Tsou-kao, XLV, 73-76. See note #10 in Chapter IV as well.

46 F.O. 17/825. Memorandum of the War Between Yakub Beg and China, 3/26/1877. The commentator noted that the terrain in Yakub Beg's area was formidable, and doubted China's ability to retake it without foreign officers. See also Ch'in, TWHKTHP, 92. Kreitner, "Die Wege," 416-422.

47 Ch'in, TWHKTHP, 90-92. C.P. Skrine, Chinese Central Asia (London, 1926), 284. The latter source indicates that the Chinese also used tax incentives to encourage the planting of trees.

48 Tso, Tsou-kao, XLV, 59-62; XLVIII, 69-72. CSLC,

LXI, 44. Hsü, "The Late Ch'ing Reconquest," 58.

[49] Tso, Tsou-kao, XLV, 79-80. Lo, TWHKNP, VII, 2. Bales, Tso Tsung-t'ang, 328-332. Henry Lansdell, Chinese Central Asia: A Ride to Little Tibet (London, 1893), 334. The latter sources point to a site where Tso's soldiers cultivated.

[50] Hsu, "The Late Ch'ing Reconquest," 59. Rutherford Alcock, "The Chinese Empire and Its Foreign Relations," Fortnitely Review, XXV (1876), 670.

[51] Teng and Fairbank, China's Response, 81. Tso, Tsou-kao, XLV, 38-52; LIV, 44-55. Tso usually submitted detailed records of his expenditures unlike many other officials as shown by David Pong, "Income and Military Expenditure of Kiangsi Province in the Last Years of the Taiping Rebellion," Journal of Asian Studies, XXVI (1966-1967), 52-57.

[52] Yang, Tso Tsung-t'ang, 11. Shen, Tso Wen-hsiang-kung, 200-206. Hsu, "The Late Ch'ing Reconquest," 53.

[53] Teng and Fairbank, China's Response, 82.

[54] Stanley, Late Ch'ing Finance, 48-51.

[55] Tso, Tsou-kao, XLV, 69-72; XLVIII, 36-42. Ch'in, TWHKTHP, 54. Stanley, Late Ch'ing Finance, 14-15.

[56] Tso, Tsou-kao, XLVIII, 34-35, 48-49. Hsu, "The Late Ch'ing Reconquest," 53.

[57] Huang, K'an-ting Hsin-chiang, III, 1. Tso, Tsou-kao, XLIX, 74. A.N. Kuropatkin, Kashgaria: A Historical and Geographical Sketch of the Country, Its Military Strength, Industries, and Trade, W.E. Gowan, trans., (Calcutta, 1882), 247-248, 254-255. F.O. 17/826. Account of the Capture of Kashgaria by the Chinese, 1876-1877, 156.

[58] Ibid. Kuropatkin, Kashgaria, 254-255.

[59] Ibid. Kuropatkin also pointed out that as far as he could tell many of the natives of Kashgaria were quite disaffected with the rule of Yakub Beg. This was on the eve of the Chinese reconquest.

[60] F.O. 17/826, Account, 156.

[61] F.O. 17/825, Fraser to Derby, 12/29/1877. NCH, XXII (1878), 604. MCH, XXIV (1879), 400. The latter account reported on an article in the German Army Gazette which stated that China would be a natural ally with Germany in a war with Russia. Tso's conquest then did temporarily at least raise foreigners opinions of China.

[62] Tso, Tsou-kao, XXII, 4-5. Bell, "The Dungan Rebellion," 58. Wu, Turkistan, 258. Tu Chung-yuan, Sheng Shih-ts'ai yu Hsin Hsin-chiang (The new Sinkiang and Sheng Shih-ts'ai) (Shanghai, 1938), 71. Tso's policy of assimilation was criticized by two generally sympathetic commentators as too harsh and chauvinistic. Sinification of the peoples of the Northwest, especially Chinese Turkestan, was viewed as important by the government in the late nineteenth century to forestall foreign domination.

[63] Tso, Tsou-kao, XXII, 4-5.

[64] I-hsin, et al., CTPTSKSKHFFL, CCXXII, 18-19; CCXXIII, 9. CSLC, LXI, 41. Yi, et al., PTKLCL, VII, 10-11. Lo, TWHKNP, V, 22-23; 34-35.

[65] Tso had many problems with "surrendered Moslems." Ma Hua-lung for example, asked the government to be allowed to surrender when he faced the aggressive troops of Liu Sung-shan; Ma claimed that the trouble in his area was started by others and that he should not be considered as a rebel. Tso investigated these charges and decided that Ma was a central figure behind the rebellions in Kansu. He therefore returned to the attack. Mu-t'u-shan, a government leader in Ma's territory had worked out a compromise arrangement with Ma and began to undermine Tso's actions by charging the general commanding the troops in Ma Hua-lung's area wity ruthless acts of aggression. A lengthy debate between Tso and Mu-t'u-shan commenced which was finally decided in Tso's favor when the latter discovered a letter written by Ma urging other Moslems to revolt. Tso also received complaints by the Alashan Mongols that Ma Hua-lung was attempting to gain domination over them. The court finally accepted Tso's arguments, and Ma's forces were eventually defeated. Chu, The Moslem Rebellion, 129-142, has the best account of this question.

[66] Tso, Tsou-kao, XLI, 14-15. Lo, TWHKNP, IV, 53-56. Thousands of Moslems who surrendered to Liu Sung-shan caused trouble later.

[67] E.H. Parker, Studies in Chinese Religion (London, 1910), 257. Tso's experience with ming-shih was helpful in carefully considering the information relating to the Moslems.

⁶⁸I-hsin, et al., CTPTSKSKHFFL, CCXXXI, 20-22. Yi, et al., PTKLCL, VII, 9-10. Ch'in, TWHKTHP, 77. Imanaga, "Lin Tse-hsü," 5-6. Lin used statistical methods to determine accurate policies for the Moslems in Northwest and Southwest China in the 1840s. Such techniques were common to the statecraft group.

⁶⁹Ch'in, TWHKTHP, 78.

⁷⁰Tso, Tsou-kao, XXXIX, 53. Ch'in, TWHKTHP, 78. Chu, The Moslem Rebellion, 150-151.

⁷¹Chang, et al., CS, 4764.

⁷²Tso, Tsou-kao, XXX, 16-18; XXXVI, 38-39. Wright, The Last Stand, 123. Ma, Hsi-pei, 77-78. The latter source discusses the negative side of Tso's relations with the Moslems. Despite his careful measures there was much suffering on their part and some died from starvation. Officials also threatened and cheated the Moslems as well.

⁷³Chu, The Moslem Rebellion, 156-158.

⁷⁴Tso, Tsou-kao, XXXVIII, 62-66.

⁷⁵Ibid., XLI, 1-2; XLIII, 73; XLV, 81-83. Chu, The Moslem Rebellion, 159-160.

⁷⁶Teng and Fairbank, China's Response, 81.

⁷⁷Tso, Tsou-kao, XXII, 4-5. Serge A. Zenkovsky, "Kulturkampf in Pre-Revolutionary Central Asia," American Slavic and East European Review, XIV (1955), 23-25, 32-41. The Russians were also unsuccessful in attempting to Russify the Moslems of Central Asia.

⁷⁸Kuo-shih pen-chuan (Biography of National history) in Tso, Ch'uan-chi 18. Hu Ch'iu-yuan, Chung-kuo ying-hsiung chuan (Biographies of Chinese heroes) (Hong Kong, 1964), III, 22. The latter author notes that Tso adhered to Lin Tse-hsü's view point in the treatment of the Moslems. Tso may have had some contact with the Moslems from his days in Hunan because as the article, "Hsiang-t'an, Hunan," Friends of Moslems, XXII (1948), 25., indicates there was a mosque in Hsian-t'an, the home of Tso's first wife. The question is when this mosque was built and cannot be determined at this time.

[79] Pai, Hui-min, IV, 308-311. Crawford, The Life and Thought, 14. Chang also strenuously applied clear, simple laws in a thorough but fair fashion.

[80] Bales, Tso Tsung-t'ang, 282. Chu, The Moslem Rebellion, 155-156. Ma, Hsi-pei, 72-73. Tsui, "Tso Tsung-t'ang," 10-11.

[81] Ch'in, TWHKTHP, 174-175. Shen, Tso Wen-hsiang-kung, 206-207.

[82] Ch'in, TWHKTHP, 15.

[83] Ho, San-ming-chen, Hu section, 29.

[84] Yang, Tso Tsung-t'ang, 11, 27. Ch'in, TWHKTHP, 160-164.

[85] Tso, Tsou-kao, XLII, 82-86; XLIII, 11013; XLIV, 71-72. Piassetsky, Russian Travelers, II, 142, 148-154.

[86] Ibid.

[87] Ch'in, TWHKTHP, 16-168.

[88] Tso, Tsou-kao, XLI, 3-4; XLV, 3-4. Ch'en, "Tso Tsung-t'ang, Farmer," 223. See also Chapter I above.

[89] Tso, Tsou-kao, LI, 21-22. "Sa So-to," 91-92.

[90] Tso, Tsou-kao, XLI, 51-52.

[91] Ibid., XLVII, 4-10. Chang, et al., CS, 4502-4503. CSLC, LXXV, 45-46. Ch'in, TWHKTHP, 125-128. See also note #12 in this chapter as well as Chapter III above.

[92] Lo, TWHKNP, VII, 43.

[93] Ch'en, "Tso Tsung-t'ang, Farmer," 216-217. Imanaga, "Lin Tse-hsü," 5. The latter noted that similar measures by Lin in 1845 opened 37,000 mou. One acre equals 6.6 mou.

[94] Tso, Tsou-kao, LVII, 42-43. NCH, XXVII (1881), 7. 305-306. Ch'en, Tso Tsung-t'ang, Pioneer, 57, 73. Ch'en, "Tso Tsung-t'ang, Farmer," 217. Taylor, Call, 23. F.C.H. Clarke, "Colonel Sosnoffsky's Expedition to China in 1874-1875," Journal of the Royal Geographic Society, XLVII

(1877), 165, 179. W.W. Rockhill, <u>The Land of the Lamas: Notes of a Journey Through China, Mongolia, and Tibet</u> (New York, 1891), 28.

[95] <u>Ibid.</u>

[96] Clarke, "Colonel Sosnoffsky's," 154. Tso, <u>Tsou-kao</u>, XLII, 38-39; XLV, 5-13. <u>CSLC</u>, LXI, 43. Ch'in, <u>TWHKTHP</u>, 149=151.

[97] <u>Ibid.</u>, 147. Hummel, <u>ECCP</u>, 282. See Chapter IV above too.

[98] Tso, <u>Tsou-kao</u>, XLII, 7-11. <u>CSLC</u>, LXI, 43. Ch'in, <u>TWHKTHP</u>, 146-149.

[99] <u>Ibid</u>. Tso, <u>Tsou-kao</u>, XLII, 38-39; XLV, 5-13.

[100] Frank H. King, <u>Money and Monetary Policy in China, 1845-1895</u> (Cambridge, 1965), 213, 223. Tso, <u>Tsou-kao</u>, XLIII, 32-33.

[101] <u>Ibid.</u>, XLV, 21-23; LIII, 8-12. Bell, "The Country," 30-31. This question will be further explored in Chapter VII.

[102] Hummel, <u>ECCP</u>, 334. Ch'en, Tso <u>Tsung-t'ang, Pioneer</u>, 88.

[103] William Mesny, "Tso Wen Hsiang," <u>Mesny's China Miscellany</u> (January 1, 1905), 7. See below as well.

[104] W.M. Davis. "Across Eastern Gobi," <u>Science</u>, I (1883), 48. This is but one of many travelers through part of Chinese Turkestan in the time of Tso's tenure of office there. Davis reported much devastation there.

[105] Tso, <u>Tsou-kao</u>, LVI, 20-25, 26-50. Tsui, "Tso Tsung-t'ang," 12. Imanaga, "Lin Tse-hsü," 5. Tsui, a generally harsh critic of Tso, applauds the latter's vigorous efforts in Chinese Turkestan. Imanaga notes that Lin did many of the same things at an earlier date.

[106] Chang Sen-dou, "The Historical Trend of Chinese Urbanization," <u>Annals of the Association of American Geographers</u>, LII (1963), 139. "Promenade a Travers L' Asie," <u>Les Missions Catholique</u>, (1884), 377-391. The latter notes many luxuriant and prosperous valleys on the road from Kansu to Chinese Turkestan.

[107] Teng and Fairbank, China's Response, 81.

[108] Hu, Chung-kuo, III, 231-232.

[109] H. Bower, "A Trip to Turkistan," The Geographical Journal, V (1895), 244. Lansdell, Chinese Central Asia, II, 64.

[110] Tso, Tsou-kao, LIII, 86-87.

[111] Ibid., XLIX, 40-42; LV, 29-30. Hsü, "The Late Ch'ing Reconquest," 62.

[112] Chang, "The Historical Trend," 139-141. Bell, "The Dungan Rebellion," 60. L.W. Golab, "A Study of Irrigation in Eastern Turkistan," Anthropos, XLVI (1951), 199. Liu En-lan, "The Ho-si Corridor," Economic Geography, XXXVIII (1952), 53-54.

[113] Tso, Tsou-kao, LII, 3-5; LIII, 30-42; LVI, 34-38; LIX, 57-62. Li, Tseng, Tso, Hu, Tso section, 53-54.

[114] Ch'ing shih-lu, (Te-tsung), CXCIV, 27-28.

[115] Ch'in, TWHKTHP, 117-119.

[116] Tso, Shu-tu, XXIV, 18.

[117] Schuyler, Turkistan, II, 185-187. Boulger, Central Asian Portraits, 217-218. Prjevalsky, Mongolia, I, 15-16. Dilke, "On the Valley," 246. Boulger noted that the Chinese monarch rewarded the Russian commander, Kolpakovsky, for the aid the latter rendered to Solon tribesmen who had fled to Russia. Prjevalsky pointed out that the Russians sent several hundred troops to protect their trade interests in Urga, Mongolia when the Dungans threatened to raid that city. Dilke commented that the Russians in 1874 still had not intended to permanently occupy the Ili area as they had refused to invest money there.

[118] See Chapter V.

[119] Hummel, ECCP, 766.

[120] E.V.G. Kiernan, "Kashgar and the Politics of Central Asia, 1868-1878," Cambridge Historical Journal, XI (1953-1955), 317-342.

[121] F.O. 17/825, Wade to Derby, 3/5. 1877. Tso, Tsou-kao, LI, 17-20.

[122] Hsü, "British Mediation," 143-144. Kiernan, "Kashgar," 331-332.

[123] Hsü, "British Mediation," 146-147. The British (Wade) were so anxious for the Kashgarians and the Chinese to come to some accommodation that they did not inform Kuo that reports of the death of Yakub Beg existed. He negotiated for a time in ignorance of that fact.

[124] Djang Chu, "War and Diplomacy over Ili," Chinese Social and Political Review, XX (1936), 371.

[125] Ibid., 360.

[126] F.C.H. Clarke, "Kuldja," Proceedings of the Geographic Society of London, VIII (August 1880), 489-491.

[127] Herold J. Wiens, "Change in the Ethnography and Land Use of the Ili Valley and Region, Chinese Turkestan," Annals of the Association of American Geographers, LIX (1969), 753.

[128] Aurel Stein, "Innermost Asia: Its Geography as a Factor in History," Geographical Journal, LXV (1925), 497.

[129] L.E. Frechtling, "Anglo-Russian Rivalry in Eastern Turkestan, 1863-1881," Journal of the Royal Central Asian Society, XXVI (1939), 474.

[130] Kiernan, "Kashgar," 341-342.

[131] Ibid.

[132] F.O. 65/1087, Plunkett to Granville, 11/2/1880, 218.

[133] Immanuel C.Y. Hsü, The Ili Crisis: A Study of Sino-Russian Diplomacy, 1871-1881 (Oxford, 1965), 96-97.

[134] Chu, "War and Diplomacy," 388.

[135] Ibid., 391. Immanuel C.Y. Hsü, "Gordon in China, 1880," Pacific Historical Review, XXXIII (1964), 166.

## CHAPTER VII

[1] NCH, XXII (1879), 237.

[2] Tsui, Tso Tsung-t'ang, 11. Nishida, Sa So-to, 158, 163.

[3] John L. Rawlinson, China's Struggle for Naval Development, 1839-1895 (Cambridge, 1967), 29, 136-137. Hsu, "The Great Policy Debate," 227-228. Imanaga, "Lin Tse-hsu," 5,, 10-11.

[4] Clarke, "Kuldja," 489-491. Henry Rawlinson, England and Russia in the East: A Series of Papers on the Political and Geographical Condition of Central Asia (London, 1875), 176.

[5] Tsui, Tso Tsung-t'ang, 11-12.

[6] Hummel, ECCP, 289.

[7] NCH, XXVI (1881), 249.

[8] Fletcher, "Central Asian Sufism," 78-79.

[9] Li Yu-ning, ed., The First Emperor of China (New York, 1975), 12. Rene Grousset, The Rise and Splendor of the Chinese Empire (Berkeley, 1962), 40-41. Albert F. Verwilghen, Mencius: The Man and His Ideas (New York, 1967), 69.

[10] F.O. 17/825, "Mayer's Memorandum of an Interview Between Himself and Members of the Tsungli Yamen," 93.

[11] NCH, XVIII (1877), 201, 229; XIX (1877), 1-2, 227.

[12] Tsui, "Tso Tsung-t'ang," 10-11. Ma, Hsi-pei, 72-73.

[13] Pai, Hui-min, IV, 306, C.G. Warren, "D'Ollone's Investigations on the Chinese Moslems," New China Review, II (1920), 276.

[14] F.O. 17/825, "Mayer's Notes on the Forsyth-Li Meeting, 9/4/1876," 61. Tsui, "Tso Tsung-t'ang," 9-12.

[15] Piassetsky, Russian Travelers, II, 154.

[16] F.O. 17/825, "Mayers' Notes on the Forsyth-Li Meeting," 61ff.

[17] Hsun K'uang, Hsun Tzu: Basic Writings, trans., Burton Watson, (New York, 1963), 67.

[18] Ibid., 68.

[19] Ibid., 69.

[20] Ibid., 13.

[21] Tso, Tsou-kao, XXII, 4-5. Ch'in, TWHKTHP, 200-226.

[22] Bellew, Kashmir, 354.

[23] F.F. von Richthofen, Baron Richthofen's Letters, 1870-1872 (Shanghai, 1903), 71-72, 99-100. David P. Ekvall, Outposts or Tibetan Border Sketches (New York, 1907), 185. Upton, Armies, 30. The latter author hypothesized that the reason for the large loss of life during the rebellion was a policy of kill sufficient numbers of rebels to prevent a renewed outbreak.

[24] Tso, Tsou-kao, XXXVIII, 63. deGroot, Sectarian and Religious, 508-510.

[25] Pai, Hui-min, IV, 308-311.

[26] NCH, XVIII (1877), 201, 229; XIX (1817), 1-2, 227. The last citation also shows that the Chinese carefully investigated the stories of 2000 Tungans caught up in the fighting at Turfan. Their story that they were forced by the rebel, Pai Yen-hu to travel with him from Hami to Turfan was verified. The Chinese then aided the Tungans who returned home to Hami.

[27] Owen Lattimore, Pivot of Asia: Sinkiang and the Inner Asian Frontiers of China and Russia (Boston, 1950), 50.

[28] Piassetsky, Russian Travelers, II, 154. There is no evidence to show that Tso either encouraged or tolera-

ted acts of violence against the Christians or their Chinese converts.

[29] Lattimore, Turkestan Reunion, 129. Her number of 130,000 Chinese deaths in Urumchi may bot be accurate but large numbers of Chinese did perish in the fighting.

[30] Fletcher, "The Naqshbandiyya," 114.

[31] Benjamin E. Wallacker, "Studies in Medieval Siegecraft: The Siege of Ch'ien-k'ang, A.D. 548-549," Journal of Asian History, V (1971), 35-53.

[32] Ibid. Pai, Hui-min, 306. Warren, "D;Ollone's Investigations," 276. Similar percentages occurred in the bitter Chin-chi-pao and Suchow sieges.

[33] Tso was in Central Kansu during the Northern campaigns of the Liu Sung-shan and Liu Chin-t'ang and in Suchow during most of the fighting in Chinese Turkestan. He nevertheless is still responsible for the general conduct of his men.

[34] See Chapter VI above.

[35] Kreitner, "Die Wege," 418-422. Kuropatkin, Kashgaria, 254-255. F.C. 17/826, "Account of the Capture of Kashgaria," 156.

[36] Kreitner, "Die Wege," 418-422.

[37] Piassetsky, Russian Travelers, II, 107, 210, 224, 254-255. C. Holcombe, "Notes Made on a Tour Through Shan-si and Shen-si," Journal of the North China Branch of the Royal Asiatic Society, X (1876), 67. Prjevalsky, Mongolia, I, 177-178.

[38] NCH, XVIII (1877), 391. Kreitner, "Die Wege," 418-422. As noted above Tso took great care to see that the troops were paid. He even contributed substantial amounts from his own salary and lived in quarters similar to theirs on many occasions. These efforts, however, could accomplish only so much to alleviate the soldiers' suffering.

[39] NCH, IXI (1877), 480. The Russian said that he was informing Tso of the treachery of his troops at Hami and urged him to take care that such instances not be repeated. Kaufman added that he felt sure that Tso would agree with this and not let his subordinates tarnish his reputation

as China's best general.

⁴⁰Ibid., XXIV (1880), 397-399.

⁴¹Eugene Schuyler, *Selected Essays with a Memoir by Evelyn Schuyler Schaeffer* ( New York, 1901), 52-54.

⁴²Boulger, *Central Asia*, 85-90. David Mackenzie, *The Lion of Tashkent: The Career of General M.G. Cherniaev, 1828-1898* (Athens, Ga., 1974), 110-112. Sokol, "The Revolt," 110, 120, 129, 181.

⁴³Tso, *Chia-shu*, II, 58.

⁴⁴*Ibid.*

⁴⁵Piassetsky, *Russian Travelers*, II, 98-99. Taylor, *The Call*, 163. Ekvall, *Gateway*, 23. R.B. Ekvall, "Revolt of the Crescent in Western China," 945.

⁴⁶Williams, *The Middle*, II, 834.

⁴⁷Ekvall, "Revolt of the Crescent in Western China," 944-945.

⁴⁸Tso, *Chia-shu*, II, 16-18.

⁴⁹*NCH*, XVIII (1877), 1-2, 77, 129; XIX (1877), 221; XX (1878), 101; XXI (1878), 281.

⁵⁰United Kingdom, House of Commons, Sessional Papers, LXXV (1878), 684.

⁵¹*NCH*, XVIII (1877), 129; XX (1878), 258; XXIII (1879); 322-323.

⁵²*Ibid.*, XXIV (1880), 57.

⁵³Tso, *Shu-tu*, I, 22.

⁵⁴Ho, *San-ming-chen*, Tso section, 22, 60, 137. Bland, *Bland Papers*, "Manchu Miscellaneous," Box 26, folder 27. This file contains a rumor that Tso Tsung-t'ang became addicted to opium in his later years. This statement is unverified and must be left in that fashion. Tso vigorously attempted to eradicate opium production and consumption in the Northwest. He did not tolerate its use by anyone. No other source has claimed that Tso had

an opium habit.

[55] Ch'in, TWHKTHP, 181-182.

[56] Ibid.

[57] Holcombe, "Notes," 67.

[58] Prjevalsky, Mongolia, I, 177-178. Richthofen, Baron Richthofen's, 109. The latter asserted that the high officials' efforts to stop opium consumption and production were thwarted by subordinates themselves involved in the process.

[59] Piassetsky, Russian Travelers, II, 13-14, 64, 107, 210, 224, 254-255.

[60] Kreitner, "Die Wege," 420-421.

[61] NCH, XX (1878), 54. House of Commons, Sessional Papers, LXXX, 179. Jonathan Spence, "Opium Smoking in Ch'ing China," in Wakeman and Grant, eds.) Conflict and Control, 170-171. The second source noted that Shensi and Kansu produced excellent grades of opium sufficient to supply the local demand and export to other provinces as well. This position came to be used as an excuse for Britain's continued importation of opium into China. The British were therefore competing in an established market (one which they had helped create for decades).

[62] Ibid., 164. NCH, XXI (1878), 337; XXVII (1881), 69-70, 144.

[63] See Chapter V.

[64] Pai, Hui-min, IV, 308-311.

[65] Ma, Hsi-pei, 77-78. Tsui, "Tso Tsung-t'ang," 9-12. These writers are very useful because they provide views sympathetic to the Muslims something difficult to obtain otherwise. Certainly the loss of life and suffering was experienced by all Northwestern groups. Many Muslims died as a result of Tso's policies especially those of the New Teaching others experienced dislocation and suffered because they were relocated elsewhere than their native places. Still it may be argued that Tso tried to be as fair as possible in his own as well as the statecraft tradition.

Notes to pages 101-103

[66] See Chapter VI.

[67] Tu, Sheng, Shih-ts-ai, 70-71.

[68] Geoffrey Wheeler, "British and Russian Imperial Attitudes in Asia," Journal of the Royal Central Asian Society, (1954), 256-260.

[69] Ibid. Michael Gillet, "The National Minorities of Western China," Central Asian Review, XVI (1968), 69-70.

[70] Warren, "D'Ollone's Investigations," 276. The man was Han Wen-hsiu.

[71] Ekvall, "Revolt," 945.

[72] O.S.S. "Peoples and Politics," R. & A. #1921, 25-32.

[73] Ch'in, TWHKTHP, 183-193.

[74] Ch'en, "Tso Tsung-t'ang, Farmer," 211, 217-218, 221-223, 225. Chang, "Historical Trend," 139.

[75] Shen, Tso Wen-hsiang-kung, 206-207.

[76] NCH, XXIII (1881), 511. Interestingly Tso and Li Hung-chang were called members of a Utilitarian "party" by the British editors of the North China Herald.

[77] Rockhill, Land, 35-36. Ch'en, Tso Tsung-t'ang, Pioneer, vide supra.

[78] NCH, XXI (1878), 231; XXIV (1880), 575.

[79] Mesny, "Tso," 5-7, NCH, XXIV (1880), 575.

[80] Kreitner, "Die Wege," 416. Mesny, "Tso," 7. NCH, XXVI (1881), 241.

[81] Mesny, "Tso," 7. NCH, XXVII (1881), 499. For some additional ching-shih programs see Tso, Tsou-kao, XLI, 30-36; XLII, 40-41; LXI, 8-9; LXIV, 6-10.

[82] NCH, XXVI (1881), 499.

[83] Ibid., XXVII (1881), 241.

[84] Ibid.

[85] Mesny, "Tso," 1-7.

[86] Rockhill, Land, 33. Bell, "The Country," 28-29.

[87] W.W. Rockhill, Journey Through Mongolia and Tibet in 1891-1892 (Washington, 1894), 60.

[88] Bell, "The Country," 28-29.

[89] Piassetsky, Russian Travelers, II, 126. Tso also purchased and had delivered a steam elevator but it was rendered inoperative because of a lack of replacement parts.

[90] NCH, XXI (1878), 131. Rockhill, Land, 35-36.

[91] MacKenzie, Lion of Tashkent, 217, 227. For some post-1880 ching-shih efforts of Tso see Tso, Tsou-kao, LIX, 11-20; 42-45; 54-56.

## CHRONOLOGY

### Important Dates and Events in Tso Tsung-t'ang's Career

1812    Born in Hsiang-yin, Hunan.

1816    The Tso Family moves to Changsha.

1823    Tso's eldest brother dies.

1827    Tso's mother dies.

1830    Tso's father dies. Tso meets Ho Ch'iang-ling.

1831    Tso enters the Ch'eng-nan Academy which is headed by Ho Hsi-ling, brother of Ho Ch'ang-ling.

1832    Tso and his elder brother, Tsung-chih attaing chü-jen status. Tso marries Chou I-tuan.

1833    Tso fails the Metropolitan Examination.

1835    Tso again fails the Metropolitan Examination.

1836    Tso develops an intense interest in geography and map making. Tso takes Chang Ju as a second wife.

1837    Tso teaches at the Lu-chiang Academy and meets T'ao Chu there.

1838    Tso fails the Metropolitan Examination for the third time and vows never again to take it. Meets T'ao Chu for a second time in Nanking. Studies agriculture intensively.

1839    T'ao Chu dies and Tso is to tutor T'ao's son.

1840    Tso moves to the T'ao household.

1842    Tso renews his acquaintance with Hu Lin-i, a son-in law of T'ao Chu.

1843    Tso buys a farm in Hsiang-yin.

1844    Tso moves his family to his new home.

1845    Tso studies and experiments with farming.

1848    Serious flooding in Hsiang-yin. Tso declines to enter Lin Tse-hsü's mu-fu.

1849    Tso meets with Lin Tse-hsü.

1852    Taiping forces in Hunan. Tso leaves his family to serve Chang Liang-chi as a military advisor.

1853    Tso resigns his post and returns home.

| | |
|---|---|
| 1854 | Tso serves with Lo Ping-chang as his military advisor. |
| 1859 | Tso is charged with unruliness and misconduct but is spared a trial through an intervention by Hu Lin-i. |
| 1860 | Tso journeys toward Peking to take the Metropolitan examination for the fourth time but is intercepted by a letter from Hu Lin-i urging him to join Tseng Kuo-fan's mu-fu. Tso does this and is finally given command of a force of Hunanese which he is to organize. |
| 1861 | Tso's force, the Ch'u-chun, fights many battles in Kiangsi, Anhwei, and Chekiang. |
| 1862 | Tso is appointed Governor of Chekiang. |
| 1863 | Tso is appointed Governor-General of Chekiang and Fukien. |
| 1866 | Tso is appointed Governor-General of Shensi and Kansu. |
| 1867 | Tso establishes a supply base at Wuhan. |
| 1867-1868 | Tso arrives in Shensi but spends most of the next year in fighting against the Nien forces. He returns to Shensi in late 1868. |
| 1869 | Shensi is cleared of Muslims and Tso moves into Kansu. |
| 1870 | Liu Sung-shan, a key commander dies and is replaced by his able nephew, Liu Chin-t'ang. Chou I-tuan dies. |
| 1871 | Chin-chi-pao, a New Sect stronghold is captured and its leader, Ma Hua-lung is executed. |
| 1872 | Hochow and Sining, two important Muslim centers fall. Tso moves his headquarters to Lanchow. Tso Tsung-chih dies. |
| 1873 | Suchow, the last major stronghold in Kansu is taken. Tso's eldest son dies. |
| 1874-1875 | The Frontier-Coastal Debate ranges in the government. Tso is appointed commander of the Chinese Turkestan Campaign (1875). |
| 1876 | Tso moves his headquarters to Suchow. The Northern Campaign in Chinese Turkestan is begun and successfully concluded. |

1877-   The Southern Campaign in Chinese Turkestan is be-
1878    gun and successfully terminated.

1880-   The Ili Crisis begins and ends.  Tso moves into
1881    Chinese Turkestan to assume personal charge of
        the campaign then is called to Peking to advise
        the court on military matters.  He reaches Peking
        in early 1881.

1885    Death of Tso.

BIBLIOGRAPHY

I. Government Documents and Collections

Britain

F.O. 17 General Correspondence between the Foreign Office and its Agents in China for the Period 1876-1878.

F.O. 65 Diplomatic Correspondence between London and British Representatives in Russia, 1880-1881.

House of Commons Sessional Papers, 1878-1882.

China

I-hsin, et al. Ch'in-ting p'ing-ting Shen-Kan Hsin-chiang Hui-fei fang-lüeh (Account of the suppression and pacification of the Moslem rebels in Shensi, Kansu, and Chinese Turkestan). Peking, 1896. (Taipei, reprint 1968). 30 v.

Pai Shou-i. ed. Hui-min ch'i-i (The Moslem uprisings). Shanghai: Shen chou kuo kuang she, 1952. 4 v.

Ta-ch'ing li-ch'ao shih-lu (veritable records of the successive reigns of the Ch'ing dynasty). Chung-chun, Manchuria: 1935-1940.

II. Works and Collections in Chinese and Japanese

Chang Ch'i-yun, et al. Ch'ing shih (History of the Ch'ing period). Taipei: Kuo-fang yen-chiu yuan, 1963. 2nd. edn. 8 v.

Ch'en Ching-lung. "Lun Pai Shan Tang (Aktaglik) yu Hei Shan Tang (Karataglik) (The White and Black Mountain sects.)," Pien-cheng Nien-pao. #2 (July 1971), 209-231.

Ch'ien Mu. Chung-kuo chin-san-pai-nien-hsüeh-shu shih (History of the academies in the last three hundred years in China). Taipei: Commercial Press, 1957, 827 p.

Ch'in Han-ts'ai. Tso Wen-hsiang-kung tsai Hsi-pei (Tso Tsung-t'ang in the Northwest). Shanghai: Commercial Press, 1946. 229 p.

Ch'ing-shih lieh-chuan (Biographies for the Ch'ing history). Shanghai: The China Bookshop, 1928. 20 chüan

Chu K'ung-chang. Chung-hsing chiang-shuai pieh-chuan (Collection of biographies of generals of the T'ung-chih era). Nanking, 1897. 30 chüan.

Fu T'ung-hsien. Chung-kuo hui-chiao shih (History of Islam in China). Changsha: Commercial Press, 1940. 240 p.

Ho Hsi-ling. Han-hsiang-kuan shih-ch'ao (Works from the Han-hsiang-kuan). N.P. 1848. 8 chüan

Ho T'ien-chu. San-ming-chen shu-tu (Letters of three famous statesmen) (Shanghai, 1908). 3 chüan.

Hsu I-shih. "Tso Tsung-t'ang yu Liang Ch'i-ch'ao (Tso Tsung-t'ang and Liang Ch'i-ch'ao," Ku-chin p'an yueh k'an. #14 (1942), 1197-1200.

Hu Ch'iu-yuan. Chung-kuo ying-hsiung chuan (Bibliographies of Chinese heroes). Hong Kong: Asian Publishers Ltd., 1964. 256 p.

Hu Lin-i. Hu Wen-chung-kung i chi (The posthumous collected works of Hu Lin-i). Taipei reprint, 1966. 86 chüan.

Huang-ch'ao ching-shih wen-hsü-pien (Supplement to the Huang-ch'ao ching-shih wen-pien). ed. Ko Shih-chun. Shanghai, 1898. 120 chüan.

Huang-ch'ao ching-shih wen-pien (Collection of useful essays about society written in the Ch'ing dynasty). ed. Ho Ch'ang-ling and Wei Yuan. Taipei reprint, 1963. 3 v.

Huang Ping-k'un, et al. K'an-ting Hsin-chiang chi (Account of the suppression of the rebellion in Sinkiang). Taipei reprint, 1963, 8 chüan.

Imanaga Seiji. "Shindai Chugoku Kaimin shakai kenkyu (A Study of the Chinese Muslim Community in the Ch'ing period)," Tohogaku, #24 (1962), 51-70.

——————. "Rin Soku-jo no Kaimin ni tsuite (Lin Tse-hsü's Moslem policy)," Shigaku kenkyu, #69 (May 1958), 1-18.

Iwamura Shinobu. Chugoku Kaikyo shakkai no kozo
(An analysis of Chinese Muslim society).
Tokyo: 1949-1950. 2 v.

Kao Teng-chih. "Ch'ing-tai nien-chien Shen-Kan Hui-min ch'i-i (The Shensi and Kansu Moslem uprisings in the T'ung-chih era of the Ch'ing dynasty)," Jen-wen k'o hsüeh ts'a-chih. #6 (1969), 19-35.

Keiseibumpen so moku-roku (General index to the editions of the writings on statecraft). comp. Kindai Chugoku Kenkyu Iinkai. Tokyo, 1956.

Kuo-Ting-i. Chin-tai Chung-kuo shih jih-chih Chronology of modern Chinese history). Taipei: Commercial Press, 1963. 2 v.

Li Huan. Kuo-ch'ao chi-hsien lei-cheng ch'u-pien (Classified collections of eminent Chinese of the Ch'ing period, first series). Taipei reprint, 1966. 25 v.

Li Shao-ling. Tseng, Tso, Hu (Tseng Kuo-fan, Tso Tsung-t'ang, and Hu Lin-i). Kaohsiung: Ta-yeh Bookstore, 1962. 248 p.

Lin Kan, et al. Ch'ing-tai hui-min ch'i-i (Moslem rebellions in the Ch'ing dynasty). Shanghai: Hsin-shih ch'u pan she, 1957. 73 p.

Ling (Lin) Chung-yung. Lin Tse-hsü chuan (A biography of Lin Tse-hsu). Taipei: Commercial Press, 1968 (revised edition). 732 p.

Lo Tse-nan. Lo Chung-chieh-kung i-chi (Posthumously collected works of Lo Tse-nan). Taipei: Wen hai ch'u pan she, 1967. 259 p.

Ma Hsiao-shih. Hsi-pei hui-tsu ko-ming chien-shih (A short history of the revolution of the Moslem peoples in the Northwest). Shanghai: Lien-yun Bookstore, 1951. 151 p.

Min-kuo ching-shih wen-pien (Collection of useful essays about society in the Republican period). Shanghai, 1914, and Taipei reprint.

Momose Hiromu. "Shimmatsu no keiseibumpen ni tsuite (On the ching-shih wen-pien of the late Ch'ing), in Ikeuchi hakushi kanreki kinen Toyoshi ronso (Essays on Oriental history collected to commemorate the 60th birthday of Dr. Ikeuchi). Tokyo: Zauho kankokai, 912 p.

Nakada Yoshinobu. "Doji nenkan no Sen-Kan no Kairan ni tsuite (The Moslem rebellion in Shensi and Kansu, 1862-1873)," Kindai Chugoku Kenkyu, III (1959), 71-159.

Nishida Tamotsu. Sa So-to to Shinkyo mondai (Tso Tsung-t'ang and Sinkiang). Tokyo, 1941. 382 p.

Pai Jui-ch'ang. Hui-chiao shih-chieh (World of Islam). Taipei: Chung-hua wen-hua ch'u pan she, 1959. 188 p.

Pai Shou-i. Chung-kuo hui-chiao hsiao-shih (A brief history of Islam in China). Chungking: Commercial Press, 1944, 46 p.

——————. Hsüeh-pu chi (Learning steps). Peking: Hsin chin san lien shu tien, 1962. 298 p.

——————. Hui-hui min-tsu ti hsin-sheng (The new life of the Moslem peoples). Shanghai: Tung-fang shu-she, 1951. 116 p.

——————. "Hui-hui min-tsu ti hsing-ch'eng ho ch'u-pu fa chan (The formation and early development of the Moslem peoples)." Hsin chien-she. #110 (1957), 34-38.

——————. ed. Hui-min ch'i-i (The Moslem uprisings). Shanghai: Shen chou kuo kuang she, 1952. 4 v.

Po Ching-wei. Feng-hsi ts'ao-t'ang-chi (Collections from the Feng-hsi-ts'ao hall) (Nanking, 1924). 8 chüan.

"Sa So-to no seihoku keiei ippan (An aspect of Tso Tsung-t'ang's administration of the Western region)," Kaikyo Jijo, III #4 (1940), 86-92.

Saguchi Toru. Juhachi to Jukyu seiki Higashi Turkestan shakkai shi kenkyu (The social history of Eastern Turkestan in the eighteenth and nineteenth centuries). Tokyo, 1963. 755 p.

——————. "A Study of Islamic Mysticism in China," Tohogaku, (October 1954), 75-92.

Tai Mu-chen. Tso Tsung-t'ang p'ing-chuan (A critical biography of Tso Tsung-t'ang). Sian, 1943. 82 p.

Tseng Kuo-ch'uan and Li Han-chang, ed. Hunan t'ung-chih (Gazetteer of Hunan province). N.P., 1885.

Tseng Kuo-ch'uan. Tseng Wen-chung-hsiang-kung ch'üan-chi (Collected works of Tseng Kuo-ch'uan). N.P., 1903. 32 chüan.

Tseng Kuo-fan. Tseng Wen-chung-kung ch'üan-chi (Collected works of Tseng Kuo-fan). Peking, 1876. 160 chüan.

Tso Tsung-chih. Shen-an shih wen ch'ao (Writings and poetry from the Shen studio). N.P., 1875. 4 chüan.

Tso Tsung-t'ang. Tso Wen-hsiang-kung chia-shu (Family letters of Tso Tsung-t'ang). ed. Tso Hsiao-t'ung. Shanghai, 1920. 2 v.

──────────. Tso Wen-hsiang-kung ch'üan-chi (Collected works of Tso Tsung-t'ang). Peking, 1888-1897. 104 chüan.

──────────. Tun-pi yu-shen (Knowledge acquired after military life). Changsha, 1881. 88 p.

Ts'ui Chi-en, "Tso Tsung-t'ang shu-p'ing (A critical narrative of Tso Tsung-t'ang)," Shih-hsüeh yueh-k'an, (July 1957), 9-12.

Tu Chung-yuan. Sheng Shih-ts'ai yu Hsin Hsin-chiang (The new Sinkiang and Sheng Shih-ts'ai). Shanghai: Sheng-huo shu-tien, 1938. 103 p.

Wan Ch'ieh-ch'ing. Li-tai ming-jen chuan-chi (Biographical stories of famous historical figures). Taipei, 1961. 2 v.

Wang Chia-chien. Wei Yüan nien-p'u (A chronological biography of Wei Yüan). Taipei: Kuo-fang yen-chiu yuan, 1967. 204 p.

Wang Hsien-ch'ien. Hsu-shou-t'ang wen-chi (Collected writings of the Hsu-shou hall). Taipei reprint, 1966. 2 v.

Wang Hung-chih. Tso Tsung-t'ang p'ing Hsi-pei Hui-luan liang-hsiang chih ch'ou-hua yu chuan-yün (A study of the logistics and supplies in Tso Tsung-t'ang's pacification of the Moslem rebellions in the Northwest). Taipei: Cheng chung shu chu, 146 p.

Wei Yüan. Hai-kuo t'u-chih (Illustrated gazetteer of the maritime countries). 1876 reprint. 100 chüan.

Wei Yüan. Sheng-wu chi (Record of imperial military exploits). Taipei reprint, 1962. 14 chüan.

Wu Ju-lun. T'ung-cheng Wu hsien-sheng ch'üan-shu Collected literary works of Wu Ju-lun). Taipei reprint, 1964.

Yang Kung-t'ao. Tso Tsung-t'ang i-shih (Anecdotes about Tso Tsung-t'ang). N.P., 1919. 84 p.

Yang Sung-kuo. Chung-kuo ku-tai ssu-hsiang shih (An intellectual history of China's ancient period). Peking: Hsin hua yin shua tien, 1954. 413 p.

Yi K'ung-chao, et al. P'ing-ting kuan-lung chi-lueh (Record of the pacification of Shensi and Kansu). Taipei reprint, 1968. 3 v.

III. Travel Accounts, Missionary Records, and Newspaper Materials

These sources largely accounts contemporary to the period of Tso Tsung-t'ang's campaigns in Northwest China add an important dimension to the official records. The success of some of his programs can be better assessed by eye witness accounts. The missionary accounts also show some of the long range effects of Tso's military and political efforts and add crucial information about the Moslem brotherhoods in Northwest China.

Bateson, William. Letters From the Steppe Written in the Years 1886-1887. London: Methuen and Co. Ltd., 1928. 222 p.

Battuta Ibn. Travels of Ibn Battuta. Trans. H.A.R. Gibb. Cambridge: Cambridge University Press, 1958-1962. 2 v.

Bell, Mark. "The Country of the Dungan Rebellions of 1861 and 1895-1896," Asian Review, 3rd series, II (1896), 23-36.

Bellew, H.W. Kashmir and Kashgar: A Narrative of the Journey of the Embassy to Kashgar in 1873-1874. London: Trubner and Co., 1875. 419 p.

Bower, H. "A Trip to Turkistan," The Geographical Journal, V (1895), 240-257.

"Brief Notice of M. Prjevalsky's Recent Journey to Lob-Nor and Tibet, and Other Russian Explorations," *Proceedings of the Royal Geographic Society*, XXII (1877-1878), 51-53.

Cable, Mildred and Francesca French. *Dispatches From Northwest Kansu*. London: China Inland Mission, 1925. 75 p.

"A Chinese Moslem Has Recently Returned From a Pilgrimage to Mecca," *Chinese Repository*, II (1833), 96.

Clarke, F.C.H. "Colonel Sosnoffsky's Expedition to China in 1874-1875," *Journal of the Royal Geographic Society*, XLVII (1877), 150-187.

——————. "Kuldja," *Proceedings of the Geographical Society of London*, VIII (August 1880), 489-499.

Dilke, Ashton W. "On the Valley of the Ili and the Water-system of Russian Turkistan," *Proceedings of the Royal Geographic Society*, XVIII (April 13, 1874), 246-253.

Ekvall, David P. *Outposts or Tibetan Border Sketches*. New York: Alliance Press, 1907, 227 p.

Ekvall, Robert B. *Cultural Relations on the Kansu-Tibetan Border*. Chicago: University of Chicago Press, 1939. 87 p.

——————. *Gateway to Tibet: The Kansu-Tibetan Border*. Harrisburg: Christian Publications, 1938. 198 p.

——————. "Revolt of the Crescent in Western China," *Asia*, XXIX (1929), 944-947, 1004-1007.

Forsyth, Douglas. *Autobiography and Reminiscences of Sir Douglas Forsyth*. ed. Ethel Forsyth. London: Richard Bentley and Son, 1887. 283 p.

Grenard, F. "Note Sur les Musulmans Solar du Kansou," *Journal Asiatique*, Series 9 (1898), 546-551.

Hayward, Harold D. "The Kansu Moslems," *The Moslem World*, XXIV (1934), 68-80.

Holcombe, C. "Notes Made on a Tour Through Shan-hsi and Shen-hsi," *Journal of the North China Branch of the Royal Asiatic Society*, X (1876), 55-70.

Huc, Evariste, and Joseph Gabet. *Travels in Tartary, Thibet, and China, During the Years, 1844-1846*. Chicago: The Open Court Publishing Company, 1898. 2 v.

Hunter, G.W. "Islam in Central Asia," *The Moslem World*, XX (1930), 20-23.

Johnson, W.H. "Report on His Journey to Ilchi, the Capital of Khotan, in Chinese Tatary," *Journal of the Royal Geographic Society*, XXXVII (1867), 1-47.

"Khotan to Kashgar," *Friends of Moslems*, V (1931), 2-3.

King, George E. "Notes on Kansu," *Journal of the North China Branch of the Royal Asiatic Society*, L (1919), 185-188.

Kreitner, G. "Die Wege von Ansifan Durch die Wuste Gobi nach Hami," *Petermann's Mittheilungen*, XXVIII (1882), 416-422.

Kuropatkin, A.N. *Kashgaria: A Historical and Geographical Sketch of the Country. Its Military Strength, Industries, and Trade*. trans. W.E. Gowan. Calcutta: Thacher, Spink, and Co., 1882. 255 p.

Lansdell, Henry. *Chinese Central Asia: A Ride to Little Tibet*. London: Samson Low, Marston and Company, 1893. 2 v.

_____. *Russian Central Asia, Including Kuldja, Bokhara, Khiva, and Merv*. Boston: Houghton Mifflin and Company, 1885. 2 v.

Lattimore, Eleanor. *Turkestan Reunion*. New York: The John Day Company, 1934.

"Letters from Colonel Prjevalsky," *Proceedings of the Royal Geographic Society*, VII (1885), 67-72, 807-815.

"Narrative of the Travels of Khwajah Ahmed Shah," *Journal of the Royal Society of Bengal*, #4 (1856), 344-358.

Nakshabandi Ahmed Shah. "Route from Kashmir Via Ladakh to Yarkand," *Journal of the Royal Society of Great Britain and Ireland*. XII (1849), 372-385.

*The North China Herald and Supreme Court and Consular Gazette*, XVIII-XXXVII (1877-1886). Shanghai.

Piassetsky, Pavel. *Russian Travelers in Mongolia and China*. trans. J. Gordon-Cumming. London: Chapman and Hall Ltd., 1884. 2 v.

Pickens, Claude L. "Hung Lo, Ninghsia," *Friends of Moslems*, XVII (October 1943), 52.

──────. "A Journey Through Northwest China," *The Moslem World*, XXVII, (1937), 112-114.

──────. "More Extracts from the Secretary's Diary," *Friends of Moslems*, X (October 1936), 71.

──────. "A Trek Through the Tangut Country," *The Moslem World*, XXXIII (1943), 9-15.

"Gregor N. Potanin's Journey Through the Altai Mountains," *The Geographical Magazine*, IV (May 1, 1877), 118-119.

Prjevalsky, Nicholas M. *Mongolia, The Tangut Country, and the Solitudes of Northern Tibet, Being a Narrative of Three Years Travel in Eastern High Asia*. Trans. E.D. Morgan. London: Samson Low, Marston, Searle, and Rivington, 1878, 2 v.

"Promenade a Travers L'Asie," *Les Missions Catholique*, (1884), 377-391.

Richthofen, Ferdinand F. *Baron Richthofen's Letters, 1870-1872*. Shanghai: North China Herald Office, 1872. 149 p.

Rockhill, William W. *Journey Through Mongolia, and Tibet in 1891-1892*. Washington: Smithsonian Institution, 1894. 413 p.

──────. *The Land of the Lamas: Notes of a Journey Through China, Mongolia and Tibet*. New York: The Century Company, 1891. 399 p.

Saunders, W.A. "Hsuan Hua Kang," *Friends of Moslems*, VIII (October 1934), 69-71.

Schram, Louis M.J. "The Monguors of the Kansu-Tibetan Frontier: Their Origin, History, and Social Organization," *Transactions of the American Philosophical Society*, new series XLIV, part 1 (1954), 1-137.

Schram, Louis M.J. "The Monguors of the Kansu-Tibetan Frontier: Records of the Monguor Clans, History of the Monguors in Huangchung, and the Chronicle of the Lu Family," <u>Transactions of the American Philosophical Society</u>, new series, LI, part 1 (1961), 3-117.

Schuyler, Eugene. <u>Turkistan: Notes of a Journey in Russian Turkistan, Bukhara, and Kuldja</u>, New York: Scribner, Armstrong, and Company, 1876. 2 v.

Street, Leonard. "Islam in Lanchow," <u>Friends of Moslems</u>, XX (October 1946), 34-37.

Taylor, Mary G. <u>The Call of China's Great Northwest: Kansu and Beyond</u>. London: China Inland Mission, N.D. 215 p.

Vambery, Arminius. <u>Travels in Central Asia</u>. New York: Praeger Press, 1970 reprint. 443 p.

Wathen, W.H. "Memoir on Chinese Tartary and Khoten," <u>Journal of the Asiatic Society of Bengal (Calcutta Journal)</u>, #48 (December 1835), 653-664.

Wessels, C. <u>Early Jesuit Travelers in Central Asia. 1603-1721</u>. The Hague: Martinus Nijhoff, 1924. 344 p.

IV. Other Western Language Materials

Abel-Remusat, Jean Pierre. <u>Histoire de la Ville de Khotan: Tiree des Annals de la Chine et Traduite du Chinois</u>. Paris: Imprimerie de Doublet, 1820. 239 p.

Ahmed Ali. "Islam in China," <u>Pakistan Horizon</u>, (1948), 171-190.

──────. <u>Muslim China</u>. Karachi: Pakistan Institute of International Affairs, 1949. 63 p.

Alcock, Rutherford. "The Chinese Empire and Its Foreign Relations," <u>Fortnightly Review</u>, XXV (1876), 652-670.

Allworth, Edward. ed. <u>Central Asia: A Century of Russian Rule</u>. New York: Columbia University Press, 1967. 552 p.

<u>The Analects of Confucius</u>. trans. Arthur Waley. London: George Allen and Unwin Ltd., 1938. 268 p.

Anderson, John. "Chinese Mohammedans," Royal Anthropological Institute of Great Britain and Ireland, I (1872), 147-162.

Andrew, George F. The Crescent in Northwest China. London: China Inland Mission, 1921. 113 p.

Arnold, Thomas Walker. The Preaching of Islam: A History of the Propagation of the Muslim Faith. Westminster: Arhibald, Constable, and Company, 1896. 388 p.

Bales, William L. Tso Tsung-t'ang: Soldier and Statesman of Old China. Shanghai: Kelly and Walsh Ltd., 1937. 436 p.

Barthold, V.V. "Kansu," Encyclopaedia of Islam, II (1927), 719-720.

──────. "Khokand," Encyclopaedia of Islam, II (1927), 963-965.

──────. "Kuldja," Encyclopaedia of Islam, II (1927), 1113.

deBary, William T. et al. Self and Society in Ming Thought. New York: Columbia University Press, 1970. 550 p.

Beasley, W.G. and E.G. Pulleyblank, eds. Historians of China and Japan. London: Oxford University Press, 1961. 351 p.

Becker, Seymour. Russia's Protectorates In Central Asia: Bukhara and Khiva, 1865-1924. Cambridge: Harvard University Press, 1968.

Bell, Mark. "China in Central Asia," Asian Review, IX (1890), 327-347.

──────. "The Dungan Rebellions and Hankow," Asian Review, 3rd series, I (1896), 55-64.

Bennigson, Alexander. "Traditional Islam in the Customs of the Turkic Peoples of Central Asia," Middle East Journal, XII (1958), 227-242.

"A Biography of Sayyid Edjell," Friends of Moslems, X (January 1936), 10.

Bland, J.O.P. The Bland Papers. Manuscript papers for the books Bland published relating to China and diaries relating to his stay in China in the nineteenth century. Toronto: University of Toronto Library.

Bland, J.O.P., and E. Backhouse. China Under the Empress Dowager: Being a History of the Life and Times of Tzu Hsi. London: William Heinemann, 1910. 523 p.

Bonin, C.E. "The Kansu Moslems and Their Last Revolt," Revue de Monde Musulman, X (1915), 210-233.

The Book of Rites. Trans. James Legge. New York: New Hyde Park University Books, 1967. 2v.

Borei, Dorothy. "Eccentricity and Dissent: The Case of Kung Tzu-chen," Ch'ing-shih wen-t'i, III (December 1975), 50-62.

Botham, Mark. "Chinese Islam as an Organism," The Moslem World, XIV (1924), 261-267.

——————. "Islam in Kansu," The Moslem World, X (1920), 377-390.

Botham, Olive. "The Djahariyeh and the Godeemi in Kansu," Friends of Moslems, V (April 1931), 16.

Boulger, Demetrius C. Central Asian Portraits: The Celebrities of the Khanates and the Neighboring States. London: W.G. Allen and Company, 1880. 310 p.

——————. A Short History of China: An Account for the General Reader of an Ancient Empire and People. London: P.F. Collier and Son, 1898, 540 p.

——————. The Life of Yakub Beg: Athalik Ghazi and Badaulet Ameer of Kashgar. London: William H. Allen and Company, 1878. 344 p.

——————. "Three Chinese Generals," Calcutta Review, LXXI (1880), 301-310.

Broomhall, Marshall. Islam in China: A Neglected Problem. New York, 1966 reprint. 322 p.

Bruk, S.I. "The Ethnography of Sinkiang and Tibet," Central Asian Review, VII (1959), 84-92.

——————. "Sinkiang," Central Asian Review, IV (1956), 433-437.

Buote, Edward L. Chu-ko Liang and the Kingdom of Shu-Han. Chicago: University of Chicago Ph.D. thesis, 1968, 254 p.

Castagne, Joseph. "Le Culte des Lieux Saints de L'Islam au Turkestan," L'Ethnographie, XLVI (1951), 46-124.

Chang Hao. "On the Ching-shih Ideal in Neo-Confucianism," Ch'ing-shih wen-t'i, III (November 1974), 36-61.

Chang Hsin-pao. Commissioner Lin and the Opium War. Cambridge: Harvard University Press, 1964. 319 p.

Chang Sen-dou. "The Historical Trend of Chinese Urbanization." Annals of the Association of American Geographers, LIII (1963), 104-143.

——————. "Some Observations on the Morphology of Chinese Walled Cities." Annals of the Association of American Geographers, LX (1970), 63-91.

Chen, C.Y. "A Review of the Hsien-T'ung Yun-nan Hui-min Shih-pien," Journal of Asian Studies, XXX (1970), 177-178.

Ch'en Chieh-hsien. ed. Proceedings of the East Asian Altaistic Conference. Tainon:

Ch'en, Gideon, "Tso Tsung-t'ang: The Farmer of Hsiangshang," Yenching Journal of Social Studies, I (1939), 211-225.

——————. Tso Tsung-t'ang. Pioneer Promoter of the Modern Dockyard and the Woolen Mill in China. New York, 1961 reprint. 93 p.

Chin Ch'i-t'ang. "The Rebellion of Ma Ming-hsin," Friends of Moslems, XVII (April 1943), 33.

"The Chinese Reconquest of Eastern Turkistan," The Spectator, LI (1878), 466-467.

Chu, Djang. "War and Diplomacy over Ili," Chinese Social and Political Science Review, XX (1936), 369-392.

Ch'u T'ung-tsu. Local Government in China Under the Ch'ing. Cambridge: Harvard University Press, 1962. 414 p.

Chu, Wen-djang. The Moslem Rebellion in Northwest China, 1862-1878: A Study of Government Minority Policy. The Hague: Mouton and Company, 1966. 232 p.

—————— The Policy of the Manchu Government in the Suppression of the Moslem Rebellion in

Shensi, Kansu, and Sinkiang from 1862-1878. Seattle: University of Washington Ph.D. thesis, 1955. 418 p.

Cohen, Paul. China and Christianity: The Missionary Movement and the Growth of Anti-Foreignism, 1860-1870. Cambridge: Harvard University Press, 1963. 392 p.

Cordier, Henri. "Turkestan," Catholic Encyclopedia. XV (1912), 95-97.

Crawford, Robert B. The Life and Thought of Chang Chu-cheng. Seattle: University of Washington Ph.D. thesis, 1961. 318 p.

Creel, H.G. "The Meaning of Hsing Ming," in Soren Egerod, Studia Serica: Bernhard Karlgren Dedicata. Copenhagen: E. Munksgaard, 1959. 282 p., 199-211.

——————. The Origins of Statecraft in China. Chicago: University of Chicago Press, 1970. 545 p.

——————. Shen Pu-hai. Chicago: University of Chicago Press, 1974. 446 p.

Dardess, John W. Conquerors and Confucians. New York: Columbia University Press, 1973. 254 p.

Davis, W.M. "Across Eastern Gobi," Science, I (1883), 48-49.

Denby, Charles. "The Chinese Conquest of Songaria," Peking Oriental Society, III, #2. 159-181.

Drew, W.J. "Sinkiang: The Land and the People," Central Asian Review, XVI (1968), 205-216.

Eastman, Lloyd. Throne and Mandarins: China's Search for a Policy During the Sino-French Controversy, 1880-1885. Cambridge: Harvard University Press, 1967. 254 p.

Fairbank, John K. ed. The Chinese World Order. Cambridge: Harvard University Press, 1968. 416 p.

Fairbank, John K. and S.Y. Teng. Ch'ing Administration: Three Studies. Cambridge: Harvard University Press, 1960. 218 p.

Fields, Lanny Bruce. "Ethnicity in Tso Tsung-t'ang's Armies, 1867-1880: The Interest-Group Perspective," Journal of Asian Affairs, (1978).

Filchner, Wilhelm. *Hui Hui: Asiens Islam Kämpfe*. Berlin: Peter J. Astergaard, 1928. 423 p.

Fletcher, Joseph. "The Naqshbandiyya and the *Dhikr-i Arra*," *Journal of Turkish Studies*, I (1977).

des Forges, Roger V. *Hsi-liang and the Chinese National Revolution*. New Haven: Yale University Press, 1973. 274 p.

*The Four Books*. Trans. James Legge. Hong Kong: Wei Tung Book Store, 1966 reprint. 351 p.

"The Four Men Huan," *Friends of Moslems*, XVI (January 1942), 6-7.

Frechtling, L.E. "Anglo-Russian Rivalry, Eastern Turkestan, 1863-1881," *Journal of the Royal Central Asian Society*, XXVI (1939), 471-489.

Gibb, H.A.R. "The Structure of Religious Thought in Islam (IV), Sufism," *The Moslem World*, XXXVIII (1948), 280-291.

Giles, Herbert A. *A Chinese Biographical Dictionary*. London: Bernard Quartich, 1898. 1022 p.

Gill, William. "The Chinese Army," *Journal of the Royal United Service Institutions*, XXIV, (1881), 358-377.

Gillet, Michael. "The National Minorities of Western China," *Central Asian Review*, XVI (1968), 69-70.

Gilsenan, Michael. *Saint and Sufi in Modern Egypt: An Essay in the Sociology of Religion*. Oxford: At the Clarendon Press, 1973. 248 p.

Giquel, Prosper. *The Foochow Shipyard and Its Results: From Commencement in 1867 to the End of the Foreign Directorate on the 16th February, 1874*. Trans. H. Lang. Shanghai: Shanghai Evening Courier, 1874. 38 p.

Golab, L.W. "A Study of Irrigation in Eastern Turkestan," *Anthropos*, XLVI (1951), 187-199.

Groot, J.J.M. de. *Sectarianism and Religious Persecution in China: A Page in the History of Religions*. Amsterdam, 1903-1904. 2 v.

Grosier, M. L'Abbe. *De la Chine ou Description Generale de Cet Empire*. Paris: Chez Pillet Aine, Imprimeur-Libraire, 1819. 4 v.

Hai Baruddin Wee-liang. *Muslim Minority in China*. New York: Columbia University M.A. thesis, 1955. 153 p.

Hinton, Harold O. *The Grain Tribute System of China: 1845-1911*. Cambridge: Harvard University Press, 1956. 163 p.

Ho Ping-ti. "The Salt Merchants of Yang-chou: A Study of Commercial Capitalism in Eighteenth Century China," *Harvard Journal of Asiatic Studies*, XVII (1950), 130-168.

——————. *Studies on the Population of China, 1368-1953*. Cambridge: Harvard University Press, 1959. 341 p.

Holdsworth, Mary. *Turkestan in the Nineteenth Century: A Brief History of the Khanates of Bukhara, Kokand, and Khiva*. Oxford: Central Asian Research Centre and St. Anthony's College, Soviet Affairs Study Group, 1959. 81 p.

"Hsiang-t'an, Hunan," *Friends of Moslems*, XXII (1848), 25.

Hsiao Kung-ch'uan. *Rural China: Imperial Control in the Nineteenth Century*. Seattle: University of Washington Press, 1960. 783 p.

Hsü, Immanuel C.Y. "British Mediation of China's War with Yakub Beg, 1877," *Central Asiatic Journal*, IX (1964), 142-149.

——————. *China's Entrance into the Family of Nations: The Diplomatic Phase, 1858-1880*. Cambridge: Harvard University Press, 1960. 255 p.

——————. "Gordon in China, 1880," *Pacific Historical Review*, XXXIII (1964), 147-166.

——————. "The Great Policy Debate in China, 1874: Maritime Defense vs. Frontier Defense," *Harvard Journal of Asiatic Studies*. XXV (1964-1965), 212-218.

——————. *The Ili Crisis: A Study of Sino-Russian Diplomacy, 1871-1881*. Oxford: At the Clarendon Press, 1965. 230 p.

——————. "The Late Ch'ing Reconquest of Sinkiang: A Reappraisal of Tso Tsung-t'ang's Role," *Central Asiatic Journal*, XII (1968), 50-63.

_____. "Russia's Special Position in China During the Early Ch'ing Period," Slavic Review, XXIII (1964), 688-700.

Huang Pei. A Study of the Yung-cheng Period, 1723-1735: The Political Phase. Bloomington: Indiana University Ph.D. thesis, 1963. 500 p.

Hummel, Arthur, ed. Eminent Chinese of the Ch'ing Period. Washington, D.C.: United States Government Printing Office, 1943-1944. 2 v.

Institute of Pacific Relations. Agrarian China: Selected Source Materials From Chinese Authors. Chicago: University of Chicago Press, N.D. 258 p.

Iwamura Shinobu. "Islamic Society on the Chinese-Mongolian Border," Islamic Review, (September 1952), 23-28.

_____. "The Structure of Moslem Society in Inner Mongolia," Far Eastern Quarterly, VIII (1948-1949), 34-44.

Jarring, Gunnar. Materials to the Knowledge of Eastern Turki: Tales, Poetry, Proverbs, Riddles, Ethnological and Historical Texts From the Southern Parts of Eastern Turkestan. Stockholm: Lunds Universitets Arsskrift, 1948-1951. 4 v.

Jones, Susan Mann. "Scholasticism and Politics in Late Eighteenth Century China," Ch'ing-shih wen-t'i, III (December 1975), 28-49.

(H.K.) "Chinese Mahometans at Mecca," The China Review, (1858), 252.

Kiernan, E.V.G. British Diplomacy in China, 1880-1885. Cambridge: Cambridge University Press, 1939. 327 p.

_____. "Kashgar and the Politics of Central Asia, 1868-1878," Cambridge Historical Journal, XI (1953-1955), 317-342.

King, Frank H.H. Money and Monetary Policy in China, 1845-1895. Cambridge: Harvard University Press, 1965. 330 p.

"Kirghizia," Asian Review, (January 1955), 70-78.

Kostenko, L.F. The Turkistan Region: Being a Military Statistical Review of the Turkistan Military District of Russia or Russian Turkistan Gazetteer. Simla: Government Central Branch Press, 1882-1884. 3 v.

Krader, Lawrence. Peoples of Central Asia. Bloomington: Indiana University Press, 1963. 319 p.

——————. Social Organization of the Mongol-Turkic Pastoral Nomads. The Hague: Mouton and Company, 1963. 412 p.

Kuhn, Philip A. Rebellion and Its Enemies in Late Imperial China: Militarization and Social Structure, 1796-1864. Cambridge: Harvard University Press, 1970. 254 p.

Kuznetsov, V.S. "British and Russian Trade in Sinkiang, 1819-1851," Central Asian Review, XIII (1965), 149-156.

"The Late Yakoob Beg of Kashgar," Westminster Review, new series, V (July 1878).

Lattimore, Owen. "Inner Asian Frontiers: China and Russian Margins of Expansion," Journal of Economic History, VII (1947), 24-52.

——————. Pivot of Asia: Sinkiang and the Inner Asian Frontiers of China and Russia. Boston: Little, Brown, and Company, 1950. 288 p.

Liang Ch'i-ch'ao. Intellectual Trends of the Ch'ing Period. Trans. Immanuel C.Y. Hsü. Cambridge: Harvard University Press, 1959. 194 p.

Lin En-lan. "The Ho-si Corridor," Economic Geography, XXVIII (1952), 51-56.

Lipman, Jonathan. "Patchwork Society, Network Society: A Study of Sino-Muslim Communities," Paper Presented at International Conference on Islam in Asia, Jerusalem, Israel (April 1977), Conference Volume in Preparation, 1-

Lowenthal, Rudolph. "Russian Contributions to the History of Islam in China," Central Asiatic Journal, VLL (1962), 312-315.

"Ma Yuan-chang," Friends of Moslems, XX (1946), 204.

Macartney, G. "Eastern Turkestan: The Chinese as Rulers Over an Alien Race," Proceedings of the Central Asian Society (March 1909), 3-23.

Mackenzie, David. The Lion of Tashkent: The Career of General M.G. Cherniaey. Athens: University of Georgia Press, 1974. 267 p.

Markovitz, Irving L. "Traditional Social Structure, the Islamic Brotherhoods and Political Development in Senegal," Journal of Modern African Studies, VIII (1970), 73-96.

Mason, Isaac. "How Islam Entered China," The Moslem World, XIX (1929), 249-263.

──────. "Notes on Chinese Mohammedan Literature," North China Branch of the Royal Asia Society, LVI (1925), 172-215.

Mesny, William. "Tso Wen Hsiang," Mesny's China Miscellany, (January 1, 1905), 1-7.

Metzger, Thomas. The Internal Organization of Ch'ing Bureaucracy. Cambridge: Harvard University Press, 1973. 469 p.

──────. "The Organizational Capabilities of the Ch'ing State in the Field of Commerce: The Liang-Huai Salt Monopoly, 1740-1840," in W.E. Willmott, Economic Organization in Chinese Society Stanford: Stanford University Press, 1972. 9-45.

──────. "T'ao Chu's Reform of the Huai-pei Salt Monopoly, 1831-1833," Papers on China, XVI (1962), 1-47.

Mikhaleva, G.A. "Diplomatic Relations Between Russia and Bukhara at the Turn of the Eighteenth Century," Central Asian Review, XI (1963), 268-273.

Mitchell, Peter M. Wei Yüan (1794-1857) and the Early Modernization Movement in China and Japan. Bloomington: Indiana University Ph.D. thesis, 1970. 321 p.

Monteil, Vincent. "The Introduction to the Voyages of Ibn Battutah," Islamic Review, LVIII (March 1970), 30-37.

"Nakshaband," Friends of Moslems, X (July 1936), 46.

Nicholson, R.A. The Mystics of Islam. Beirut: Khayats Book and Publishing Company, 1966. 178 p.

d'Ollone, H.M.G. Recherches sur les Musulmans Chinois. Paris: E. Leroux, 1911. 470 p.

Palladius, Archimandrite, "The Mohammedans of China," The Chinese Recorder, XLIX (July 1918), 436-442.

Parker, E.H. "Islam in China," *Asian Review*, XXIV (1908), 63-84.

———. "Kashgar," *Asian Review*, XX (1905), 328-337.

———. "Manchu Relations with Turkestan," *The China Review*, XVI (1888), 321-326.

———. "The Salt Revenue of China," *Journal of the North China Branch of the Royal Asiatic Society*, new series, XXII (1887), 67-80.

———. *Studies in Chinese Religion*. London: Chapman and Hall Ltd., 1910. 308 p.

Pettus, W.B. "Chinese Mohammedanism," *The Chinese Recorder and Missionary Journal*, XLIV (February 1913), 88-94.

Phillips, G. "Marco Polo and Ibn Batuta in Fookien," *The Chinese Recorder and Missionary Journal*, III (June 1870-May 1871), 73.

Pierce, Richard A. *Russian Central Asia, 1867-1917: A Study in Colonial Rule*. Berkeley: University of California Press, 1960. 359 p.

Pipes, Richard. "Muslims of Central Asia," *Middle East Journal*, IX (1955), 295-308.

Pong, David. "Income and Military Expenditure of Kiangsi Province in the Last Years (1860-1864) of the Taiping Rebellion," *Journal of Asian Studies*, XXVI (1966-1967), 49-65.

Poppe, Nicholas. "Remarks on the Salar Language," *Harvard Journal of Asiatic Studies*, XVI (1953), 438-477.

Porter, Johnathan. *Tseng Kuo-fan's Private Bureaucracy*. Berkeley: University of California Press, 1972. 151 p.

Rawlinson, Henry. *England and Russia in the East: A Series of Papers on the Political and Geographical Condition of Central Asia*. London: John Murray, 1875. 412 p.

Rawlinson, John L. *China's Struggle for Naval Development, 1839-1895*. Cambridge: Harvard University Press, 1967. 318 p.

Rockhill, W.W. "The Dungan Rebellion and the Muhammedans in China," *Asian Review*, XII (1896), 414-418.

Rossabi, Morris. *China and Inner Asia: From 1368 to the Present Day.* London: Thames and Hudson, Ltd., 1975. 320 p.

——————. "Muslim and Central Asian Revolts in Late Ming and Early Ch'ing," Unpublished paper.

——————. "The Muslims in the Early Yuan Dynasty," Paper presented at International Conference on Islam in Asia, Jerusalem, Israel (April 1977), Conference Volume in Preparation.

Saguchi, Toru. "The Eastern Trade of the Koqand Khanate," *Memoirs of the Research Department of the Toyo Bunko,* XXIV (1965), 47-114.

——————. "The Revival of the White Mountain Khwajas, 1760-1820 (From Sarimsaq to Jihangir)," *Acta Asiatica,* XIV (1968), 7-20.

Samolin, William. *The Turkisation of the Tarim Basin up to the Qara-Qytay: A Preliminary Survey of the Problems Involved.* New York: Columbia University Ph.D. thesis, 1953, 373 p.

Savitsky, A.P. "Tsarist Policy Towards Islam: The Soviet Version," *Central Asian Review,* VI (1958), 242-252.

Sheehy, Ann. "Russia and China in the Pamirs: Eighteenth and Nineteenth Centuries," *Central Asian Review,* XVI (1969), 4-14.

Shen Han-yin Chen. "Tseng Kuo-fan in Peking, 1840-1852: His Ideas on Statecraft and Reform," *Journal of Asian Studies,* XXVII (1967), 61-80.

Skrine, C.P. *Chinese Central Asia.* London: Methuen and Company, 1926, 306 p.

Sokol, Edward Dennis. "The Revolt of 1916 in Russian Central Asia," *The Johns Hopkins University Studies in Historical and Political Science,* series LXXI (1953), 13-188.

Stanley, Charles Johnson. *Late Ch'ing Finance: Hu Kuang-yung as an Innovator.* Cambridge: Harvard University Press, 1961, 117 p.

Subham, John A. *Sufism: Its Saints and Shrines: An Introduction to the Study of Sufism with Special Reference to India.* Lucknow: Lucknow Publishing House, 1938, 412 p.

Sushanlo, M. "The Dungans in China," Central Asian Review, IX (1961), 201-205.

_____, "The Migration of the Dungans, 1877-1882," Central Asian Review, VI (1958), 264-271.

Teng, S.Y. "Some New Light on the Nien Movement and Its Effect on the Fall of the Manchu Dynasty," Symposium on Chinese Studies Commemorating the Golden Jubilee of the University of Hong Kong, 1911-1961, III (1968), 50-69.

_____. The Taiping Rebellion and the Western Powers: A Comprehensive Survey. Oxford: The Clarendon Press, 1971. 458 p.

Thiersant, P. Dabry de. Le Mahometisme en Chine et dans le Turkestan Oriental. Paris: Ernest Leroux, 1878, 2 v.

Tikhonov, D. "The Internal Policies of Yakub Beg of Kashgar," Central Asian Review, VII (1959), 403-408.

Trimingham, J. Spencer. The Sufi Orders in Islam. Oxford: The Clarendon Press, 1971. 333 p.

United States, Office of Strategic Services, Research and Analysis Branch, "Peoples and Politics of China's Northwest," R. and A. #1921 (July 1, 1945), 1-60.

Upton, Emery. Armies of Asia and Europe: Embassy Official Reports on the Armies of Japan, China, India, Persia, Italy, Russia, Austria, Germany, France and England. New York: Greenwood Press, 1928, 376 p.

Vambery, Arminius. Central Asia and the Anglo-Russian Frontier Question: A series of Political Papers. London: Smith, Elder, and Company, 1874. 385 p.

Wakeman, Frederick Jr. and Carolyn Grant, eds. Conflict and Control in Late Imperial China. Berkeley: University of California Press, 1975. 328 p.

Walshe, W. Gilbert. "Religious Toleration in China, Mohammedanism," Contemporary Review, LXXXVI (July 1904), 127-133.

Warren, G.G. "D'Ollone's Investigations on the Chinese Moslems," New China Review, II (1920), 267-289; 398-414.

"Western China," *Edinburgh Review*, CXXVI-CXXVII (1868), 182-202.

Wheeler, Geoffrey. "British and Russian Imperial Attitudes in Asia," *Royal Central Asian Society* (March 1970), 256-264, 318.

Wiens, Harold J. "Change in the Ethnography and Land Use of the Ili Valley and Region, Chinese Turkestan," *Annals of the Association of American Geographers*, LIX (1969), 753-775.

——————. "The Historical and Geographical Role of Urumchi, Capital of Chinese Central Asia," *Annals of the Association of American Geographers*, LIII (1963), 441-464.

Wilhelm, Helmut. "The Heresies of Ch'en Liang," *Asiatische Studien*, XI (1957), 102-111.

Williams, S.W. *The Middle Kingdom: A Survey of the Geography, Government, Literature, Social Life, Arts, and History of the Chinese Empire and Its Inhabitants*. New York: Charles Scribners Sons, 1883. 2 v.

Wingate, R.O. "Education in Chinese Turkestan," *Journal of the Royal Central Asian Society*. XVI (1929). 319-327.

Wright, Arthur F. *Buddhism in Chinese History*. New York: Antheneum Press, 1965. 144 p.

——————. ed. *Confucianism and Chinese Civilization*. Stanford: Stanford University Press, 1964. 362 p.

——————, and Denis Twitchett. eds. *Confucian Personalities*. Stanford: Stanford University Press, 1962. 411 p.

Wright, Mary O. *The Last Stand of Chinese Conservatism: The T'ung-chih Restoration, 1862-1874*. Stanford: Stanford University Press, 1957. 429 p.

Wu, Aitchen K. "The Fourteen Peoples of Chinese Turkestan," *Journal of the West China Border Research Society*, XV (1944), 83-93.

——————. *Turkistan Tumult*. London: Methuen and Company Limited, 1940. 278 p.

Wulsin, Frederick R. "Non-Chinese Inhabitants of the Province of Kansu, China," *American Journal of Physical Anthropology*, VIII (1925), 293-320.

Yang, Richard. "Sinkiang Under the Administration of Yang Tseng-hsin, 1911-1928," *Central Asiatic Journal*, VI (1961), 270-316.

Yuan, Tsing. "Yakub Beg (1820-1877) and the Moslem Rebellion in Chinese Turkestan," *Central Asiatic Journal*, VI (1961), 134-167.

Yudin, V.P. "Sinkiang: The Revolt of 1864," *Central Asian Review*, XI (1963), 168-180.

Zenkovsky, Serge A. *Pan-Turkism and Islam in Russia*. Cambridge: Harvard University Press, 1960. 345 p.

"Kulturkampf in Pre-Revolutionary Central Asia," *The American Slavic and East European Review*, XIV (1955), 15-41.

Zwemer, S.M. "The Four Religions of China," *The Moslem World*, XXVI (1936), 1-12.

## Addendum

Teng, S.Y. and John K. Fairbank. *China's Response to the West: A Documentary Survey, 1839-1923*. Cambridge: 1954.

INDEX

Afaqiyya (White Mountain Faction), 66, 67
Ahmad Kasani (Makhdum-i A'zam), Muslim leader, 65
akhunds, Muslim religious leaders, 59
Alti Shahr (the Six Cities, or Kashgaria), 45, 47, 53, 54, 66, 84, 89
An Lu-shan rebellion (775-763 A.D.), 57
Arsenals, 80

Baha Naqshband, 68
Bell, Mark, Colonel (1880s), 104
Bellew, H. W., traveller to Yakub Beg's area, 95
Bland, J. O. P., 4
Boulger, Demetrius C., 97
British, 84; support of Yakub Beg, 89; support of Chinese, 90
Brutality in warfare, 97
Buddhism, 56, 57
Bughra Khan Ghazi, Sultan, Kashgarian leader, 65
Bukhara emirate, 53
Bureaucracy, control of, 30

Camels, 47, 83
Chang Chu-cheng, Ming dynasty Fa-chia reformer, commander, 5, 6, 33, 34, 37, 38, 41, 77
Chang-Ju, second wife of Tso, 5
Chang Liang-chi, Hunan governor, 22, 26, 42
Chang P'eng-fei, 19th c. statecraft editor, 36
Changsha, cap. of Hunan, 10, 20
Chang Yueh, Tso subordinate, 84, 88
Ch'ao Tso (2nd c. B.C.), 31, 33, 34
Ch'en Fu-liang (1141-1207), mil. historian, 33, 37, 38
Ch'eng-nan Academy, 8, 24
Chen Tzŭ-lung (1608-1647), Confucian scholar, compiler of Huang-ming ching-shih wen-pien, 34-35, 38
Ch'en Tu-hsiu, and New Culture movement, 36
Cherniaev, M. G., Russian general, 97
Chia I (2nd c. B.C.), 31, 34
Chiang I-Li, Kwangtung governor, 78
Ch'iang-ling (1758-1838), Hupeh governor, fighter of Miao tribesmen, 41
Ch'ien-lung emperor (r. 1736-1795), 19, 45, 50, 51, 52, 55, 56, 57, 58, 67, 69, 82
Chin-chi-pao, Hunan, Muslim revolt center, 26, 71, 73, 81
Chinese Turkestan, vi, vii, 11, 20, 46-47; resources, 50; 53; becomes Sinkiang province (1884), 88
Ch'ing dynasty, 53, 56
Ching-lien, 82
Chin-shih degree, 1, 15
Ching-shih (statecraft), v, 106, passim.
Chin-shun, 82
Chou Hsuan-wang (8th c. A.D.), 34
Chou I-tuan, first wife of Tso, 5, 14

Ch'u Army, 25
Chu-ko Liang, chief minister (221-234 A.D.), 5, 6, 11-12, 13, 22, 31, 38, 39, 43, 77
Chung-hou, envoy to Russia during Ili crisis, 90
Ch'u-t'ien method, 106
Clarke, F. C. H., 93
Colonization, in Han period, 88, 105
Comprehensive Mirror for Aid in Government, 34
Confucianism, vi, 1, 6, 7, 20, 37, 57
Cotton, 88
Crawford, Robert, 33
Creel, H. G., v, 30=31, 39
Crops, planted by armies, 47

Deserts, of Northwest China, 47
Dungans. See Tungans

Economic programs, 102-104
Ekvall, R. B., 98
Examination system, 2, 9, 19, 22, 30; in Kansu, 85

Fa-chia (school of law and statecraft), v, 7, 9, 30, 32, 33, 34
Famine in Northwest China (1877-1878), 98
Fletcher, Joseph, 68
Foochow Arsenal (1860s), 42
Forsyth, Douglas, and Yakub Beg regime, 89, 95
Friend of India, 99

Germans, influence of, 80, 103
Grain planting, 83
Great Britain, 54, 84, 89, 90

Hami, 90
Ho Ch'ang-ling, Hunan scholar, Ch'ing official, 8, 9, 10, 15, 16, 17, 18, 19, 23; and cotton textile production, 16; and opium, 17, 18, 19, 23; editor of Huang-ch'ao.., 30
Hochow, Hunan, revolt center, 26, 48
Ho Hsi-ling, Hunan scholar-official, 4, 8, 9, 13, 15, 16, 17, 20, 24, 41
Ho Kuei-ling, Hunan scholar-official, 15
Ho-shen, corrupt influence of, 52
Hsian R., 9
Hsiang Army, led by Wang Chin against Taipings, 25
Hsiao Ta-heng, Kansu official, end of Ming dyn., 55
Hsiao-t'ung, son of Tso, 25
Hsiao-wei, son of Tso, 3-4
Hsia Yun-i (17th c.), 38
Hsien-feng emperor (19th c.), 22
Hsi Hsia kingdom, 50
Hsin Chiao, Muslim movement (1760s), 62, 68. See New Teaching
Hsing-ming, merit rating, v, 31, 32
Hsu Chan-piao, military commander, 84
Hsu Fu-yuan (17th c.), 38
Hsun Tzu, Confucian thinker, 94

Hsu Sung, topographer, W. Turkestan, 25-26, 41, 48, 77
Huang, Ray, 37
Huang Ch'ao rebellion (874-884 A.D.), 58
<u>Huang-ch'ao ching-shih wen-pien</u> (1827), 8, 12, 15, 19, 24, 29, 34, 35. See also Ho Ch'ang-ling
<u>Huang-ch'ao ching'shih wen-hsu-pien</u> (1880s), 36
<u>Huang-ming ching-shih wen-pien</u> (17th c.), 19, 24, 29, 35, 38
Huc, Evariste (1840s), 73
Hui-hui. See Tungans
Hu Kuang-yung, comprador, 83
Hu Lin-i, Hunan scholar-general, 15, 17, 18, 20, 22, 23, 25, 30, 42, 43, 77, 83
Hunan statecraft group, passim

Ili Valley, 47, 49, 53, 61, 82, 89, 90, 93, 97; crisis, 98
Interest groups, 55; perspective, 73
Irrigation, 48
Ishan-i Kalan (Muhammad Amin), 66
Ishaqiyya (Black Mountain Faction), 66, 67

Jao Yü-cheng (19th c.), statecraft editor, 36
Jahriyya group, 67, 68

Kalmyk Mongols, 56
K'ang-hsi emperor (r. 1662-1722), 19, 51, 82
Kansu, vi, 50
Kashgar, 66
Kashgaria, 47. See Alti Shahr
Kaufman, Konstantin Petrovich von, Russian general, 97, 104
Kazakhs, 56
Khiva khanate, 53
Khoja Burhan-al-din (d. 1758), Muslim rebel, 53
Khoja Jehangir, Muslim leader, 53
Kiangsu region, 16, 17, 19
Kirgiz, 56
Kokand khanate, 51, 53, 54
Kokonor region, 87
Kolpakovsky, G. A., Russian general, in Ili Valley, 90
Kuldja Trade Agreement (1850), 54
Kung, Prince, 34
Kung Tzu-chen, 7
Kuo Sung-t'ao, 24
Ku Tsu-yu (17th c.) geographer, 7, 10-11
Ku Yen-wu (17th c.), geographer, 10

Lanchow, 68; woolen mill, 42, 88
Land reclamation, 49, 87
Land shortage, 51
<u>Lao Chiao</u> (old teaching), 62
Lattimore, Owen, 96
Li Hung-chang, 82, 92, 94
Liu Jung, Hunanese, governor of Shensi, 26
Lin Tse-hsü (early 19th c.), Ch'ing statesman, statecraft advocate, 15, 17, 18, 19, 22, 26, 41, 42, 48, 49, 51, 77
Liu Chin-t'ang, commander, governor-gen. of Sinkiang, 88, 89, 102

Liu Pei, ruler of Shu-Han state (3rd c. A.D.), 11
Liu Sung-shan, Tso subordinate, 79, 80, 81
Lo Ping-chang, gov. of Hunan (1853), 22, 36, 42
Lo Tse-nan, 24, 25, 29, 34

Ma An-liang, 81
Ma Chan-ao, Hochow Muslim leader, 75, 81, 95, 102
Ma Chung-ying, 71
MacKenzie, David, 97
Ma Hua-lung, Tungan New Teaching leader, vi, 52, 58, 62, 70, 71; descendants, 72; 73, 74, 81, 95, 101
Ma Ming-hsin (Muhammad Amin), Muslim leader (1760s), 67, 68, 69, 70, 73, 96
Manchus, 56
Mandl, German employee, 97, 100
Mesny, William (ca. 1881), 103
Metzger, Thomas, 29
Miao peoples, 41, 42
Military colonies, 41
Ming dynasty, 56
Ming-shih doctrine, 8, 9; technique, 44; 106
Min-kuo ching-shih wen-pien (1913), 36
Mongols, and Muslims, 56
Monguors, tribe, 56
Moorcroft, William, British agent, 54
Mountains, of Northwest China, 46-47
Mu Sheng-hua (Mu Pa-pa), 70
Muslims, 19, 41, 45, 51, 55, 57, 58; rebellions, 18, 25, 46, 52, 101, 102; veneration of saints, 67; segregation of, 60, 85; Chinese treatment of, 58-59; rehabilitation, 101; in 1930s and 1940s, 102; revolt effect on government finance, 94

Naqshbandiyya tariquat (brotherhood), 53
Neo-Confucian metaphysics, 37
Network-interest group concept, vii, 73
New Teaching (Hsin chiao) movement, vii, 19, 52, 59, 62, 67, 85, 101; Tso's hatred for, 95
Nien rebellion, 25, 52, 78, 93
Ninghsia, Kansu, 48, 50, 52, 70, 74, 75
Ni Yuan-lu, 37
North China Plain, 45
Northwest campaigns, 77-84
Northwest China, 18, 45, 46; economic decline, 50; population pressure, 51; reconstruction of, 84-91; famine, 98
North China Herald, 97, 99, 104

Opium, 16, 98, 99, 100, 101
Opium War, 12, 18
Ordos Mongols, 55
Oyirad (Kalmyk Mongol) empire, 53

Piassetsky, Pavel, Russian traveller, 10, 100
Polachek, James, 105
Porter, Johnathan, 39
Prjevalsky, N. M., Russian explorer, 98

Rockhill, W. W., traveller
Russia, 45, 54, 89, 93, 104

Salars, 62, 67, 73
Salt monopoly, 19
Schuyler, Eugene, American diplomat, 68, 97
Secret societies, 80
Segregation of ethnic groups, 60, 85
Sericulture, 5, 10, 18, 88
Shang Yang (4th c. B.C.), 31, 33
Shaw, Robert, British merchant, 73
Sheep herding, 88
Shen Pu-hai (4th c. B.C.), statecraft theorist, 5, 6, 31, 33, 39, 77
Shensi, 40
Shrines, 64
Sinification of Moslems, 101, 105
Sinkiang, province formation (1884), 106
Sino-French War, 98
Social ties, 14-15
Soil rotation, 9
Ssu-ma Kuang, writer, 34
Statecraft (ching-shih), 8, 12; groups, 14-15, 30, 37-38, 40, 77
Suchow, siege (1871-1873), 82; destruction of, 93
Sufi brotherhoods, 46, 61, 63
Sung-Cheng-pi (17th c.), 38
Sun Tzu, early Chou strategist, 12

Taiping rebellion, 10, 12, 20, 22, 30, 42, 46, 51, 52, 93
Talas River, battle on (8th c. A.D.), 45
Tamerlane, 65
T'ang Chen-yu, 68
T'ang Su-tsung (8th c. A.D.), 34
T'ao Chu, Hunanese bureaucrat, reformer in Kiangsu, 13, 15, 19 22, 23, 35, 36, 77, 83, 87
Tao-kuang period, 15
T'ao Kuang, Tso's son-in-law, 17
Tarim Basin, 48
Tea culture, 10
T'ien Shan Mountains, 47
T'ien Wu, New Teaching leader (d. 1784), 69, 70
Toghto, Yuan period, 33, 38
To-lung-a, commander, 80
T'o-ming, Muslim leader, 72
Tributary system, 52-54
Trimingham, J. Spencer, 63
Tseng Kuo-ch'uan, 23
Tseng Kuo-fan, statecraft advocate, 15, 22, 30, 34, 39, 86
Tso Tsung-t'ang, family influence, 1-6; education of, 6-9; and examinations, 2, 9, 22, 29; as farmer, 9-10; and geography, 10-11, 16, 79; and military matters, 11-12, 92; early int. in statecraft, 12-13; and social ties, 14 ff.; condemns 'liquidation policy", 81; economic measures, 16, 86, 87; famine relief, 86; anti-foreign sentiments, 6, 98; and opium trade, 16, 98, 99, 100; in Hunan admin., 22; high cost of achievements, 105

Tsui Ch-en, Communist writer, 105
T'ung-chih restoration, 33-34, 106
Tungans (Dungans, Hui-hui, or Sino-Moslems), vi, 46, 56, 58, 96
Tung Fu-hsiang, bandit leader, 81, 82
Tung-hsiang Muslims (Mongol group), 56
Tun-lin statecraft faction (1630s), 38
T'un-t'ien system, 41, 43
Turfan, 67
Tz'u-hsi, Empress Dowager, 6

Uighurs (Taranchi), Muslim group, 57, 61

Wahhabi movement, 68
Wang An-shih, Sung era Confucian reformer, v, 33, 34
Wang Chin, mil. leader against Taiping rebels, 25
Wang Po-hsin, expert on Muslims, advisor to Tso, 26, 41, 48
Weber, Max, 39
Wei Yuan, Hunan statecraft notable, 19, 77, 87, 89, editor of Huang-ch'ao..., 30
Wen-ti (2d c. B.C.), 31
Western Chou era, 30
White Lotus revolt, 52
Williams, S. W., 98
Woolen mill, Lanchow, 102-103
Wright, Mary, 33-34

Yakub Beg (d. 1877), 48, 65, 72, 84, 89, 90, 99
Yang Ch'ang-chun, Chekiang fin. commissioner, 78
Yangchow, 57
Yasawi, Ahmad, 68
Yeh Shih (1150-1223), 37
Yellow River, 48
Yen Ju-i (1759-1826), Hunanese scholar strategist, 41, 42
Yoshinobu, Nakada, 68
Yuan dynasty, 45, 57
Yueh Fei (12th c.), army leader, 38
Yueh-lu Academy, Hunanese statecraft center, 24
Yung-cheng emperor (1722-1735), 19, 50, 51, 59
Yung-chia school, Chekiang, 37

Zungharia, 45, 47, 54, 73, 84, 89, 90, 96, 97
Zungharia Oyirad (Kalmyk Mongol) empire, 45, 53, 58, 67

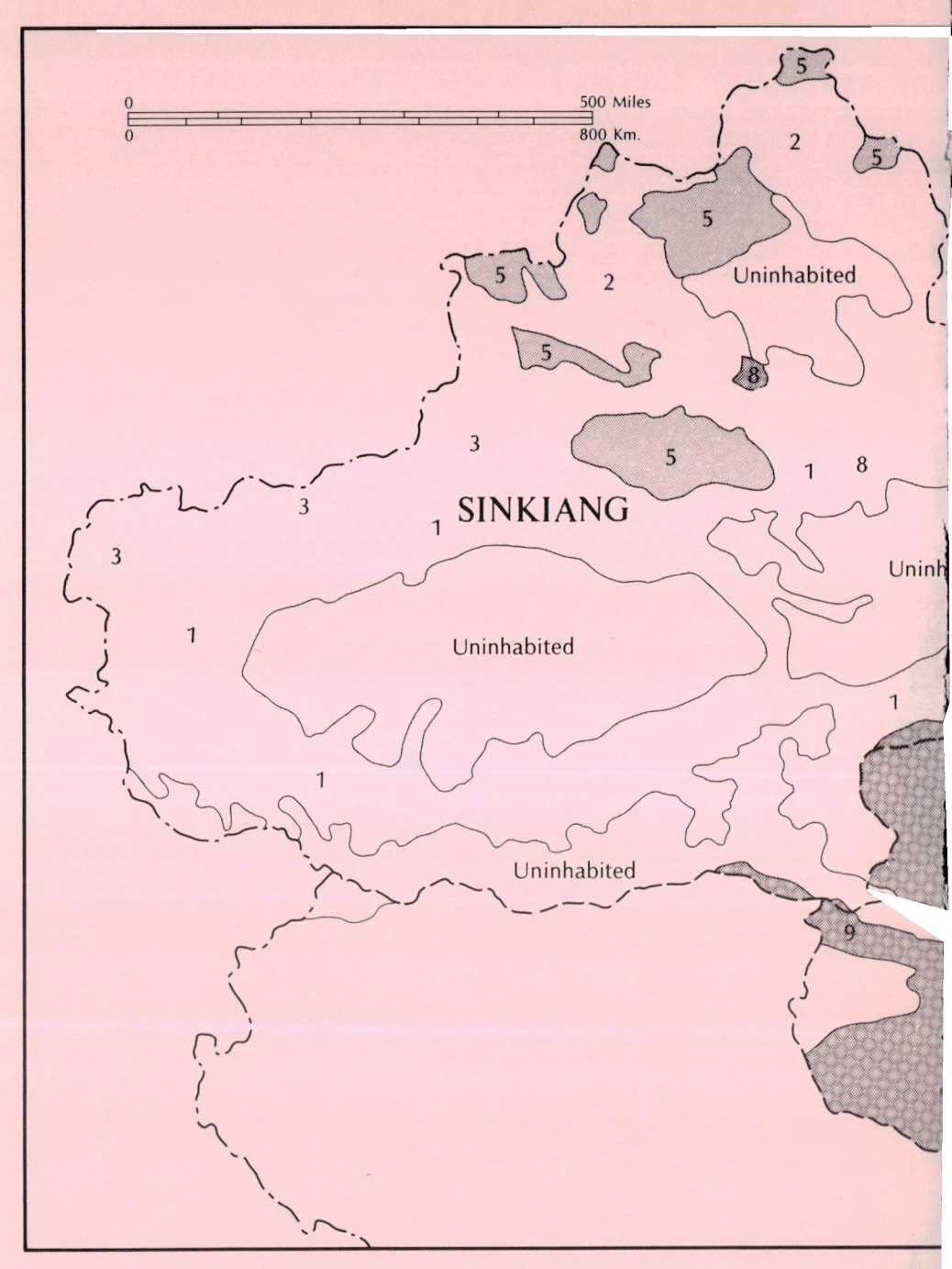